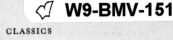

PENGUIN CLASSICS

THE BERNARD SHAW LIBRARY

PLAYS UNPLEASANT

'He did his best in redressing the fateful unbalance between truth and reality, in lifting mankind to a higher rung of social maturity. He often pointed a scornful finger at human frailty, but his jests were never at the expense of humanity' Thomas Mann

'Shaw will not allow complacency; he hates second-hand opinions; he attacks fashion; he continually challenges and unsettles, questioning and provoking us even when he is making us laugh. And he is still at it. No cliché or truism of contemporary life is safe from him' Michael Holroyd

'In his works Shaw left us his mind ... Today we have no Shavian wizard to awaken us with clarity and paradox, and the loss to our national intelligence is immense' John Carey, *Sunday Times*

'An important writer and an interesting socialist and critic ... Thank God he lived' Peter Levi, *Independent*

'He was a Tolstoy with jokes, a modern Dr Johnson, a universal genius who on his own modest reckoning put even Shakespeare in the shade' John Campbell, *Independent*

'His plays were superb exercises in high-level argument on every issue under the sun, from feminism and God, to war and eternity, but they were also hits – and still are' Paul Johnson, *Daily Mail*

BERNARD SHAW was born in Dublin in 1856. Although essentially shy, he created the persona of G.B.S., the showman, satirist, controversialist, critic, pundit, wit, intellectual buffoon and dramatist. Commentators brought a new adjective into English: Shavian, a term used to embody all his brilliant qualities.

After his arrival in London in 1876 he became an active Socialist and a brilliant platform speaker. He wrote on many social aspects of the day: on *Common Sense about the War* (1914), *How to Settle the Irish Question* (1917) and *The Intelligent Woman's Guide to Socialism and Capitalism* (1928). He undertook his own education at the British Museum and consequently became keenly interested in cultural subjects. Thus his prolific output included music, art and theatre reviews, which were collected into several volumes, such as *Music In London 1890–1894* (3 vols., 1931), *Pen Portraits and Reviews* (1931); and *Our Theatres in the Nineties* (23 vols., 1931). He also wrote five novels, including *Cashel Byron's Profession* (published by Penguin), and a collection of shorter works issued as *A Black Girl in Search of God and Some Lesser Tales* (also in Penguin).

Shaw conducted a strong attack on the London Theatre and was closely associated with the intellectual revival of British Theatre. His many plays (the full canon runs to 52) fall into several categories: 'Plays Pleasant'; 'Plays Unpleasant'; 'Plays for Puritans'; political plays; chronicle plays; 'metabiological Pentateuch' (*Back to Methuselah*) in five plays; extravaganzas; romances; and fables. He died in 1950.

DAVID EDGAR was Britain's first professor of Playwriting Studies, at the University of Birmingham. He has written widely on theatre, most recently editing and introducing *State of Play*, a study of contemporary British playwriting. His original plays include *Destiny* (1976), *Maydays* (1983) and *Pentecost* (1994) for the Royal Shakespeare Company and *Entertaining Strangers* (1987) and *The Shape of the Table* (1990) for the National Theatre. His adaptations include Dickens' *Nicholas Nickleby* (RSC, 1980) and *Albert Speer* (National Theatre, 2000), based on Gitta Sereny's biography.

DAN H. LAURENCE, editor of Shaw's *Collected Letters*, his *Collected Plays with their Prefaces*, *Shaw's Music* and (with Daniel Leary) *The Complete Prefaces*, was Literary Adviser to the Shaw Estate until his retirement in 1990. He is Series Editor for the works of Shaw in Penguin.

BERNARD SHAW

PLAYS UNPLEASANT

WIDOWERS' HOUSES
THE PHILANDERER
MRS WARREN'S PROFESSION

Definitive text under the editorial supervision of
DAN H. LAURENCE
with an Introduction by DAVID EDGAR

PENGUIN BOOKS

PENGUIN BOOKS

Published by the Penguin Group
Penguin Books Ltd, 27 Wrights Lane, London w8 5TZ, England
Penguin Putnam Inc., 375 Hudson Street, New York, New York 10014, USA
Penguin Books Australia Ltd, Ringwood, Victoria, Australia
Penguin Books Canada Ltd, 10 Alcorn Avenue, Toronto, Ontario, Canada M4V 3B2
Penguin Books (NZ) Ltd, Private Bag 102902, NSMC, Auckland, New Zealand

Penguin Books Ltd, Registered Offices: Harmondsworth, Middlesex, England

Published in Penguin Books 26 July 1946
Reprinted with a new Introduction in Penguin Classics 2000
1 3 5 7 9 10 8 6 4 2

'Widowers' House' first produced in London, 1892; in New York, 1907
'The Philanderer' first produced in London, 1905 (West End, 1917); in New York,
1913; in Berlin, 1908
'Mrs Warren's Profession' first performed (privately) in London, 1902; (publicly
Birmingham, 1925; London, 1925; first produced in America, 1905; in Berlin, 1907.

Printed in England by Clays Ltd, St Ives plc
Set in Monotype Baskerville

All business connected with Bernard Shaw's plays is in the hands of The Society of Authors,
84 Drayton Gardens, London SW10 9SD (Telephone 020-7373 6642/3), to which all inquiries
and applications for licences should be addressed and fees paid. Dates and places
of contemplated performances must be precisely specified in all applications.
Accounts showing the receipts at each performance should accompany payments.

Applications for permission to give stock and amateur performances of Bernard Shaw's
plays in the United States of America and Canada should be made to Samuel French, Inc.,
25 West 45th Street, New York, New York 10036. In all other cases, whether for stage, radio, or
television, application should be made to The Society of Authors, 84 Drayton Gardens,
London SW10 9SD, England.

CONTENTS

Introduction   vii

Preface   7
PLAYS UNPLEASANT
Widowers' Houses   29
The Philanderer   97
Mrs Warren's Profession   179

Principal Works of Bernard Shaw   290

Shaw claimed that he wrote *Widowers' Houses* with the sole purpose of inducing people to vote on the progressive side at the next London County Council elections. For many critics (and some devotees) of Shaw's work, this boldly utilitarian statement of aims applies to most of the canon. But, for Shaw himself, *Widowers' Houses*, *The Philanderer* and *Mrs Warren's Profession* stand apart from his later plays, in purpose, content and form. Indeed, in defining these three plays as 'unpleasant' he was seeking to make a firm distinction between plays that exposed social evils (slum landlordism, the marriage laws and prostitution) from the 'pleasant' plays which he published simultaneously, and which deal with 'romantic follies' and the individuals who struggle against them. In this he anticipates critics who regard the plays unpleasant as, at best, an apprenticeship and, at worst, a false start.

Certainly, the writing and production history of these plays was disagreeably tortuous. *Widowers' Houses* was conceived as a collaboration between Shaw and the critic William Archer to rework a recent Parisian success (Emile Augier's *Ceinture Doree*), on the principle that Archer could do the story and Shaw the dialogue. Claiming to have run out of plot by the beginning of Act III, Shaw read out the story so far to Archer, who hated its construction, characterization and jokes, and washed his hands of it. There things remained, until seven years later, when J. T. Grein's Independent Theatre was looking for a follow-up to its brave British premiere of Ibsen's *Ghosts*. For this purpose, Shaw dusted off, completed and titled *Widowers' Houses*, which premiered in December 1892 to the cheers of the politicos in the audience, and the boos of everyone else.

The second play in this volume also suffered from an

ending problem; having read out the first draft, Shaw was advised by Lady Colin Campbell to burn the third act on the grounds of the moral outrage it would undoubtedly provoke[1]. Even revised, Shaw couldn't find a producer for the play (Grein, for whom it was written, was the first to turn it down). The play was eventually produced by the amateur New Stage Club in 1905, going on to receive its professional premiere at the Royal Court Theatre two years later, to indifferent reviews.

But the problems with *The Philanderer* were as nothing to those of the third play. Although the word prostitute does not appear in *Mrs Warren's Profession* (any more than the word 'syphylis' appears in *Ghosts*), Shaw knew perfectly well that the play would be denied a licence by the Lord Chamberlain, whose power to censor plays in the English theatre, granted by Sir Robert Walpole to suppress the political satires of Henry Fielding, is the subject of his specific preface. (Shaw's proposed alternative to this arcane system – control by local authority licensing – seems a risky strategy, particularly if the voters failed on all occasions to take Shaw's electoral advice).

Thus it was not until 1902 that *Mrs Warren's Profession* received two private club performances in London, to an apparently bemused audience (Grein reporting that some of the audience failed to pick up what the Profession was[2]). According to Shaw's preface, those who were not confused were outraged (William Archer accusing Shaw of wallowing in pitch, Grein himself announcing that Shaw had shattered his ideals). Subsequently, the play was performed in New Haven (where the theatre's license was revoked), New York (where half the cast were arrested) and in Kansas City (where the actress playing Mrs Warren was summoned to the police court for indecency). The play was eventually performed professionally in England in 1924.[3] Because of – or despite – this checkered history, none of the *Plays Unpleasant* has entered the main Shavian canon. True, the fiftieth anniversary of Shaw's death in 2000 saw revivals of both *Widowers'*

Houses and *Mrs Warren's Profession*; and a version of *The Philanderer* with the original last act was presented at the Hampstead Theatre in 1990. But compared to three of the four *Plays Pleasant* – *Arms and the Man, Candida* and *You Never Can Tell* – *Plays Unpleasant* could be retitled 'Plays Undone'.

Why should this be? Is it, as conventional wisdom has it (and the preface appears to confirm), that the *Plays Unpleasant* are arid agitprop while the *Plays Pleasant* (and the string of subsequent successes, from *Major Barbara* via *Man and Superman* to *Pygmalion*) are essentially agreeable if quirky romantic comedies, from which – in Egon Friedell's phrase – you can suck the theatrical sugar from the pill of propaganda, and put the pill itself back on the plate?[4] Or is it, as I believe, that Shaw's mistaken view of his own work led him to accept a fundamentally false dichotomy between the didactic and dramatic elements of his plays, rejecting what he had learnt in at least two of the *Plays Unpleasant*, and thus confirming the 'false start' thesis which has consigned one partially and one almost entirely successful political play to the fringes of the repertoire?

Shaw's mission statement as a dramatist was an essay about another one. The 'Quintessence of Ibsenism' was initially written as a paper for the Fabian Society, delivered in July 1890. As revised over the years, it became certainly the best essay by one playwright about another; it is actually one of the best pieces of sustained dramatic criticism ever written. Shaw defines Ibsenism as a confrontation with Idealism, which he defines as the tendency to mask the shortcomings of existing institutions by pretending that they are perfect and celebrating them as such (we might more easily call this 'conservatism' or 'traditionalism'). In *A Doll's House*, the idealized institution is marriage, the idealizer Torvald Helmer, and the 'realist' (Ibsen's term for the anti-idealist) is Nora, who realizes that her family life has been a fiction and so walks out on it, slamming the door behind her. In *The Wild*

Duck, the idealist is a man who believes that honesty is always the best policy, and thereby destroys a family and kills a child.

In addition to describing what Ibsen is saying, Shaw also describes how he thinks it is done. He argues that Ibsen's great innovation as a playwright was the discussion: while pre-Ibsenite (and by implication pre-Shavian) plays consisted of exposition, situation and unravelling, he argues, 'now you have exposition, situation and discussion; and the discussion is the test of the playwright'.

In fact, this argument seems a little dubious in Ibsen – if (as Shaw argues) the final argument between Nora and Telvig is a 'discussion', then this applies to every non-violent climactic scene in dramatic literature. But much more importantly, it implies that the discussion as a dramatic element is distinct from the traditional dramaturgical tools of emplotment, that somehow all the storytelling stops for the discussion to take place (as when Shaw contentiously claims that Nora unexpectedly stops her emotional acting and says: 'we must sit down and discuss all this that has been happening between us').

Now, of course, the discussion in this sense happens in Shaw, but it doesn't always happen, and when it is fully integrated into the plot it is almost always better. And this misunderstanding of Ibsen and his own art implies an even more profound mistake in Shaw's thinking: the idea that great drama is an escape from and not a development of pulp drama; so that, for example, 'Shakespeare survives by what he has in common with Ibsen, and not by what he has in common with Webster'. In the political theatre, this misconception leads to the idea of the sugar of entertainment somehow being suckable off the pill of propaganda (or, as T. S. Eliot put it, 'If the audience gets its strip tease it will swallow the poetry'). It is doubly surprising that Shaw would think this, as when he wrote 'The Quintessence', he was just about to embark (or in the case of *Widowers' Houses*) had already

x

embarked on, the creation of plays in which the political message was integral to the plot.

Shaw was (on occasion) happy to acknowledge Ibsen's influence on his work; he was less happy to admit the influence of the well-made play. One immediate effect of this influence is the location, look and milieu of the plays: although the settings are intriguingly various (moving from outside to inside, cleverly exploiting different times of day) the dominant milieu is the familiar one of the servanted classes at home. Despite their subjects, we never visit a slum tenement or a brothel in *Widowers' Houses* or *Mrs Warren's Profession*; we never meet a victim of Sartorius' or Kitty Warren's grisly trades. But more fundamentally, the influence of contemporary popular drama gave Shaw a template of emplotment into which he could insert a contrary set of meanings, by the simple device of denying the audience's expectations of where the plot would lead. In all of the *Plays Unpleasant*, Shaw sets up a moral dilemma for his central characters, absolutely in the manner of the Scribean well-made play, if not in two of the three cases with its usual matter. What he then nearly does in *Widowers' Houses*, fails to do in *The Philanderer*, and triumphantly succeeds in doing in *Mrs Warren's Profession* is to defy the audience's expectations of how the plot will be resolved, without losing plausibility or denying its own terms.

Before seeing how Shaw does this, it's worth looking at the opening of the plays, to see how skilfully – even at the outset of his career – Shaw establishes his characters, their situation and their dilemmas. Again, his beginnings distinguish Shaw from his mentor: however brilliantly he manages his denouements, Ibsen was usually pretty hamfisted with his exposition (*The Wild Duck* is by no means the only play in which the first act consists largely of one central character telling another central character what they both already know). The opening of *Widowers' Houses* on the other hand tells us within seconds who Cokane and Trench are by the simple expedient of hearing them discuss what sights they wish to visit on the current stage of their improving continental tour ('There is a very graceful female statue in the private house of a nobleman in Frankfurt. Also a zoo. Next day, Nuremberg! Finest collection of instruments of torture in the world'), in the same way that, in *Candida*, we learn all we need initially to know about the politics and personality of the Rev. James Morrell by hearing him finalize his upcoming diary engagements. This cunning use of Baedeker as a clue to character is then reiterated, not only to establish the next set of characters, but also to remove two of the subsequent assembly from the stage so that a proposal of marriage can take place under the pressure of their imminent return. And just as this device is in danger of wearing thin, Shaw introduces another, when Sartorius (for reasons about which we are already intrigued) asks that Trench write a letter to his relatives soliciting approval of his engagement to Sartorius' daughter, a task which falls to Cokane, who then calls upon Sartorius' assistance to complete it. Thus Shaw can map both the spoken and unspoken assumptions of three of the main characters concerning an as-yet-unrevealed skeleton in one of their closets, by the expedient of having one draft a letter on behalf of another in collaboration with the third.

Shaw does not pose himself nearly as much of an expositional challenge in *The Philanderer*, though it has to be said that he none the less starts the show with a bang. The initial stage direction reads 'A lady and gentleman are making love to one another in the drawing room of a flat in Ashley Gardens', from which Shaw goes on to chart Leonard Charteris' politics, attitude to marriage and questionably-concluded liaison with a third party, in preparation for the entry of that third party, whose opening line unconsciously expresses the very attitudes that Charteris has been repudiating a few moments before. But most elegant of all is the opening duologue of *Mrs Warrren's Profession*, in which a middle-aged man attempts to find common intellectual and cultural ground with what he and we see as 'an attractive specimen of the sensible, able, highly-educated young middle-class Englishwoman', who chooses to defy his expectations of such a person, thereby effortlessly establishing not only what sort of person she is, but (via his assumptions) what sort of person he is as well. In addition, Shaw has set up a series of vital trails and teasers for the future (including Vivie Warren's ignorance of her mother's occupation and intention to become an actuary).

By the end of the first act of both *Widowers' Houses* and *Mrs Warren's Profession*, then, Shaw has established his agenda, not by stating it, but by posing what is in fact the same question: how does one of the central characters earn their living and what effect will the answer have on the rest? Because he is more skilful by then, Shaw has inserted a false trail into his third play: for a moment, we are fooled into thinking that the big secret is not Mrs Warren's profession but Miss Warren's parenthood (and if we're really clever we note that 'profession' can mean assertion as well as occupation, and thus could well apply to both scenarios). But, in fact, the third play like the first is about a presumably virtuous younger character having to confront their dependence on the wickedness of an older one, and the question Shaw poses at the end of each play is how they and the rest respond to this knowledge in practical terms.

For it is in the endings that Shaw's meaning is revealed. The whole art of the stage is dedicated to concealing a single dirty little secret: that we know how most plays end before they begin. In tragedy, this is because the audience typically know the story already; in comedy it is because, from V century Athens to the end of the nineteenth century, the vast majority of comedies consisted of two young people overcoming parental or quasi-parental obstacles to their union, and getting married. Even in our century, with its bewildering array of new genres, we find that while we may not know the outcome of the story (who did it) we certainly know the ending of the plot (the murderer will be unmasked). Be the milieu the western, the thriller, the spy story or the romance, we will know from the outset who is the villain, who is the victim, and who is the hero, and thereby pretty much how the thing will turn out.

What Shaw took from Ibsen was the blindingly simple idea that this doesn't have to be the case. As he put it in the 'Quintessence', the new drama 'arises through a conflict of unsettled ideals', and the question which makes the play interesting 'is which is the villain and which the hero'. But by setting his plays within familiar theatrical milieus, Shaw gave himself an additional theatrical weapon. In Ibsen, there are no familiar landmarks to help us decide what kind of territory we're in. In Shaw, we think we know where we are (six of the seven *Plays Pleasant* and *Plays Unpleasant* appear to promise a betrothal) but in fact we find we are somewhere else. In Ibsen we don't know who the hero or the villain is, so we have to work it out for ourselves; in Shaw, we think we know but we find we've been deceived.

No wonder then that the inexperienced Shaw had trouble with his endings. Only in his third play does he bring off the reversal he has been striving for in both the others. In *The Philanderer*, his first, implausible but dynamic, ending was jettisoned in favour of a kind of evasion. In *Widowers' Houses*, his ending took him seven years.

As stated, *Widower's Houses* began life as a collaboration between Shaw and William Archer to adapt a French comedy, whose inciting incident is the discovery by a young man that the inheritance of the woman he loves was acquired immorally. In the original, his dilemma was resolved by the intervention of a major national economic crisis, so that the heroine's father might be ruined and the problem removed. In the first Archer–Shaw version (originally titled 'The Way to a Woman's Heart') the hero has to confront his problem, which he does by literally pitching the father's money into the river at Remagen (hence the

second Shaw–Archer title 'Rhinegold'). In the final and completed Shaw version, however, the hero does not behave
heroically, not least because the heroine chooses to behave in
a most surprising way.

By the end of the first act of *Widowers' Houses*, young Harry
Trench has become engaged to Blanche Sartorius, whose
brisk and unsentimental attitude to things (including Dr
Trench himself) we have learnt to enjoy and admire. We
have also discovered that there is a problem with the means
by which Blanche's father amassed his fortune. In the second
act, Trench discovers that Sartorius is a slum landlord, and,
like the heroes of both *Ceinture Doree* and 'Rhinegold', pro-
claims that he cannot possibly accept this tainted treasure,
proposing to his fiancée (without, being a Victorian gentleman, entirely explaining why) that they live off his income
alone.

Then two unexpected, but by no means implausible,
things happen. The first is that Blanche refuses to abandon
her inheritance, on the impeccably feminist grounds that it's
her money not his, that she does not wish to be absolutely
dependent on her husband, and that if (as she suspects) this
is an excuse to renege on his commitment to her then this is
'so like a man'. The second is that Sartorius reveals that
Trench's own income comes from mortgages on Sartorius'
property – in order to free himself of it he would have not
only to impoverish his wife but bankrupt himself.

This situation is left unresolved at the second interval, but
given a further twist in Act III, when Sartorius is faced with
a choice rich in irony – if he improves his hellish properties
he might make a killing from compulsory purchases by (yes,
here they are again) the London County Council, but he can
only do so by risking Trench's capital and thus his livelihood.
The only way this conundrum can be resolved is if Trench
overcomes his scruples and marries Blanche after all.

Now this doesn't *quite* work in plot terms; basically, Trench
faces the same moral dilemma twice, though in the second

case it is not so much a dilemma as a *fait accompli*. But anyone who has attempted to make such material work will recognize that Shaw has presented a complicated financial plot in a way that is plausible, intriguing of itself, and consistently clear; at each stage, the plotting faces the characters with unavoidable practical choices rich in moral meaning; and at the climax of the play he has complicated an already potent situation with a surprising, ironical, and yet plausible twist (the fact that in order to make an even fatter profit out of compulsory purchase, it suddenly becomes in Sartorius' interests to become a model landlord). All of which communicates Shaw's message, that capitalism has made everyone complicit in its evils whether they like it or not; and that the alternative is not to attempt to live an individually moral life, but to change society. Which Trench cannot do, so we, by implication, must take on the task.

Having brought that off, there is a sense of Shaw giving up: in order to top and tail Trench's surrender, he must bring Trench and Blanche back together, which he does in a long speech by Blanche in which the text is abuse and the subtext animal sexuality ('It suddenly flashes on him', Shaw instructs the Trench actor disarmingly, 'that all this ferocity is erotic: that she is making love to him'). Silent until the embrace, Trench informs her re-entering father that he'll 'stand in, compensation or no compensation'. So the challenge that in *Ceinture Doree* is avoided, and in 'Rhinegold' confronted, is here surrendered, from which Shaw invites us to draw the obvious conclusion.

The Philanderer is different from the other two *Plays Unpleasant*, but less different in its first version than the one Shaw published. The opening love triangle was drawn from Shaw's own life, with the current lover (Grace Tranfield) based on the actress Florence Farr (who played Blanche in *Widowers' Houses*), and the spurned ex-lover, Julia Craven, being an unflattering portrait of Jenny Patterson (who had taken Shaw's virginity eight years before). By the end of the second act, Grace has rejected the idea of marriage to Charteris on good 'New Womanly' grounds ('I will never marry a man I love too much. It would give him a terrible advantage over me: I should be utterly in his power'). While in order to evade his earlier entanglement, Charteris is busily organizing the marriage of Julia into the sub plot (a Dr Paramore, whose main function is to diagnose Julia's father as terminally ill with a liver disease of his own discovery, and to be most put out when he discovers that there's nothing wrong with his patient after all).

The original third act is four years later. Paramore has indeed married Julia, but fallen out of love with her, and wants a divorce so he can marry Grace. Shaw assembles the characters (rather clumsily) for precisely the kind of detached discussion of the iniquity of the marriage laws which he ascribes erroneously to Ibsen and (on his good days) equally erroneously to himself. It is agreed that Dr and Mrs Paramore should be divorced abroad, and there is a neat (if psychologically implausible) coda between Julia Paramore and Charteris, in which it is revealed that they have been having a secret liaison for most of the course of her marriage. Now she is free of Paramore, she insists that if Charteris wants to continue the affair, they will have to wed ('No more philandering and advanced views for me'). But Charteris' magnetism is too much for her, and despite his refusal, she ends the play in his arms.

Assured by Lady Campbell that this wouldn't wash, Shaw's substitute last act is continous with the second. Again, all the characters assemble at Dr Paramore's consulting rooms, but this time merely to witness the success of Charteris' scheme to marry Julia off to the doctor. Grace repeats her refusal to marry Charteris, Shaw half heartedly offers and withdraws the possibility of Charteris marrying Julia's sister, and the final question posed by the play is whether Charteris will congratulate Julia on her engagement (why would he not?). And like *Widowers' Houses*, the play ends with a virtually impossible stage direction: 'Charteris, amused and untouched, shakes his head laughingly. The rest look at Julia with concern, and even a little awe, feeling for the first time the presence of a keen sorrow'.[5]

So for the second time in a row, Shaw has the problem of a denouement of which the whole point is that a situation *doesn't* change. In both cases – though to a much greater extent in *The Philanderer* – this makes for an unsatisfactory and strangely perfunctory close. In his third play, one would expect Shaw at the very least not to make the same mistake again. But for whatever reason, that is precisely what he does do – with the significant difference that, on this occasion, he makes it work.

Like *Widowers' Houses*, *Mrs Warren's Profession* was based on two previous stabs at the same story. In his first version of what was to become *Yvette*, Maupassant has a girl respond to the discovery that her mother is a courtesan by suicide. In the actual *Yvette*, the girl becomes a kept woman herself. Armed with these two alternatives, Shaw was again eager to come up with a third.

As in *Widowers' Houses*, Shaw saves his major revelation for the second act, with the third providing another turn to the screw. In Act II, Kitty Warren tells her daughter that she was forced by circumstance into prostitution, thus converting Vivie from a conservative contempt for such self-serving excuses to a wholehearted acceptance of her mother's argument that society offered her no choice (or rather that the only other choices were worse). In Act III, however, Vivie discovers a new piece of information – that Mrs Warren is still running brothels, even though there is no longer any material imperative for her to do so. Sickened by this revelation, Vivie runs off to London and the small accountancy firm she now runs with her friend Honoria Fraser, in Chancery Lane, to make her own way in the world.

Having written two last acts without enough material to fill them, one might expect Shaw to end it there. In fact he adds a fourth act, in which Mrs Warren follows Vivie to London, to plead for acceptance from her daughter once again. The difference of course is that, unlike Harry Trench, Vivie Warren has actually spurned the tainted treasure, and this act is about the cost, not of doing the wrong thing, but of doing the right one. For that reason it can be, and is, driven not by plot but by character. In Act II, Mrs Warren's arguments are cogent and convincing; in Act IV they are neither, but they are compelling, because they are about her limits as a human being and her fears of growing old alone. In Act II, Vivie can respond joyously to her mother's strength and courage; now, rejecting her, she must be sarcastic and cruel. Modern as well as contemporary critics have seen Vivie transformed (in Chesterton's words) into 'an iceberg of contempt'[6]. But this surely is Shaw's point: that if the logic of capitalism traps all but the bravest into complicity, then the price of escape is the sacrifice of the best bits of oneself.

Shaw was not the last political writer to explore this paradox. At the end of her last scene with her daughter, Mrs Warren cries 'Lord help the world if everybody took to doing the right thing!', in direct anticipation of the message of Brecht's *Caucasian Chalk Circle* and *The Good Person of Setzuan*. In fact, Brecht wrote a rather silly essay on Shaw in 1926, in which he described him as a terrorist and said that he agreed with Shaw's opinions about evolution even though he didn't know what they were.[7] He was not to know the debt he would owe to Shaw as a political writer.

As Eric Bentley points out, Shaw's claim that 'my procedure is to imagine characters and let them rip' is disingenuous; in *Widowers' Houses* and *Mrs Warren's Profession*, the plot was a given, and Shaw's procedure was not to destroy but to upend it.[8] The crucial discovery that Shaw made in his early plays was that by placing realistic political content into recognizable theatrical structures he could effect the reversals he sought by allowing his characters to stage a double revolt – against their allocated office in life (as wife, daughter, servant) but also their expected role in the plot (as hero, victim or villain). When Shaw's great argument scenes work, they do so because both things are happening – the story is forcing the character to question their office, while at the same time the character is challenging their role in the plot. This is what Shaw means when he writes in the Mrs Warren preface that 'the real secret of the cynicism and inhumanity of which shallower critics accuse me is the un-expectedness with which my characters behave like human beings, instead of conforming to the romantic logic of the stage'. So, in *Arms and the Man*, Raina's failure to sustain the role of sensitive heroine allows Bluntschli to prise her away from her office as dutiful fiancée. But something even more complicated and interesting occurs at the end of *Mrs Warren's Profession*.

As I pointed out above, the plot of *Mrs Warren's Profession* is effectively concluded by the end of Act III. Not only romantic but also structural logic demands therefore that something else will happen in Act IV, which can only be that Vivie Warren changes her mind and returns to her mother's corrupt embrace. The fact that she refuses to do so is a dramatic surprise as well as a psychological shock. Vivie Warren's refusal to accept the office of daughter to a woman she despises is underlined by the heroine's refusal to do what the structure expects of her, which is to turn again. It is the last act which makes *Mrs Warren's Profession* not only a great but also a complete political play.

Shaw's current charge against his polemical plays was that by dealing with the pressing political issues of his day, they inevitably date. By 1895, he resolved to write no more 'blue-book' plays on current social problems, arguing that in periods when political institutions lagged behind cultural changes, it was natural for the imagination of dramatists to be set in action on behalf of social reform, but that even then 'the greatest dramatists shew a preference for the non-political drama ... for subjects in which the conflict is between man and his apparently inevitable and eternal rather than his political temporal circumstances'.[9]

For me this dichotomy is false. In all three *Plays Unpleasant*, but particularly in *Mrs Warren's Profession*, Shaw wrote of the conflict between youthful ideals and economic realities, the drawbacks of promiscuity and the perils of matrimony, the duties of women to others and themselves, the necessity for and the costs of revolt. What could be more eternal than that?

Notes

1. Michael Holroyd, *Bernard Shaw: The Search for Love*, p283.
2. Quoted in Margery M. Morgan, *The Shavian Playground* (1972), p37.
3. Having finally abolished stage censorship in 1968, we can feel agreeably superior to the censors on both sides of the Atlantic from the turn of the last century. But the device used by the Kansas City authorities was the same as that used by Mary Whitehouse to prosecute Howard Brenton's *The Romans in Britain* in 1981, a campaign supported by the then leader of – as it happens – the Greater London Council. And as I write, the Mayor of New York is threatening to withdraw funds from an art gallery presenting the British exhibition *Sensation*, and the state of Kansas has removed the Darwinian theory of evolution from the state education curriculum.
4. Quoted in Eric Bentley, 'The Making of a Dramatist', in R. J. Kaufmann (ed.), *G. B. Shaw: A Collection of Critical Essays* (1965), p57.
5. Shaw was not alone in over-estimating the power of the silent actor: directing one of his own plays, Granville Barker advised an actress that 'From the moment you come in you must make the audience understand that you live in a small town in the provinces and visit a great deal with the local clergy; you make slippers for the curate and go to dreary tea-parties'. Her one line in the scene was 'How do you do'. (Michael Holroyd, *Bernard Shaw: The Pursuit of Power*, p151.)
6. G. K. Chesterton, *George Bernard Shaw* (1909), p138.

7. Bertolt Brecht, 'Ovation for Shaw', in Kaufmann, op cit., p18.
8. Bentley in Kaufmann, op cit., p60–61.
9. Quoted in Holroyd: *The Search for Love*, op cit., p340.

PLAYS UNPLEASANT

Contents

PREFACE: *Mainly About Myself*   7

WIDOWERS' HOUSES: *A Play*   29

THE PHILANDERER: *A Topical Comedy*   97
   Prefatory Note   98

MRS WARREN'S PROFESSION: *A Play*   179
   Preface   181

Mainly About Myself

THERE is an old saying that if a man has not fallen in love before forty, he had better not fall in love after. I long ago perceived that this rule applied to many other matters as well: for example, to the writing of plays; and I made a rough memorandum for my own guidance that unless I could produce at least half a dozen plays before I was forty, I had better let playwriting alone. It was not so easy to comply with this provision as might be supposed. Not that I lacked the dramatist's gift. As far as that is concerned, I have encountered no limit but my own laziness to my power of conjuring up imaginary people in imaginary places, and finding pretexts for theatrical scenes between them. But to obtain a livelihood by this insane gift, I must have conjured so as to interest not only my own imagination, but that of at least some seventy or a hundred thousand contemporary London playgoers. To fulfil this condition was hopelessly out of my power. I had no taste for what is called popular art, no respect for popular morality, no belief in popular religion, no admiration for popular heroics. As an Irishman I could pretend to patriotism neither for the country I had abandoned nor the country that had ruined it. As a humane person I detested violence and slaughter, whether in war, sport, or the butcher's yard. I was a Socialist, detesting our anarchical scramble for money, and believing in equality as the only possible permanent basis of social organisation, discipline, subordination, good manners, and selection of fit persons for high functions. Fashionable life, open on indulgent terms to unencumbered 'brilliant' persons, I could not endure, even if I had not feared its demoralizing effect on a character which required looking after as much as my own. I was neither a sceptic nor a cynic in these matters: I simply understood life differently from the average respectable man; and as I certainly enjoyed myself more – mostly in ways which would have made him unbearably miserable – I was not splenetic over our variance.

Judge then, how impossible it was for me to write fiction that should delight the public. In my nonage I had tried to obtain a foothold in literature by writing novels, and had actually produced five long works in that form without getting further than an encouraging compliment or two from the most dignified of the London and American publishers, who unanimously declined to venture their capital upon me. Now it is clear that a novel cannot be too bad to be worth publishing, provided it is a novel at all, and not merely an ineptitude. I was not convinced that the publishers' view was commercially sound until I got a clue to my real condition from a friend of mine, a physician who had devoted himself specially to ophthalmic surgery. He tested my eyesight one evening, and informed me that it was quite uninteresting to him because it was normal. I naturally took this to mean that it was like everybody else's; but he rejected this construction as paradoxical, and hastened to explain to me that I was an exceptional and highly fortunate person optically, normal sight conferring the power of seeing things accurately, and being enjoyed by only about ten per cent of the population, the remaining ninety per cent being abnormal. I immediately perceived the explanation of my want of success in fiction. My mind's eye, like my body's, was 'normal': it saw things differently from other people's eyes, and saw them better.

This revelation produced a considerable effect on me. At first it struck me that I might live by selling my works to the ten per cent who were like myself; but a moment's reflection shewed me that these must all be as penniless as I, and that we could not live by taking in oneanother's literary washing. How to earn daily bread by my pen was then the problem. Had I been a practical commonsense moneyloving Englishman, the matter would have been easy enough: I should have put on a pair of abnormal spectacles and aberred my vision to the liking of the ninety per cent of potential book-buyers. But I was so prodigiously self-satisfied with my superiority, so flattered by my abnormal normality, that the resource of hypocrisy never occurred to me. Better see rightly on a pound a week than squint on a million. The question was, how to get the pound a week. The matter, once I gave up writing novels, was not so very difficult. Every despot must have one disloyal subject to keep him sane. Even Louis the Eleventh had to tolerate his confessor, standing for the eternal against the temporal throne. Democracy has now handed the sceptre of the despot to the sovereign people; but they, too, must have their confessor, whom they call Critic. Criticism is not only medicinally salutary: it has positive popular attractions in its cruelty, its gladiatorship, and the gratification given to envy by its attacks on the great, and to enthusiasm by its praises. It may say things which many would like to say, but dare not, and indeed for want of skill could not even if they durst. Its iconoclasms, seditions, and blasphemies, if well turned, tickle those whom they shock; so that the critic adds the privileges of the court jester to those of the confessor. Garrick, had he called Dr Johnson Punch, would have spoken profoundly and wittily; whereas Dr Johnson, in hurling that epithet at him, was but picking up the cheapest sneer an actor is subject to.

It was as Punch, then, that I emerged from obscurity. All I had to do was to open my normal eyes, and with my utmost literary skill put the case exactly as it struck me, or describe the thing exactly as I saw it, to be applauded as the most humorously extravagant paradoxer in London. The only reproach with which I became familiar was the ever-lasting 'Why can you not be serious?' Soon my privileges were enormous and my wealth immense. I had a prominent place reserved for me on a prominent journal every week to say my say as if I were the most important person in the kingdom. My pleasing toil was to report upon all the works of fine art the capital of the world can attract to its exhibitions, its opera house, its concerts and its theatres. The classes eagerly read my essays: the masses patiently listened to my harangues. I enjoyed the immunities of impecuniosity with the opportunities of a millionaire. If ever there was a man without a grievance, I was that man.

But alas! the world grew younger as I grew older: its vision cleared as mine dimmed: it began to read with the naked eye the writing on the wall which now began to remind me that the age of spectacles was at hand. My opportunities were still there: nay, they multiplied tenfold; but the strength and youth to cope with them began to fail, and to need eking out with the shifty cunning of experience. I had to shirk the platform; to economize my health; even to take holidays. In my weekly columns, which I once filled full from a magic well that never ran dry or lost its sparkle provided I pumped hard enough, I began to repeat myself; to fall into a style which, to my great peril, was recognized as at least partly serious; to find the pump tiring me and the water lower in the well; and, worst symptom of all, to reflect with little tremors on the fact that my mystic wealth could not, like the money for which other men threw it away, be stored up against my second childhood. The younger generation, reared in an enlightenment unknown to my schooldays, came knocking at the door too: I glanced back at my old columns and realized that I had timidly botched at thirty what newer men do now with gay confidence in their cradles. I listened to their vigorous knocks with exultation for the race, with penurious alarm for my own old age. When I talked to this generation, it called me Mister, and, with its frank, charming humanity, respected me as one who had done good work in my time. A famous playwright wrote a long play to shew that people of my age were on the shelf; and I laughed at him with the wrong side of my mouth.

It was at this bitter moment that my fellow citizens, who had previously repudiated all my offers of political service, contemptuously allowed me to become a vestryman: *me*, the author of Widowers' Houses! Then, like any other harmless useful creature, I took the first step rearward. Up to that fateful day I had never penuriously spooned up the spilt drops of my well into bottles. Time enough for that when the well was empty. But now I listened to the voice of the publisher for the first time since he had refused to listen to mine. I turned over my articles again; but to serve up the weekly paper of five years ago as a novelty! no: I had not yet fallen so low, though I see that degradation looming before me as an agricultural laborer sees the workhouse. So I said 'I will begin with small sins; I will publish my plays.'

How! you will cry: plays! What plays?

Let me explain. One of the worst privations of life in London for persons of serious intellectual and artistic interests is the want of a suitable playhouse. I am fond of the play, and am, as intelligent readers of this preface will have observed, myself a bit of an actor. Consequently, when I found myself coming across projects of all sorts for the foundation of a theatre which should be to the newly gathered intellectual harvest of the nineteenth century what Shakespear's theatre was to the harvest of the Renascence, I was warmly interested. But it soon appeared that the languid demand of a small and uppish group for a form of entertainment which it had become thoroughly accustomed to do without, could never provide the intense energy necessary for the establishment of the New Theatre (we of course called everything advanced 'the New' at that time: see The Philanderer, the second play in this volume). That energy could be set free only by the genius of the actor and manager finding in the masterpieces of the New Drama its characteristic and necessary mode of expression, and revealing their fascination to the public. Clearly the way to begin was to pick up a masterpiece or two. Masterpieces, however, do not grow on the bushes. The New Theatre would never have come into existence but for the plays of Ibsen, just as the

Bayreuth Festival Playhouse would never have come into existence but for Wagner's Nibelungen tetralogy. Every attempt to extend the repertory proved that it is the drama that makes the theatre and not the theatre the drama. Not that this needed fresh proof, since the whole difficulty had arisen through the drama of the day being written for the theatres instead of from its own inner necessity. Still, a thing that nobody believes cannot be proved too often.

Ibsen, then, was the hero of the new departure. It was in 1889 that the first really effective blow was struck by the production of A Doll's House by Charles Charrington and Janet Achurch. Whilst they were taking that epoch making play round the world, Mr Grein followed up the campaign in London with his Independent Theatre. It got on its feet by producing Ibsen's Ghosts; but its search for unacted native dramatic masterpieces was so complete a failure that in the autumn of 1892 it had not yet produced a single original piece of any magnitude by an English author. In this humiliating national emergency, I proposed to Mr Grein that he should boldly announce a play by me. Being an extraordinarily sanguine and enterprising man, he took this step without hesitation. I then raked out, from my dustiest pile of discarded and rejected manuscripts, two acts of a play I had begun in 1885, shortly after the close of my novel writing period, in collaboration with my friend William Archer.

Archer has himself described how I proved the most impossible of collaborators. Laying violent hands on his thoroughly planned scheme for a sympathetically romantic 'well made play' of the Parisian type then in vogue, I perversely distorted it into a grotesquely realistic exposure of slum landlordism, municipal jobbery, and the pecuniary and matrimonial ties between them and the pleasant people with 'independent' incomes who imagine that such sordid matters do not touch their own lives. The result was revoltingly incongruous; for though I took my theme seriously enough, I did not then take the theatre quite seriously, even in taking it more seriously than it took itself. The farcical trivialities in which I followed the fashion of the times became silly and irritating beyond all endurance when intruded upon a subject of such depth, reality, and force as that into which I had plunged my drama. Archer, perceiving that I had played the fool both with his plan and my own theme, promptly disowned me; and the project, which neither of us had much at heart, was dropped, leaving me with two abortive acts of an unfinished and condemned play. Exhuming this as aforesaid seven years later, I saw that the very qualities which had made it impossible for ordinary commercial purposes in 1885 might be exactly those needed by the Independent Theatre in 1892. So I completed it by a third act; gave it the farfetched Scriptural title of Widowers' Houses; and handed it over to Mr Grein, who launched it at the public in the Royalty Theatre with all its original tomfooleries on its head. It made a sensation out of all proportion to its merits or even its demerits; and I at once became infamous as a playwright. The first performance was sufficiently exciting: the Socialists and Independents applauded me furiously on principle; the ordinary playgoing firstnighters hooted me frantically on the same ground; I, being at that time in some practice as what is impolitely called a mob orator, made a speech before the curtain; the newspapers discussed the play for a whole fortnight not only in the ordinary theatrical notices and criticisms, but in leading articles and letters; and finally the text of the play was published with an introduction by Mr Grein, an amusing account by Archer of the original collaboration, and a long preface and several elaborate controversial appendices in my most energetically egotistic fighting style. The volume, forming number one of the Independent Theatre series of plays, now extinct, is a curious relic of that nine days wonder; and as it contains the original text of the play with all its silly pleasantries, I can recommend it to collectors of quarto

Hamlets, and of all those scarce and superseded early editions which the unfortunate author would so gladly annihilate if he could.

I had not achieved a success; but I had provoked an uproar; and the sensation was so agreeable that I resolved to try again. In the following year, 1893, when the discussion about Ibsenism, 'the New Woman', and the like, was at its height, I wrote for the Independent Theatre the topical comedy called The Philanderer. But even before I finished it, it was apparent that its demands on the most expert and delicate sort of high comedy acting went beyond the resources then at the disposal of Mr Grein. I had written a part which nobody but Charles Wyndham could act, in a play which was impossible at his theatre: a feat comparable to the building of Robinson Crusoe's first boat. I immediately threw it aside, and, returning to the vein I had worked in Widowers' Houses, wrote a third play, Mrs Warren's Profession, on a social subject of tremendous force. That force justified itself in spite of the inexperience of the playwright. The play was everything that the Independent Theatre could desire: rather more, if anything, than it bargained for. But at this point I came upon the obstacle that makes dramatic authorship intolerable in England to writers accustomed to the freedom of the Press. I mean, of course, the Censorship.

In 1737, Henry Fielding, the greatest practising dramatist, with the single exception of Shakespear, produced by England between the Middle Ages and the nineteenth century, devoted his genius to the task of exposing and destroying parliamentary corruption, then at its height. Walpole, unable to govern without corruption, promptly gagged the stage by a censorship which is in full force at the present moment. Fielding, driven out of the trade of Molière and Aristophanes, took to that of Cervantes; and since then the English novel has been one of the glories of literature, whilst the English drama has been its disgrace. The extinguisher which Walpole dropped on Fielding descends on me in the form of the Lord Chamberlain's Examiner of Plays, a gentleman who robs, insults and suppresses me as irresistibly as if he were the Tsar of Russia and I the meanest of his subjects. The robbery takes the form of making me pay him two guineas for reading every play of mine that exceeds one act in length. I do not want him to read it (at least officially; personally he is welcome) on the contrary, I strenuously resent that impertinence on his part. But I must submit in order to obtain from him an insolent and insufferable document, which I cannot read without boiling of the blood, certifying that in his opinion – *his* opinion! – my play 'does not in its general tendency contain anything immoral or otherwise improper for the stage,' and that the Lord Chamberlain therefore 'allows' its performance (confound his impudence!). In spite of this certificate he still retains his right, as an ordinary citizen, to prosecute me, or instigate some other citizen to prosecute me, for an outrage on public morals if he should change his mind later on. Besides, if he really protects the public against my immorality, why does not the public pay him for the service? The policeman does not look to the thief for his wages, but to the honest man whom he protects against the thief. And yet, if I refuse to pay, this tyrant can practically ruin any manager who produces my play in defiance of him. If, having been paid, he is afraid to license the play: that is, if he is more afraid of the clamor of the opponents of my opinions than of their supporters, then he can suppress it, and impose a mulct of £50 on everybody who takes part in a representation of it, from the callboy to the principal tragedian. And there is no getting rid of him. Since he lives, not at the expense of the taxpayer, but by blackmailing the author, no political party would gain ten votes by abolishing him. Private political influence cannot touch him; for such private influence, moving only at the promptings of individual benevolence to individuals, makes nice little places to jog nice little people into instead of doing away with them. Nay, I myself, though I know that the Examiner is necessarily an odious and mischievous official, and that if I were appointed to his post (which I shall probably apply for at the next vacancy) I could no more help being odious and mischievous than a ramrod could if it were stuck into the wheels of a steam engine, am loth to stir up the question lest the Press, having now lost all tradition of liberty, and being able to conceive no alternative to the Lord Chamberlain's Examiner than a Home Secretary's Examiner or some other sevenheaded devil to replace the oneheaded one, should make the remedy worse than the disease. Thus I cling to the Censorship as many Radicals cling to the House of Lords or the Throne, or as domineering women shun masterful men, and marry weak and amiable ones. Until the nation is prepared for Freedom of The Stage on the same terms as it now enjoys Freedom of The Press, by allowing the playwright and manager to perform anything they please and take the consequences before the ordinary law as authors and editors do, I shall cherish the Lord Chamberlain's Examiner as the apple of my eye. I once thought of organizing a Petition of Right from all the managers and authors to the Prime Minister; but as it was obvious that nine out of ten of these victims of oppression, far from daring to offend their despot, would promptly extol him as the most salutary of English institutions, and spread themselves with unctuous flattery on the perfectly irrelevant question of his estimable personal character, I abandoned the notion. What is more, many of them, in taking this safe course, would be pursuing a sound business policy, since the managers and authors to whom the existing system has brought success not only have no incentive to change it for another which would expose them to wider competition, but have for the most part the greatest dread of the 'New' ideas which the abolition of the Censorship would let loose on the stage. And so long live the Lord Chamberlain's Examiner!

In 1893 this post was occupied by a gentleman, now deceased, whose ideas had in the course of nature become quite obsolete. He was openly hostile to the New movement; and his evidence before the Select Committee of the House of Commons on Theatres and Places of Entertainment in 1892 (Blue Book No. 240, pp. 328–335) is probably the best compendium in existence of every fallacy that can make a Censor obnoxious. In dealing with him Mr Grein was at a heavy disadvantage. Without a license, Mrs Warren's Profession could only be performed in some building not a theatre, and therefore not subject to reprisals from the Lord Chamberlain. The audience would have to be invited as guests only; so that the support of the public paying money at the doors, a support with which the Independent Theatre could not afford to dispense, was out of the question. To apply for a license was to court a practically certain refusal, entailing the £50 penalty on all concerned in any subsequent performance whatever. The deadlock was complete. The play was ready; the Independent Theatre was ready; and the case was ready; but the mere existence of the Censorship, without any action or knowledge of the play on its part, was sufficient to paralyze all these forces. So I threw Mrs Warren's Profession aside too, and, like another Fielding, closed my career as playwright in ordinary to the Independent Theatre.

Fortunately, though the Stage is bond, the Press is free. And even if the Stage was freed, none the less would it be necessary to publish plays as well as perform them. Had the two performances of Widowers' Houses achieved by Mr Grein been multiplied by fifty, it would still have remained unknown to those who either dwell out of reach of a theatre, or, as a matter of habit, prejudice, comfort, health or age, abstain altogether from playgoing. Many people who read with delight all the classic dramatists, from Eschylus to Ibsen, only go to the theatre on the rare occasions when they are offered a play by an author whose work they have already learnt to value as literature, or a performance by an actor of the first rank. Even our habitual playgoers have no true habit of playgoing. If on any night at the busiest part of the theatrical season in London, the audiences were cordoned by the police and examined individually as to their views on the subject, there would probably not be a single house-owning native among them who would not conceive a visit to the theatre, or indeed to any public assembly, artistic or political, as an exceptional way of spending an evening, the normal English way being to sit in separate families in separate houses, each person silently occupied with a book, a paper, or a game of halma, cut off equally from the blessings of society and solitude. You may make the acquaintance of a thousand streets of middle-class English families without coming on a trace of any consciousness of citizenship, or any artistic cultivation of the senses. The condition of the men is bad enough, in spite of their daily escape into the city, because they carry the exclusive and unsocial habits of 'the home' with them into the wider world of their business. Amiable and companionable enough by nature, they are, by home training, so incredibly ill-mannered, that not even their interest as men of business in welcoming a possible customer in every inquirer can correct their habit of treating everybody who has not been 'introduced' as a stranger and intruder. The women, who have not even the city to educate them, are much worse: they are positively unfit for civilized intercourse: graceless, ignorant, narrow-minded to a quite appalling degree. In public places these homebred people cannot be taught to understand that the right they are themselves exercising is a common right. Whether they are in a second-class railway carriage or in a church, they receive every additional fellow-passenger or worshipper as a Chinaman receives the 'foreign devil' who has forced him to open his ports.

In proportion as this horrible domestic institution is broken up by the active social circulation of the upper classes in their own orbit, or its stagnant isolation made impossible by the conditions of working class life, manners improve enormously. In the middle classes themselves the revolt of a single clever daughter (nobody has yet done justice to the modern clever Englishwoman's loathing of the very word Home), and her insistence on qualifying herself for an independent working life, humanizes her whole family in an astonishingly short time; and such communal enjoyments as a visit to the suburban theatre once a week, or to the Monday Popular Concerts, or both, softens the worst symptoms of its unsociableness. But none of these breaches in the English survival of the hareem can be made without a cannonade of books and pianoforte music. The books and music cannot be kept out, because they alone can make the hideous boredom of the hearth bearable. If its victims may not live real lives, they may at least read about imaginary ones, and perhaps learn from them to doubt whether a class that not only submits to home life, but actually boasts about it, is really a class worth belonging to. For the sake of the unhappy prisoners of the home, then, let my plays be printed as well as acted.

But the dramatic author has reasons for publishing his plays which would hold good even if English families went to the theatre as regularly as they take in the newspaper. A perfectly adequate and successful stage representation of a play requires a combination of circumstances so extraordinarily fortunate that I doubt whether it has ever occurred in the history of the world. Take the case of the most successful English dramatist of the first rank: Shakespear. Although he wrote three centuries ago, he still holds his own so well that it is not impossible to meet old playgoers who have witnessed public performances of more than thirty out of his thirty-seven reputed plays, a dozen of them fairly often and half a dozen over and over again. I myself, though I have by no means availed myself of all my opportunities, have seen twenty-three of his plays publicly acted. But if I had not read them as well, my impression of them would be not merely incomplete, but violently distorted and falsified. It is only within the last few years that some of our younger actor-managers have been struck with the idea, quite novel in their profession, of performing Shakespear's plays as he wrote them, instead of using them as a cuckoo uses a sparrow's nest. In spite of the success of these experiments, the stage is still dominated by Garrick's conviction that the manager and actor must adapt Shakespear's plays to the modern stage by a process which no doubt presents itself to the adapter's mind as one of masterly amelioration, but which must necessarily be mainly one of debasement and mutilation whenever, as occasionally happens, the adapter is inferior to the author. The living author can protect himself against this extremity of misrepresentation; but the more unquestioned his authority is on the stage, and the more friendly and willing the co-operation of the manager and the company, the more completely does he get convinced of the impossibility of achieving an authentic representation of his piece as well as an effective and successful one. It is quite possible for a piece to enjoy the most sensational success on the basis of a complete misunderstanding of its philosophy; indeed, it is not too much to say that it is only by a capacity for succeeding in spite of its philosophy that a dramatic work of serious poetic import can become popular. In the case of the first part of Goethe's Faust we have this frankly avowed by the extraction from the great original of popular entertainments like Gounod's opera or the Lyceum version, in which poetry and philosophy are replaced by romance, which is the recognized spurious substitute for both and is destructive of them. Not even when a drama is performed without omission or alteration by actors who are enthusiastic disciples of the author does it escape transfiguration. We have lately seen some remarkably sympathetic stage interpretations of poetic drama, from the experiments of Charles Charrington with Ibsen and of Lugné Po with Maeterlinck,

under comparatively inexpensive conditions, to those of the
Wagner Festival Playhouse at Bayreuth on the costliest
scale; and readers of Ibsen and Maeterlinck, and pianoforte
students of Wagner are rightly warned that they cannot fully
appreciate the force of a dramatic masterpiece without the
aid of the theatre. But I have never found an acquaintance
with a dramatist founded on the theatre alone, or with a
composer founded on the concert room alone, a really intimate and accurate one. The very originality and genius of
the performers conflicts with the originality and genius of
the author. Imagine Shakespear confronted with Sir Henry
Irving at a rehearsal of The Merchant of Venice, or Sheridan
with Miss Ada Rehan at one of The School for Scandal. It is
easy to imagine the speeches that might pass on such occasions. For example 'As I look at your playing, Sir Henry,
I seem to see Israel mourning the Captivity and crying,
"How long, O Lord, how long?" It is a little startling to see
Shylock's strong feelings operating through a romantic intellect instead of through an entirely commercial one; but
pray dont alter your conception, which will be abundantly
profitable to us both.' Or 'My dear Miss Rehan: let me congratulate you on a piece of tragic acting which has made me
ashamed of the triviality of my play, and obliterated Sir
Peter Teazle from my consciousness, though I meant him to
be the hero of the scene. I foresee an enormous success for
both of us in this fortunate misrepresentation of my intention.' Even if the author had nothing to gain pecuniarily by
conniving at the glorification of his play by the performer,
the actor's excess of power would still carry its own authority
and win the sympathy of the author's histrionic instinct,
unless he were a Realist of fanatical integrity. And that
would not save him either; for his attempts to make powerful
actors do less than their utmost would be as futile as his
attempts to make feeble ones do more.

In short, the fact that a skilfully written play is infinitely
more adaptable to all sorts of acting than available acting is

to all sorts of plays (the actual conditions thus exactly reversing the desirable ones) finally drives the author to the conclusion that his own view of his work can only be conveyed by himself. And since he could not act the play single-handed even if he were a trained actor, he must fall back on his powers of literary expression, as other poets and fictionists do. So far, this has hardly been seriously attempted by dramatists. Of Shakespear's plays we have not even complete prompt copies: the folio gives us hardly anything but the bare lines. What would we not give for the copy of Hamlet used by Shakespear at rehearsal, with the original stage business scrawled by the prompter's pencil? And if we had in addition the descriptive directions which the author gave on the stage: above all, the character sketches, however brief, by which he tried to convey to the actor the sort of person he meant him to incarnate, what a light they would shed, not only on the play, but on the history of the sixteenth century! Well, we should have had all this and much more if Shakespear, instead of merely writing out his lines, had prepared the plays for publication in competition with fiction as elaborate as that of Meredith. It is for want of this elaboration that Shakespear, unsurpassed as poet, storyteller, character draughtsman, humorist, and rhetorician, has left us no intellectually coherent drama, and could not afford to pursue a genuinely scientific method in his studies of character and society, though in such unpopular plays as All's Well, Measure for Measure, and Troilus and Cressida, we find him ready and willing to start at the twentieth century if the seventeenth would only let him.

Such literary treatment is much more needed by modern plays than by Shakespear's, because in his time the acting of plays was very imperfectly differentiated from the declamation of verses; and descriptive or narrative recitation did what is now done by scenery, furniture, and stage business. Anyone reading the mere dialogue of an Elizabethan play understands all but half a dozen unimportant lines of it without difficulty; whilst many modern plays, highly successful on the stage, are not merely unreadable but positively unintelligible without visible stage business. Recitation on a platform, with the spectators seated round the reciter in the Elizabethan fashion, would reduce them to absurdity. The extreme instance is pure pantomime, like L'Enfant Prodigue, in which the dialogue, though it exists, is not spoken. If a dramatic author were to publish a pantomime, it is clear that he could make it intelligible to a reader only by giving him the words which the pantomimist is supposed to be uttering. Now it is not a whit less impossible to make a modern practical stage play intelligible to an audience by dialogue alone, than to make a pantomime intelligible to a reader without it.

Obvious as this is, the presentation of plays through the literary medium has not yet become an art; and the result is that it is very difficult to induce the English public to buy and read plays. Indeed, why should they, when they find nothing in them except the bare words, with a few carpenter's and costumier's directions as to the heroine's father having a grey beard, and the drawing room having three doors on the right, two doors and an entrance through the conservatory on the left, and a French window in the middle? It is astonishing to me that Ibsen, devoting two years to the production of a three-act play, the extraordinary quality of which depends on a mastery of character and situation which can only be achieved by working out a good deal of the family and personal history of the individuals represented, should nevertheless give the reading public very little more than the technical memorandum required by the carpenter, the electrician, and the prompter. Who will deny that the resultant occasional mysteriousness of effect, enchanting though it may be, is produced at the cost of intellectual obscurity? Ibsen, interrogated as to his meaning, replied 'What I have said, I have said.' Precisely; but the point is that what he hasnt said, he hasnt said. There are perhaps people (though I doubt it, not being one of them myself) to whom Ibsen's plays, as they stand, speak sufficiently for themselves. There are certainly others who could not understand them on any terms. Granting that on both these classes further explanations would be thrown away, is nothing to be done for the vast majority to whom a word of explanation makes all the difference?

Finally, may I put in a plea for the actors themselves? Born actors have a susceptibility to dramatic emotion which enables them to seize the moods of their parts intuitively. But to expect them to be intuitive as to intellectual meaning and circumstantial conditions as well, is to demand powers of divination from them: one might as well expect the Astronomer Royal to tell the time in a catacomb. And yet the actor generally finds his part full of emotional directions which he could supply as well or better than the author, whilst he is left quite in the dark as to the political or religious conditions under which the character he impersonates is supposed to be acting. Definite conceptions of these are always implicit in the best plays, and are often the key to their appropriate rendering; but most actors are so accustomed to do without them that they would object to being troubled with them, although it is only by such educative trouble that an actor's profession can place him on the level of the lawyer, the physician, the churchman, and the statesman. Even as it is, Shylock as a Jew and usurer, Othello as a Moor and a soldier, Caesar, Cleopatra and Anthony as figures in defined political circumstances, are enormously more real to the actor than the countless heroes as to whom nothing is ever known except that they wear nice clothes, love the heroine, baffle the villain, and live happily ever after.

The case, then, is overwhelming not only for printing and publishing the dialogue of plays, but for a serious effort to convey their full content to the reader. This means the institution of a new art; and I daresay that before these two volumes are ten years old, the bald attempt they make at it will be left far behind, and that the customary brief and unreadable scene specification at the head of an act will have expanded into a chapter, or even a series of chapters. No doubt one result of this will be the production, under cover of the above arguments, of works of a mixture of kinds, part narrative, part homily, part description, part dialogue, and (possibly) part drama; works that could be read, but not acted. I have no objection to such works; but my own aim has been that of the practical dramatist: if anything my eye has been too much on the stage. At all events, I have tried to put down nothing that is irrelevant to the actor's performance, and, through it, to the audience's comprehension of the play. I have of course been compelled to omit many things that a stage representation could convey, simply because the art of letters, though highly developed grammatically, is still in its infancy as a technical speech notation: for example, there are fifty ways of saying Yes, and five hundred of saying No, but only one way of writing them down. Even the use of spaced letters instead of italics for underlining, though familiar to foreign readers, will have to be learned by the English public before it becomes effective. But if my readers do their fair share of the work, I daresay they will understand nearly as much of the plays as I do myself.

Finally, a word as to why I have labelled the three plays in this volume Unpleasant. The reason is pretty obvious: their dramatic power is used to force the spectator to face unpleasant facts. No doubt all plays which deal sincerely with humanity must wound the monstrous conceit which it is the business of romance to flatter. But here we are confronted, not only with the comedy and tragedy of individual character and destiny, but with those social horrors which arise from the fact that the average homebred Englishman, however honorable and goodnatured he may be in his private capacity, is, as a citizen, a wretched creature who, whilst clamoring for a gratuitous millennium, will shut his eyes to the most villainous abuses if the remedy threatens to add another penny in the pound to the rates and taxes which he has to be half cheated, half coerced into paying. In Widowers' Houses I have shewn middle-class respectability and younger son gentility fattening on the poverty of the slum as flies fatten on filth. That is not a pleasant theme.

In The Philanderer I have shewn the grotesque sexual compacts made between men and women under marriage laws which represent to some of us a political necessity (especially for other people), to some a divine ordinance, to some a romantic ideal, to some a domestic profession for women, and to some that worst of blundering abominations, an institution which society has outgrown but not modified, and which 'advanced' individuals are therefore forced to evade. The scene with which The Philanderer opens, the atmosphere in which it proceeds, and the marriage with which it ends, are, for the intellectually and artistically conscious classes in modern society, typical; and it will hardly be denied, I think, that they are unpleasant.

In Mrs Warren's Profession I have gone straight at the fact that, as Mrs Warren puts it, 'the only way for a woman to provide for herself decently is for her to be good to some man that can afford to be good to her.' There are certain questions on which I am, like most Socialists, an extreme Individualist. I believe that any society which desires to found itself on a high standard of integrity of character in its units should organize itself in such a fashion as to make it possible for all men and all women to maintain themselves in reasonable comfort by their industry without selling their affections and their convictions. At present we not only condemn women as a sex to attach themselves to breadwinners, licitly or illicitly, on pain of heavy privation and disadvantage; but we have great prostitute classes of men: for instance, the playwrights and journalists, to whom I myself belong, not to mention the legions of lawyers, doctors, clergymen, and platform politicians who are daily using their highest faculties to belie their real sentiments; a sin compared to which that of a woman who sells the use of her person for a few hours is too venial to be worth mentioning; for rich men without conviction are more dangerous in modern society than poor women without chastity. Hardly a pleasant subject, this!

I must, however, warn my readers that my attacks are directed against themselves, not against my stage figures. They cannot too thoroughly understand that the guilt of defective social organization does not lie alone on the people who actually work the commercial makeshifts which the defects make inevitable, and who often, like Sartorius and Mrs Warren, display valuable executive capacities and even high moral virtues in their administration, but with the whole body of citizens whose public opinion, public action, and public contribution as ratepayers, alone can replace Sartorius's slums with decent dwellings, Charteris's intrigues with reasonable marriage contracts, and Mrs Warren's profession with honorable industries guarded by a humane industrial code and a 'moral minimum' wage.

How I came, later on, to write plays which, dealing less with the crimes of society, and more with its romantic follies and with the struggles of individuals against those follies, may be called, by contrast, Pleasant, is a story which I shall tell on resuming this discourse for the edification of the readers of the second volume.

1898

WIDOWERS' HOUSES
A Play

WIDOWERS' HOUSES

ACT I

In the garden restaurant of a hotel at Remagen on the Rhine, on a fine afternoon in August in the eighteen-eighties. Looking down the Rhine towards Bonn, the gate leading from the garden to the riverside is seen on the right. The hotel is on the left. It has a wooden annexe with an entrance marked Table d'Hôte. A waiter is in attendance.

A couple of English tourists come out of the hotel. The younger, Dr Harry Trench, is about 24, stoutly built, thick in the neck, close-cropped and black in the hair, with undignified medical-student manners, frank, hasty, rather boyish. The other, Mr William de Burgh Cokane, is probably over 40, possibly 50: an ill-nourished, scanty-haired gentleman, with affected manners: fidgety, touchy, and constitutionally ridiculous in uncompassionate eyes.

COKANE [*on the threshold of the hotel, calling peremptorily to the waiter*] Two beers for us out here. [*The waiter goes for the beer. Cokane comes into the garden*]. We have secured the room with the best view in the hotel, Harry, thanks to my tact. We'll leave in the morning, and do Mainz and Frankfurt. There is a very graceful female statue in the private house of a nobleman in Frankfurt. Also a zoo. Next day, Nuremberg! finest collection of instruments of torture in the world.

TRENCH. All right. You look out the trains, will you? [*He takes a Continental Bradshaw from his pocket, and tosses it on one of the tables*].

COKANE [*baulking himself in the act of sitting down*] Pah! the seat is all dusty. These foreigners are deplorably unclean in their habits.

TRENCH [*buoyantly*] Never mind: it dont matter, old chappie. Buck up, Billy, buck up. Enjoy yourself. [*He throws Cokane*

*into the chair, and sits down opposite him, taking out his pipe, and
singing noisily]*

> Pour out the Rhine wine: let it flow
> Like a free and bounding river –

COKANE [*scandalized*] In the name of common decency,
Harry, will you remember that you are a Gentleman, and
not a coster on Hampstead Heath on Bank Holiday?
Would you dream of behaving like this in London?

TRENCH. Oh, rot! Ive come abroad to enjoy myself. So
would you if youd just passed an examination after four
years in the medical school and walking the hospital. [*He
again bursts into song*].

COKANE [*rising*] Trench: either you travel as a gentleman,
or you travel alone. This is what makes Englishmen unpopular on the Continent. It may not matter before the
natives; but the people who came on board the steamer at
Bonn are English. I have been uneasy all the afternoon
about what they must think of us. Look at our appearance.

TRENCH. Whats wrong with our appearance?

COKANE. Négligé, my dear fellow, négligé. On the steamboat a little négligé was quite en règle; but here, in this
hotel, some of them are sure to dress for dinner; and you
have nothing but that Norfolk jacket. How are they to
know that you are well connected if you do not shew it by
your costume?

TRENCH. Pooh! the steamboat people were the scum of the
earth: Americans and all sorts. They may go hang themselves, Billy. I shall not bother about them. [*He strikes a
match, and proceeds to light his pipe*].

COKANE. Do drop calling me Billy in public, Trench. My
name is Cokane. I am sure they were persons of consequence: you were struck with the distinguished appearance of the father yourself.

TRENCH [*sobered at once*] What! those people? [*He blows out
the match and puts up his pipe*].

COKANE [*following up his advantage triumphantly*] Here, Harry, here: at this hotel. I recognised the father's umbrella in the hall.

TRENCH [*with a touch of genuine shame*] I suppose I ought to have brought a change. But a lot of luggage is such a nuisance; and [*rising abruptly*] at all events we can go and have a wash. [*He turns to go into the hotel, but stops in consternation, seeing some people coming up to the riverside gate*]. Oh, I say! Here they are.

A lady and gentleman, followed by a porter with some light parcels, not luggage, but shop purchases, come into the garden. They are apparently father and daughter. The gentleman is 50, tall, well preserved, and of upright carriage. His incisive, domineering utterance and imposing style, with his strong aquiline nose and resolute clean-shaven mouth, give him an air of importance. He wears a light grey frock-coat with silk linings, a white hat, and a field-glass slung in a new leather case. A self-made man, formidable to servants, not easily accessible to anyone. His daughter is a well-dressed, well-fed, good-looking, strongminded young woman, presentably ladylike, but still her father's daughter. Nevertheless fresh and attractive, and none the worse for being vital and energetic rather than delicate and refined.

COKANE [*quickly taking the arm of Trench, who is staring as if transfixed*] Recollect yourself, Harry: presence of mind, presence of mind! [*He strolls with him towards the hotel. The waiter comes out with the beer*]. Kellner: ceci-là est notre table. Est-ce que vous comprenez Français?

WAITER. Yes, zare. Oll right, zare.

THE GENTLEMAN [*to his porter*] Place those things on that table. [*The porter does not understand*].

WAITER [*interposing*] Zese zhentellmenn are using zis table, zare. Vould you mind –

THE GENTLEMAN [*severely*] You should have told me so before. [*To Cokane, with fierce condescension*] I regret the mistake, sir.

COKANE. Dont mention it, my dear sir: dont mention it. Retain the place, I beg.

THE GENTLEMAN [*coldly turning his back on him*] Thank you. [*To the porter*] Place them on that table. [*The porter makes no movement until the gentleman points to the parcels and peremptorily raps on another table, nearer the gate*].

PORTER. Ja wohl, gnäd'g' Herr. [*He puts down the parcels*].

THE GENTLEMAN [*taking out a handful of money*] Waiter.

WAITER [*awestruck*] Yes, zare.

THE GENTLEMAN. Tea. For two. Out here.

WAITER. Yes, zare. [*He goes into the hotel*].

> *The gentleman selects a small coin from his handful of money, and gives it to the porter, who receives it with a submissive touch to his cap, and goes out, not daring to speak. His daughter sits down and opens a parcel of photographs. The gentleman takes out a Baedeker; places a chair for himself; and then, before sitting down, looks truculently at Cokane, as if waiting for him to take himself off. Cokane, not at all abashed, resumes his place at the other table with an air of modest good breeding, and calls to Trench, who is prowling irresolutely in the background.*

COKANE. Trench, my dear fellow: your beer is waiting for you. [*He drinks*].

TRENCH [*glad of the excuse to come back to his chair*] Thank you, Cokane. [*He also drinks*].

COKANE. By the way, Harry, I have often meant to ask you: is Lady Roxdale your mother's sister or your father's?

> *This shot tells immediately. The gentleman is perceptibly interested.*

TRENCH. My mother's, of course. What put that into your head?

COKANE. Nothing. I was just thinking – hm! She will expect you to marry, Harry: a doctor ought to marry.

TRENCH. What has she got to do with it?

COKANE. A great deal, dear boy. She looks forward to floating your wife in society in London.

TRENCH. What rot!

COKANE. Ah, you are young, dear boy: you dont know the importance of these things; apparently idle ceremonial trifles, really the springs and wheels of a great aristocratic system. [*The waiter comes back with the tea things, which he brings to the gentleman's table. Cokane rises and addresses the gentleman*]. My dear sir, excuse my addressing you; but I cannot help feeling that you prefer this table, and that we are in your way.

THE GENTLEMAN [*graciously*] Thank you. Blanche: this gentleman very kindly offers us his table, if you would prefer it.

BLANCHE. Oh, thanks: it makes no difference.

THE GENTLEMAN [*to Cokane*] We are fellow travellers, I believe, sir.

COKANE. Fellow travellers and fellow countrymen. Ah, we rarely feel the charm of our own tongue until it reaches our ears under a foreign sky. You have no doubt noticed that?

THE GENTLEMAN [*a little puzzled*] Hm! From a romantic point of view, possibly, very possibly. As a matter of fact, the sound of English makes me feel at home; and I dislike feeling at home when I am abroad. It is not precisely what one goes to the expense for. [*He looks at Trench*]. I think this gentleman travelled with us also.

COKANE [*acting as master of the ceremonies*] My valued friend, Dr Trench. [*The gentleman and Trench rise*]. Trench, my dear fellow, allow me to introduce you to – er – ? [*He looks inquiringly at the gentleman, waiting for the name*].

THE GENTLEMAN. Permit me to shake your hand, Dr Trench. My name is Sartorius; and I have the honor of being known to Lady Roxdale, who is, I believe, a near relative of yours. Blanche. [*She looks up*]. Dr Trench. [*They bow*].

TRENCH. Perhaps I should introduce my friend Cokane to you, Mr Sartorius: Mr William de Burgh Cokane. [*Cokane*

*makes an elaborate bow. Sartorius accepts it with dignity. The
waiter meanwhile returns with the tea things*].

SARTORIUS [*to the waiter*] Two more cups.

WAITER. Yes, zare. [*He goes into the hotel*].

BLANCHE. Do you take sugar, Mr Cokane?

COKANE. Thank you. [*To Sartorius*] This is really too kind.
Harry: bring your chair round.

SARTORIUS. You are very welcome. [*Trench brings his chair
to the tea table; and they all sit round. The waiter returns with
two more cups*].

WAITER. Table d'hôte at alf pass zeex, zhentellmenn.
Somesing else now, zare?

SARTORIUS. No. You can go. [*The waiter goes*].

COKANE [*very agreeably*] Do you contemplate a long stay
here, Miss Sartorius?

BLANCHE. We were thinking of going on to Rolandseck. Is
it as nice as this place?

COKANE. Harry: the Baedeker. [*Trench produces it from the
other pocket*]. Thank you. [*He consults the index for Rolandseck*].

BLANCHE. Sugar, Dr Trench?

TRENCH. Thanks. [*She hands him the cup, and looks meaningly
at him for an instant. He looks down hastily, and glances apprehensively at Sartorius, who is preoccupied with the bread and
butter*].

COKANE. Rolandseck appears to be an extremely interesting place. [*He reads*] 'It is one of the most beautiful and
frequented spots on the river, and is surrounded with
numerous villas and pleasant gardens, chiefly belonging to
wealthy merchants from the Lower Rhine, and extending
along the wooded slopes at the back of the village.'

BLANCHE. That sounds civilized and comfortable. I vote
we go there.

SARTORIUS. Quite like our place at Surbiton, my dear.

BLANCHE. Quite.

COKANE. You have a place down the river? Ah, I envy you.

SARTORIUS. No: I have merely taken a furnished villa at Surbiton for the summer. I live in Bedford Square. I am a vestryman, and must reside in the parish.

BLANCHE. Another cup, Mr Cokane?

COKANE. Thank you, no. [*To Sartorius*] I presume you have been round this little place. Not much to see here, except the Apollinaris Church.

SARTORIUS [*scandalized*] The what!

COKANE. The Apollinaris Church.

SARTORIUS. A strange name to give a church. Very continental, I must say.

COKANE. Ah, yes, yes, yes. That is where our neighbors fall short sometimes, Mr Sartorius. Taste! taste is what they occasionally fail in. But in this instance they are not to blame. The water is called after the church, not the church after the water.

SARTORIUS [*as if this were an extenuating circumstance, but not a complete excuse*] I am glad to hear it. Is the church a celebrated one?

COKANE. Baedeker stars it.

SARTORIUS [*respectfully*] Oh, in that case I should like to see it.

COKANE [*reading*] '– erected in 1839 by Zwirner, the late eminent architect of the cathedral of Cologne, at the expense of Count Fürstenberg-Stammheim.'

SARTORIUS [*much impressed*] We must certainly see that, Mr Cokane. I had no idea that the architect of Cologne cathedral lived so recently.

BLANCHE. Dont let us bother about any more churches, papa: theyre all the same. I'm tired to death of them.

SARTORIUS. Well, my dear, if you think it sensible to take a long and expensive journey to see what there is to be seen, and then go away without seeing it –

BLANCHE. Not this afternoon, papa, please.

SARTORIUS. My dear: I should like you to see everything. It is part of your education –

WIDOWERS' HOUSES

BLANCHE [*rising, with a petulant sigh*] Oh, my education!
Very well, very well: I suppose I must go through with it.
Are you coming, Dr Trench? [*With a grimace*] I'm sure the
Johannis Church will be a treat for you.

COKANE [*laughing softly and archly*] Ah, excellent, excellent:
very good indeed. [*Seriously*] But do you know, Miss
Sartorius, there actually are Johannis churches here –
several of them – as well as Apollinaris ones?

SARTORIUS [*sententiously, taking out his field-glass and leading
the way to the gate*] There is many a true word spoken in
jest, Mr Cokane.

COKANE [*accompanying him*] How true! How true!

*They go out together, ruminating profoundly. Blanche makes no
movement to follow them. She watches until they are safely out of
sight, and then posts herself before Trench, looking at him with an
enigmatic smile, which he returns with a half sheepish, half
conceited grin.*

BLANCHE. Well! So you have done it at last.

TRENCH. Yes. At least Cokane's done it. I told you he'd
manage it. He's rather an ass in some ways; but he has
tremendous tact.

BLANCHE [*contemptuously*] Tact! Thats not tact: thats in-
quisitiveness. Inquisitive people always have a lot of
practice in getting into conversation with strangers. Why
didnt you speak to my father yourself on the boat? You
were ready enough to speak to me without any introduction.

TRENCH. I didnt particularly want to talk to him.

BLANCHE. It didnt occur to you, I suppose, that you put me
in a false position by that.

TRENCH. Oh, I dont see that, exactly. Besides, your father
isnt an easy man to tackle. Of course, now that I know
him, I see that he's pleasant enough; but then youve got
to know him first, havnt you?

BLANCHE [*impatiently*] Everybody is afraid of papa: I'm sure
I dont know why. [*She sits down again, pouting a little*].

38

TRENCH [*tenderly*] However, it's all right now: isnt it? [*He sits near her*].

BLANCHE [*sharply*] I dont know. How should I? You had no right to speak to me that day on board the steamer. You thought I was alone, because [*with false pathos*] I had no mother with me.

TRENCH [*protesting*] Oh, I say! Come! It was you who spoke to me. Of course I was only too glad of the chance; but on my word I shouldnt have moved an eyelid if you hadnt given me a lead.

BLANCHE. I only asked you the name of a castle. There was nothing unladylike in that.

TRENCH. Of course not. Why shouldnt you? [*With renewed tenderness*] But it's all right now: isnt it?

BLANCHE [*softly, looking subtly at him*] Is it?

TRENCH [*suddenly becoming shy*] I – I suppose so. By the way, what about the Apollinaris Church? Your father expects us to follow him, doesnt he?

BLANCHE [*with suppressed resentment*] Dont let me detain you if you wish to see it.

TRENCH. Wont you come?

BLANCHE. No. [*She turns her face away moodily*].

TRENCH [*alarmed*] I say: youre not offended, are you? [*She looks round at him for a moment with a reproachful film on her eyes*]. Blanche. [*She bristles instantly; overdoes it; and frightens him*]. I beg your pardon for calling you by your name; but I – er – [*She corrects her mistake by softening her expression eloquently. He responds with a gush*] You dont mind, do you? I felt sure you wouldnt, somehow. Well, look here. I have no idea how you will receive this: it must seem horribly abrupt; but the circumstances do not admit of – the fact is, my utter want of tact – [*he flounders more and more, unable to see that she can hardly contain her eagerness*]. Now, if it were Cokane –

BLANCHE [*impatiently*] Cokane!

TRENCH [*terrified*] No, not Cokane. Though I assure you I

was only going to say about him that –

BLANCHE. That he will be back presently with papa.

TRENCH [*stupidly*] Yes: they cant be very long now. I hope I'm not detaining you.

BLANCHE. I thought you were detaining me because you had something to say.

TRENCH [*totally unnerved*] Not at all. At least, nothing very particular. That is, I'm afraid you wouldnt think it very particular. Another time, perhaps –

BLANCHE. What other time? How do you know that we shall ever meet again? [*Desperately*] Tell me now. I want you to tell me now.

TRENCH. Well, I was thinking that if we could make up our minds to – or not to – at least – er – [*His nervousness deprives him of the power of speech*].

BLANCHE [*giving him up as hopeless*] I dont think theres much danger of your making up your mind, Dr Trench.

TRENCH [*stammering*] I only thought – [*He stops and looks at her piteously. She hesitates a moment, and then puts her hands into his with calculated impulsiveness. He snatches her into his arms with a cry of relief*]. Dear Blanche! I thought I should never have said it. I believe I should have stood stuttering here all day if you hadnt helped me out with it.

BLANCHE [*indignantly trying to break loose from him*] I didnt help you out with it.

TRENCH [*holding her*] I dont mean that you did it on purpose, of course. Only instinctively.

BLANCHE [*still a little anxious*] But you havnt said anything.

TRENCH. What more can I say than this? [*He kisses her again*].

BLANCHE [*overcome by the kiss, but holding on to her point*] But Harry –

TRENCH [*delighted at the name*] Yes.

BLANCHE. When shall we be married?

TRENCH. At the first church we meet: the Apollinaris Church, if you like.

BLANCHE. No, but seriously. This is serious, Harry: you mustnt joke about it.

TRENCH [*looking suddenly round to the riverside gate and quickly releasing her*] Sh! Here they are back again.

BLANCHE. Oh, d – [*The word is drowned by the clangor of a bell from within the hotel. The waiter appears on the steps, ringing it. Cokane and Sartorius are seen returning by the river gate*].

WAITER. Table d'hôte in dwendy minutes, ladies and zhentellmenn. [*He goes into the hotel*].

SARTORIUS [*gravely*] I intended you to accompany us, Blanche.

BLANCHE. Yes, papa. We were just about to start.

SARTORIUS. We are rather dusty: we must make ourselves presentable at the table d'hôte. I think you had better come in with me, my child. Come.

He offers Blanche his arm. The gravity of his manner overawes them all. Blanche silently takes his arm and goes into the hotel with him. Cokane, hardly less momentous than Sartorius himself, contemplates Trench with the severity of a judge.

COKANE [*with reprobation*] No, my dear boy. No, no. Never. I blush for you. I was never so ashamed in my life. You have been taking advantage of that unprotected girl.

TRENCH [*hotly*] Cokane!

COKANE [*inexorable*] Her father seems to be a perfect gentleman. I obtained the privilege of his acquaintance: I introduced you: I allowed him to believe that he might leave his daughter in your charge with absolute confidence. And what did I see on our return? what did her father see? Oh, Trench, Trench! No, my dear fellow, no, no. Bad taste, Harry, bad form!

TRENCH. Stuff! There was nothing to see.

COKANE. Nothing to see! She, a perfect lady, a person of the highest breeding, actually in your arms; and you say there was nothing to see! with a waiter there actually ringing a heavy bell to call attention to his presence! [*Lecturing him with redoubled severity*] Have you no principles,

Trench? Have you no religious convictions? Have you no acquaintance with the usages of society? You actually kissed –

TRENCH. You didnt see me kiss her.

COKANE. We not only saw but h e a r d it: the report positively reverberated down the Rhine. Dont condescend to subterfuge, Trench.

TRENCH. Nonsense, my dear Billy. You –

COKANE. There you go again. D o n t use that low abbreviation. How am I to preserve the respect of fellow travellers of position and wealth, if I am to be Billied at every turn? My name is William: William de Burgh Cokane.

TRENCH. Oh, bother! There: dont be offended, old chap. Whats the use of putting your back up at every trifle? It comes natural to me to call you Billy: it suits you, somehow.

COKANE [*mortified*] You have no delicacy of feeling, Trench: no tact. I never mention it to any one; but nothing, I am afraid, will ever make a true gentleman of you. [*Sartorius appears on the threshold of the hotel*]. Here is my friend Sartorius, coming, no doubt, to ask you for an explanation of your conduct. I really should not have been surprised to see him bring a horsewhip with him. I shall not intrude on the painful scene.

TRENCH. Dont go, confound it. I dont want to meet him alone just now.

COKANE [*shaking his head*] Delicacy, Harry, delicacy! Good taste! Savoir faire! [*He walks away. Trench tries to escape in the opposite direction by strolling off towards the garden entrance*].

SARTORIUS [*mesmerically*] Dr Trench.

TRENCH [*stopping and turning*] Oh, is that you, Mr Sartorius? How did you find the church?

Sartorius, without a word, points to a seat. Trench, half hypnotized by his own nervousness and the impressiveness of Sartorius, sits down helplessly.

SARTORIUS [*also seating himself*] You have been speaking to my daughter, Dr Trench.

42

TRENCH [*with an attempt at ease of manner*] Yes: we had a conversation – quite a chat, in fact – while you were at the church with Cokane. How did you get on with Cokane, Mr Sartorius? I always think he has such wonderful tact.

SARTORIUS [*ignoring the digression*] I have just had a word with my daughter, Dr Trench; and I find her under the impression that something has passed between you which it is my duty as a father – the father of a motherless girl – to inquire into at once. My daughter, perhaps foolishly, has taken you quite seriously; and –

TRENCH. But –

SARTORIUS. One moment, if you will be so good. I have been a young man myself: younger, perhaps, than you would suppose from my present appearance. I mean, of course, in character. If you were not serious –

TRENCH [*ingenuously*] But I was perfectly serious. I want to marry your daughter, Mr Sartorius. I hope you dont object.

SARTORIUS [*condescending to Trench's humility from the mere instinct to seize an advantage, and yet deferring to Lady Roxdale's relative*] So far, no. I may say that your proposal seems to be an honorable and straightforward one, and that it is very gratifying to me personally.

TRENCH [*agreeably surprised*] Then I suppose we may consider the affair as settled. It's really very good of you.

SARTORIUS. Gently, Dr Trench, gently. Such a transaction as this cannot be settled off-hand.

TRENCH. Not off-hand, no. There are settlements and things, of course. But it may be regarded as settled between ourselves, maynt it?

SARTORIUS. Hm! Have you nothing further to mention?

TRENCH. Only that – that – No: I dont know that I have, except that I love –

SARTORIUS [*interrupting*] Anything about your family, for example? You do not anticipate any objection on their part, do you?

TRENCH. Oh, they have nothing to do with it.

SARTORIUS [*warmly*] Excuse me, sir: they have a great deal to do with it. [*Trench is abashed*]. I am resolved that my daughter shall approach no circle in which she will not be received with the full consideration to which her education and her breeding [*here his self-control slips a little: and he repeats, as if Trench has contradicted him*] — I say, her breeding — entitle her.

TRENCH [*bewildered*] Of course not. But what makes you think my family wont like Blanche? Of course my father was a younger son; and Ive had to take to a profession and all that; so my people wont expect us to entertain them: theyll know we cant afford it. But theyll entertain us: they always ask me.

SARTORIUS. That wont do for me, sir. Families often think it due to themselves to turn their backs on newcomers whom they may not think quite good enough for them.

TRENCH. But I assure you my people arnt a bit snobbish. Blanche is a lady: thatll be good enough for them.

SARTORIUS [*moved*] I am glad you think so. [*He offers his hand. Trench, astonished, takes it*]. I think so myself. [*He presses Trench's hand gratefully and releases it*]. And now, Dr Trench, since you have acted handsomely, you shall have no cause to complain of me. There shall be no difficulty about money: you shall entertain as much as you please: I will guarantee all that. But I must have a guarantee on my side that she will be received on equal terms by your family.

TRENCH. Guarantee!

SARTORIUS. Yes, a reasonable guarantee. I shall expect you to write to your relatives explaining your intention, and adding what you think proper as to my daughter's fitness for the best society. When you can shew me a few letters from the principal members of your family, congratulating you in a fairly cordial way, I shall be satisfied. Can I say more?

TRENCH [*much puzzled, but grateful*] No indeed. You are really very good. Many thanks. Since you wish it, I'll write to my people. But I assure you youll find them as jolly as possible over it. I'll make them write by return.

SARTORIUS. Thank you. In the meantime, I must ask you not to regard the matter as settled.

TRENCH. Oh! Not to regard the – I see. You mean between Blanche and –

SARTORIUS. I mean between you and Miss Sartorius. When I interrupted your conversation here some time ago, you and she were evidently regarding it as settled. In case difficulties arise, and the match – you see I call it a match – is broken off, I should not wish Blanche to think that she had allowed a gentleman to – to – [*Trench nods sympathetically*] Quite so. May I depend on you to keep a fair distance, and so spare me the necessity of having to restrain an intercourse which promises to be very pleasant to us all?

TRENCH. Certainly; since you prefer it. [*They shake hands on it*].

SARTORIUS [*rising*] You will write today, I think you said?

TRENCH [*eagerly*] I'll write now, before I leave here: straight off.

SARTORIUS. I will leave you to yourself then. [*He hesitates, the conversation having made him self-conscious and embarrassed; then recovers himself with an effort, and adds with dignity, as he turns to go*] I am pleased to have come to an understanding with you. [*He goes into the hotel; and Cokane, who has been hanging about inquisitively, emerges from the shrubbery*].

TRENCH [*excitedly*] Billy, old chap: youre just in time to do me a favor. I want you to draft a letter for me to copy out.

COKANE. I came with you on this tour as a friend, Trench: not as a secretary.

TRENCH. Well, youll write as a friend. It's to my Aunt Maria, about Blanche and me. To tell her, you know.

COKANE. Tell her about Blanche and you! Tell her about

your conduct! Betray you, my friend; and forget that I am writing to a lady? Never!

TRENCH. Bosh, Billy: dont pretend you dont understand. We're engaged: engaged, my boy! what do you think of that? I must write by tonight's post. You are the man to tell me what to say. Come, old chap [*coaxing him to sit down at one of the tables*]: heres a pencil. Have you a bit of – oh, here: thisll do: write it on the back of the map. [*He tears the map out of his Baedeker and spreads it face downwards on the table. Cokane takes the pencil and prepares to write*]. Thats right. Thanks awfully, old chap. Now fire away. [*Anxiously*] Be careful how you word it though, Cokane.

COKANE [*putting down the pencil*] If you doubt my ability to express myself becomingly to Lady Roxdale –

TRENCH [*propitiating him*] All right, old fellow, all right: theres not a man alive who could do it half so well as you. I only wanted to explain. You see, Sartorius has got it into his head, somehow, that my people will snub Blanche; and he wont consent unless they send letters and invitations and congratulations and the deuce knows what not. So just put it in such a way that Aunt Maria will write by return saying she is delighted, and asking us – Blanche and me, you know – to stay with her, and so forth. You know what I mean. Just tell her all about it in a chatty way; and –

COKANE [*crushingly*] If you will tell me all about it in a chatty way, I daresay I can communicate it to Lady Roxdale with becoming delicacy. What is Sartorius?

TRENCH [*taken aback*] I dont know: I didnt ask. It's a sort of question you cant very well put to a man – at least a man like him. Do you think you could word the letter so as to pass all that over? I really dont like to ask him.

COKANE. I can pass it over if you wish. Nothing easier. But if you think Lady Roxdale will pass it over, I differ from you. I may be wrong: no doubt I am. I generally am wrong, I believe; but that is my opinion.

46

TRENCH [*much perplexed*] Oh, confound it! What the deuce am I to do? Cant you say he's a gentleman: that wont commit us to anything. If you dwell on his being well off, and Blanche an only child, Aunt Maria will be satisfied.

COKANE. Henry Trench: when will you begin to get a little sense? This is a serious business. Act responsibly, Harry: act responsibly.

TRENCH. Bosh! Dont be moral!

COKANE. I am not moral, Trench. At least I am not a moralist: that is the expression I should have used. Moral, but not a moralist. If you are going to get money with your wife, doesnt it concern your family to know how that money was made? Doesnt it concern you – you, Harry? [*Trench looks at him helplessly, twisting his fingers nervously. Cokane throws down the pencil and leans back with ostentatious indifference*]. Of course it is no business of mine: I only throw out the suggestion. Sartorius may be a retired burglar for all I know. [*Sartorius and Blanche, ready for dinner, come from the hotel*].

TRENCH. Sh! Here they come. Get the letter finished before dinner, like a good old chappie: I shall be awfully obliged to you.

COKANE [*impatiently*] Leave me, leave me: you disturb me. [*He waves him off, and begins to write*].

TRENCH [*humbly and gratefully*] Yes, old chap. Thanks awfully. [*By this time Blanche has left her father, and is strolling off towards the riverside. Sartorius comes down the garden, Baedeker in hand, and sits near Cokane, reading. Trench addresses him*]. You wont mind my taking Blanche in to dinner, I hope, sir?

SARTORIUS. By all means, Dr Trench. Pray do so. [*He graciously waves him off to join Blanche. Trench hurries after her through the gate. The light reddens as the Rhenish sunset begins. Cokane, making wry faces in the agonies of composition, is disconcerted to find Sartorius's eye upon him*].

SARTORIUS. I do not disturb you, I hope, Mr Cokane.

COKANE. By no means. Our friend Trench has entrusted me with a difficult and delicate task. He has requested me, as a friend of the family, to write to them on a subject that concerns you.

SARTORIUS. Indeed, Mr Cokane! Well, the communication could not be in better hands.

COKANE [*with an air of modesty*] Ah, that is going too far, my dear sir, too far. Still, you see what Trench is. A capital fellow in his way, Mr Sartorius, an excellent young fellow. But family communications like these require good manners. They require tact; and tact is Trench's weak point. He has an excellent heart, but no tact: none whatever. Everything depends on the way the matter is put to Lady Roxdale. But as to that, you may rely on me. I understand the sex.

SARTORIUS. Well, however she may receive it – and I care as little as any man, Mr Cokane, how people may choose to receive me – I trust I may at least have the pleasure of seeing you sometimes at my house when we return to England.

COKANE [*overwhelmed*] My dear sir! You express yourself in the true spirit of an English gentleman.

SARTORIUS. Not at all. You will always be most welcome. But I fear I have disturbed you in the composition of your letter. Pray resume it. I shall leave you to yourself. [*He pretends to rise, but checks himself to add*] Unless indeed I can assist you in any way? by clearing up any point on which you are not informed, for instance? or even, if I may so far presume on my years, giving you the benefit of my experience as to the best way of wording the matter? [*Cokane looks a little surprised at this. Sartorius looks hard at him, and continues deliberately and meaningly*] I shall always be happy to help any friend of Dr Trench's, in any way, to the best of my ability and of my means.

COKANE. My dear sir: you are really very good. Trench and I were putting our heads together over the letter just now; and there certainly were one or two points on which we were a little in the dark. [*Scrupulously*] But I would not permit Harry to question you. No. I pointed out to him that, as a matter of taste, it would be more delicate to wait until you volunteered the necessary information.

SARTORIUS. Hm! May I ask what you have said, so far?

COKANE. 'My dear Aunt Maria.' That is, Trench's dear Aunt Maria, my friend Lady Roxdale. You understand that I am only drafting a letter for Trench to copy.

SARTORIUS. Quite so. Will you proceed; or would it help you if I were to suggest a word or two?

COKANE [*effusively*] Your suggestions will be most valuable, my dear sir, most welcome.

SARTORIUS. I think I should begin in some such way as this. 'In travelling with my friend Mr Cokane up the Rhine —'

COKANE [*murmuring as he writes*] Invaluable, invaluable. The very thing. '— my friend Mr Cokane up the Rhine—'

SARTORIUS. 'I have made the acquaintance of' — or you may say 'picked up', or 'come across', if you think that would suit your friend's style better. We must not be too formal.

COKANE. 'Picked up'! oh no: too dégagé, Mr Sartorius, too dégagé. I should say 'had the privilege of becoming acquainted with.'

SARTORIUS [*quickly*] By no means: Lady Roxdale must judge of that for herself. Let it stand as I said. 'I have made the acquaintance of a young lady, the daughter of —' [*He hesitates*].

COKANE [*writing*] 'acquaintance of a young lady, the daughter of' — yes?

SARTORIUS. 'of' — you had better say a 'gentleman.'

COKANE [*surprised*] Of course.

SARTORIUS [*with sudden passion*] It is not of course, sir. [*Cokane, startled, looks at him with dawning suspicion. Sartorius recovers himself somewhat shamefacedly*]. Hm! '— of a gentle-

49

man of considerable wealth and position –'

COKANE [*echoing him with a new note of coldness in his voice as he writes the last words*] '– and position.'

SARTORIUS. 'which, however, he has made entirely for himself.' [*Cokane, now fully enlightened, stares at him instead of writing*]. Have you written that?

COKANE [*expanding into an attitude of patronage and encouragement*] Ah, indeed. Quite so, quite so. [*He writes*] '– entirely for himself.' Just so. Proceed, Sartorius, proceed. Very clearly expressed.

SARTORIUS. 'The young lady will inherit the bulk of her father's fortune, and will be liberally treated on her marriage. Her education has been of the most expensive and complete kind obtainable; and her surroundings have been characterized by the strictest refinement. She is in every essential particular –'

COKANE [*interrupting*] Excuse the remark; but dont you think this is rather too much in the style of a prospectus of the young lady? I throw out the suggestion as a matter of taste.

SARTORIUS [*troubled*] Perhaps you are right. I am of course not dictating the exact words;–

COKANE. Of course not: of course not.

SARTORIUS. – but I desire that there may be no wrong impression as to my daughter's – er – breeding. As to myself –

COKANE. Oh, it will be sufficient to mention your profession, or pursuits, or – [*He pauses; and they look pretty hard at one another*].

SARTORIUS [*very deliberately*] My income, sir, is derived from the rental of a very extensive real estate in London. Lady Roxdale is one of the head landlords; and Dr Trench holds a mortgage from which, if I mistake not, his entire income is derived. The truth is, Mr Cokane, I am quite well acquainted with Dr Trench's position and affairs; and I have long desired to know him personally.

COKANE [*again obsequious, but still inquisitive*] What a remarkable coincidence! In what quarter is the estate situated, did you say?

SARTORIUS. In London, sir. Its management occupies as much of my time as is not devoted to the ordinary pursuits of a gentleman. [*He rises and takes out his card case*]. The rest I leave to your discretion. [*He leaves a card on the table*]. That is my address at Surbiton. If it should unfortunately happen, Mr Cokane, that this leads to nothing but a disappointment for Blanche, probably she would rather not see you afterwards. But if all turns out as we hope, Dr Trench's best friends will then be our best friends.

COKANE [*rising and confronting Sartorius confidently, pencil and paper in hand*] Rely on me, Mr Sartorius. The letter is already finished here [*pointing to his brain*]. In five minutes it will be finished there [*He points to the paper: nods to emphasize the assertion; and begins to pace up and down the garden, writing, and tapping his forehead from time to time as he goes, with every appearance of severe intellectual exertion*].

SARTORIUS [*calling through the gate after a glance at his watch*] Blanche.

BLANCHE [*replying in the distance*] Yes?

SARTORIUS. Time, my dear. [*He goes into the table d'hôte*].

BLANCHE [*nearer*] Coming. [*She comes back through the gate, followed by Trench*].

TRENCH [*in a half whisper, as Blanche goes towards the table d'hôte*] Blanche: stop. One moment. [*She stops*]. We must be careful when your father is by. I had to promise him not to regard anything as settled until I hear from my people at home.

BLANCHE [*chilled*] Oh, I see. Your family may object to me; and then it will be all over between us. They are almost sure to.

TRENCH [*anxiously*] Dont say that, Blanche: it sounds as if you didnt care. I hope you regard it as settled. You havnt made any promise, you know.

BLANCHE [*earnestly*] Yes, I have: *I* promised papa too. But I have broken my promise for your sake. I suppose I am not so conscientious as you. And if the matter is not to be regarded as settled, family or no family, promise or no promise, let us break it off here and now.

TRENCH [*intoxicated with affection*] Blanche, on my most sacred honor, family or no family, promise or no promise – [*The waiter reappears at the table d'hôte entrance, ringing his bell*]. Damn that noise!

COKANE [*as he comes to them, flourishing the letter*] Finished, dear boy, finished. Done to a turn, punctually to the second. C'est fini, mon cher garçon, c'est fini. [*Sartorius returns*].

SARTORIUS. Will you take Blanche in, Dr Trench? [*Trench takes Blanche in to the table d'hôte*]. Is the letter finished, Mr Cokane?

COKANE [*with an author's pride, handing his draft to Sartorius*] There! [*Sartorius reads it, nodding gravely over it with complete approval*].

SARTORIUS [*returning the draft*] Thank you, Mr Cokane. You have the pen of a ready writer.

COKANE [*as they go in together*] Not at all, not at all. A little tact, Mr Sartorius, a little knowledge of the world, a little experience of women – [*They disappear into the annexe*].

ACT II

In the library of a handsomely appointed villa at Surbiton on a sunny forenoon in September. Sartorius is busy at a writing table littered with business letters. The fireplace, decorated for summer, is close behind him: the window is in the opposite wall. Between the table and the window Blanche, in her prettiest frock, sits reading The Queen. The door is in the middle. All the walls are lined with shelves of smartly tooled books, fitting into their places like bricks.

SARTORIUS. Blanche.

BLANCHE. Yes, papa.

SARTORIUS. I have some news here.

BLANCHE. What is it?

SARTORIUS. I mean news for you – from Trench.

BLANCHE [*with affected indifference*] Indeed?

SARTORIUS. 'Indeed?'! Is that all you have to say to me? Oh, very well.

He resumes his work. Silence.

BLANCHE. What do his people say, papa?

SARTORIUS. His people? I dont know. [*Still busy*].

Another pause.

BLANCHE. What does he say?

SARTORIUS. He! He says nothing. [*He folds a letter leisurely, and looks at the envelope*]. He prefers to communicate the result of his – where did I put? – oh, here. Yes: he prefers to communicate the result in person.

BLANCHE [*springing up*] Oh, papa! When is he coming?

SARTORIUS. If he walks from the station, he may arrive in the course of the next half-hour. If he drives, he may be here at any moment.

BLANCHE [*making hastily for the door*] Oh!

SARTORIUS. Blanche.

BLANCHE. Yes, papa.

SARTORIUS. You will of course not meet him until he has spoken to me.

BLANCHE [*hypocritically*] Of course not, papa. I shouldnt have thought of such a thing.

SARTORIUS. That is all. [*She is going, when he puts out his hand, and says with fatherly emotion*] My dear child. [*She responds by going over to kiss him. A tap at the door*]. Come in.

Lickcheese enters, carrying a black handbag. He is a shabby, needy man, with dirty face and linen, scrubby beard and whiskers, going bald. A nervous, wiry, pertinacious human terrier, judged by his mouth and eyes, but miserably apprehensive and servile before Sartorius. He bids Blanche 'Good morning, miss'; *and she passes out with a slight and contemptuous recognition of him.*

LICKCHEESE. Good morning, sir.

SARTORIUS [*harsh and peremptory*] Good morning.

LICKCHEESE [*taking a little sack of money from his bag*] Not much this morning, sir. I have just had the honor of making Dr Trench's acquaintance, sir.

SARTORIUS [*looking up from his writing, displeased*] Indeed?

LICKCHEESE. Yes, sir. Dr Trench asked his way of me, and was kind enough to drive me from the station.

SARTORIUS. Where is he, then?

LICKCHEESE. I left him in the hall, with his friend, sir. I should think he is speaking to Miss Sartorius.

SARTORIUS. Hm! What do you mean by his friend?

LICKCHEESE. There is a Mr Cokane with him, sir.

SARTORIUS. I see you have been talking to him, eh?

LICKCHEESE. As we drove along: yes, sir.

SARTORIUS [*sharply*] Why did you not come by the nine o'clock train?

LICKCHEESE. I thought –

SARTORIUS. It cannot be helped now; so never mind what you thought. But do not put off my business again to the last moment. Has there been any further trouble about the St Giles property?

LICKCHEESE. The Sanitary Inspector has been complaining again about No. 13 Robbins's Row. He says he'll bring it before the vestry.

SARTORIUS. Did you tell him that I am on the vestry?

LICKCHEESE. Yes, sir.

SARTORIUS. What did he say to that?

LICKCHEESE. Said he supposed so, or you wouldnt dare to break the law so scand'lous. I only tell you what he said.

SARTORIUS. Hm! Do you know his name?

LICKCHEESE. Yes, sir. Speakman.

SARTORIUS. Write it down in the diary for the day of the next meeting of the Health Committee. I will teach Mr Speakman his duty to members of the vestry.

LICKCHEESE [*doubtfully*] The vestry cant hurt him, sir. He's under the Local Government Board.

SARTORIUS. I did not ask you that. Let me see the books. [*Lickcheese produces the rent book, and hands it to Sartorius; then makes the desired entry in the diary on the table, watching Sartorius with misgiving as the rent book is examined. Sartorius rises, frowning*]. One pound four for repairs to number thirteen! What does this mean?

LICKCHEESE. Well, sir, it was the staircase on the third floor. It was downright dangerous: there werent but three whole steps in it, and no handrail. I thought it best to have a few boards put in.

SARTORIUS. Boards! Firewood, sir, firewood! They will burn every stick of it. You have spent twenty-four shillings of my money on firewood for them.

LICKCHEESE. There ought to be stone stairs, sir: it would be a saving in the long run. The clergyman says –

SARTORIUS. What! Who says?

LICKCHEESE. The clergyman, sir, only the clergyman. Not that I make much account of him; but if you knew how he has worried me over that staircase –

SARTORIUS. I am an Englishman; and I will suffer no priest to interfere in my business. [*He turns suddenly on Lickcheese*]. Now look here, Mr Lickcheese! This is the third time this year that you have brought me a bill of over a pound for repairs. I have warned you repeatedly against

dealing with these tenement houses as if they were
mansions in a West-End square. I have had occasion to
warn you too against discussing my affairs with strangers.
You have chosen to disregard my wishes. You are discharged.

LICKCHEESE [*dismayed*] Oh, sir, dont say that.

SARTORIUS [*fiercely*] You are discharged.

LICKCHEESE. Well, Mr Sartorius, it is hard, so it is. No
man alive could have screwed more out of them poor
destitute devils for you than I have, or spent less in doing
it. I have dirtied my hands at it until theyre not fit for
clean work hardly; and now you turn me –

SARTORIUS [*interrupting him menacingly*] What do you mean
by dirtying your hands? If I find that you have stepped an
inch outside the letter of the law, Mr Lickcheese, I will
prosecute you myself. The way to keep your hands clean
is to gain the confidence of your employers. You will do
well to bear that in mind in your next situation.

THE PARLORMAID [*opening the door*] Mr Trench and Mr
Cokane.

*Cokane and Trench come in: Trench festively dressed and in
buoyant spirits: Cokane highly self-satisfied.*

SARTORIUS. How do you do, Dr Trench? Good morning,
Mr Cokane. I am pleased to see you here. Mr Lickcheese:
you will place your accounts and money on the table: I
will examine them and settle with you presently.

*Lickcheese retires to the table, and begins to arrange his accounts,
greatly depressed. The parlormaid withdraws.*

TRENCH [*glancing at Lickcheese*] I hope we're not in the way.

SARTORIUS. By no means. Sit down, pray. I fear you have
been kept waiting.

TRENCH [*taking Blanche's chair*] Not at all. Weve only just
come in. [*He takes out a packet of letters, and begins untying
them*].

COKANE [*going to a chair nearer the window, but stopping to look
admiringly round before sitting down*] You must be happy

here with all these books, Mr Sartorius. A literary atmosphere.

SARTORIUS [*resuming his seat*] I have not looked into them. They are pleasant for Blanche occasionally when she wishes to read. I chose the house because it is on gravel. The death-rate is very low.

TRENCH [*triumphantly*] I have any amount of letters for you. All my people are delighted that I am going to settle. Aunt Maria wants Blanche to be married from her house. [*He hands Sartorius a letter*].

SARTORIUS. Aunt Maria?

COKANE. Lady Roxdale, my dear sir: he means Lady Roxdale. Do express yourself with a little more tact, my dear fellow.

TRENCH. Lady Roxdale, of course. Uncle Harry –

COKANE. Sir Harry Trench. His godfather, my dear sir, his godfather.

TRENCH. Just so. The pleasantest fellow for his age you ever met. He offers us his house at St Andrews for a couple of months, if we care to pass our honeymoon there. [*He hands Sartorius another letter*]. It's the sort of house nobody can live in, you know; but it's a nice thing for him to offer. Dont you think so?

SARTORIUS [*dissembling a thrill at the titles*] No doubt. These seem very gratifying, Dr Trench.

TRENCH, Yes, arnt they? Aunt Maria has really behaved like a brick. If you read the postscript youll see she spotted Cokane's hand in my letter. [*Chuckling*] He wrote it for me.

SARTORIUS [*glancing at Cokane*] Indeed! Mr Cokane evidently did it with great tact.

COKANE [*returning the glance*] Dont mention it.

TRENCH [*gleefully*] Well, what do you say now, Mr Sartorius? May we regard the matter as settled at last?

SARTORIUS. Quite settled. [*He rises and offers his hand. Trench, glowing with gratitude, rises and shakes it vehemently, unable to find words for his feelings*].

COKANE [*coming between them*]. Allow me to congratulate you both. [*He shakes hands with the two at the same time.*]

SARTORIUS. And now, gentlemen, I have a word to say to my daughter. Dr Trench: you will not, I hope, grudge me the pleasure of breaking this news to her: I have had to disappoint her more than once since I last saw you. Will you excuse me for ten minutes?

COKANE [*in a flush of friendly protest*] My dear sir: can you ask?

TRENCH. Certainly.

SARTORIUS. Thank you. [*He goes out*].

TRENCH [*chuckling again*] He wont have any news to break, poor old boy: she's seen all the letters already.

COKANE. I must say your behavior has been far from straightforward, Harry. You have been carrying on a clandestine correspondence.

LICKCHEESE [*stealthily*] Gentlemen –

TRENCH } [*turning: they had forgotten his presence*] Hallo!
COKANE }

LICKCHEESE [*coming between them very humbly, but in mortal anxiety and haste*] Look here, gentlemen. [*To Trench*] You, sir, I address myself to more particlar. Will you say a word in my favor to the guvnor? He's just given me the sack; and I have four children looking to me for their bread. A word from you, sir, on this happy day, might get him to take me on again.

TRENCH [*embarrassed*] Well, you see, Mr Lickcheese, I dont see how I can interfere. I'm very sorry, of course.

COKANE. Certainly you cannot interfere. It would be in the most execrable taste.

LICKCHEESE. Oh, gentlemen, youre young; and you dont know what loss of employment means to the like of me. What harm would it do you to help a poor man? Just listen to the circumstances, sir. I only –

TRENCH [*moved, but snatching at an excuse for taking a high tone in avoiding the unpleasantness of helping him*] No: I had rather not. Excuse my saying plainly that I think Mr Sartorius is not a man to act hastily or harshly. I have always found him very fair and generous; and I believe he is a better judge of the circumstances than I am.

COKANE [*inquisitive*] I think you ought to hear the circumstances, Harry. It can do no harm. Hear the circumstances by all means.

LICKCHEESE. Never mind, sir: it aint any use. When I hear that man called generous and fair! – well, never mind.

TRENCH [*severely*] If you wish me to do anything for you, Mr Lickcheese, let me tell you that you are not going the right way about it in speaking ill of Mr Sartorius.

LICKCHEESE. Have I said one word against him, sir? I leave it to your friend: have I said a word?

COKANE. True: true. Quite true. Harry: be just.

LICKCHEESE. Mark my words, gentlemen: he'll find what a man he's lost the very first week's rents the new man'll bring him. Youll find the difference yourself, Dr Trench, if you or your children come into the property. Ive took money there when no other collector alive would have wrung it out. And this is the thanks I get for it! Why, see here, gentlemen! Look at that bag of money on the table. Hardly a penny of that but there was a hungry child crying for the bread it would have bought. But I got it for him – screwed and worried and bullied it out of them. I – look here, gentlemen: I'm pretty seasoned to the work; but theres money there that I couldnt have taken if it hadnt been for the thought of my own children depending on me for giving him satisfaction. And because I charged him four-and-twenty shillin to mend a staircase that three women have been hurt on, and that would have got him prosecuted for manslaughter if it had been let go much longer, he gives me the sack. Wouldnt listen to a word, though I would have offered to make up the money out of my own pocket: aye, and am willing to do it still if you will only put in a word for me.

TRENCH [*aghast*] You took money that ought to have fed

starving children! Serve you right! If I had been the father of one of those children, I'd have given you something worse than the sack. I wouldnt say a word to save your soul, if you have such a thing. Mr Sartorius was quite right.

LICKCHEESE [*staring at him, surprised into contemptuous amusement in the midst of his anxiety*] Just listen to this! Well, you a r e an innocent young gentleman. Do you suppose he sacked me because I was too hard? Not a bit on it; it was because I wasnt hard enough. I never heard him say he was satisfied yet: no, nor he wouldnt, not if I skinned em alive. I dont say he's the worst landlord in London: he couldnt be worse than some; but he's no better than the worst I ever had to do with. And, though I say it, I'm better than the best collector he ever done business with. Ive screwed more and spent less on his properties than anyone would believe, that knows what such properties are. I know my merits, Dr Trench, and will speak for myself if no one else will.

COKANE. What description of properties? Houses?

LICKCHEESE. Tenement houses, let from week to week by the room or half room: aye, or quarter room. It pays when you know how to work it, sir. Nothing like it. It's been calculated on the cubic foot of space, sir, that you can get higher rents letting by the room than you can for a mansion in Park Lane.

TRENCH. I hope Mr Sartorius hasnt much of that sort of property, however it may pay.

LICKCHEESE. He has nothing else, sir; and he shews his sense in it, too. Every few hundred pounds he could scrape together he bought old houses with: houses that you wouldnt hardly look at without holding your nose. He has em in St Giles's: he has em in Marylebone: he has em in Bethnal Green. Just look how he lives himself, and youll see the good of it to him. He likes a low deathrate and a gravel soil for himself, he does. You come down with me to Robbins's Row; and I'll shew you a soil and a deathrate, I will! And, mind you, it's me that makes it pay him so well. Catch him going down to collect his own rents! Not likely!

TRENCH. Do you mean to say that all his property – all his means – come from this sort of thing?

LICKCHEESE. Every penny of it, sir.

Trench, overwhelmed, has to sit down.

COKANE [*looking compassionately at him*] Ah, my dear fellow, the love of money is the root of all evil.

LICKCHEESE. Yes, sir; and we'd all like to have the tree growing in our garden.

COKANE [*revolted*] Mr Lickcheese: I did not address myself to you. I do not wish to be severe with you; but there is something peculiarly repugnant to my feelings in the calling of a rent collector.

LICKCHEESE. It's no worse than many another. I have my children looking to me.

COKANE. True: I admit it. So has our friend Sartorius. His affection for his daughter is a redeeming point – a redeeming point, certainly.

LICKCHEESE. She's a lucky daughter, sir. Many another daughter has been turned out upon the streets to gratify his affection for her. Thats what business is, sir, you see. Come, sir: I think your friend will say a word for me now he knows I'm not in fault.

TRENCH [*rising angrily*] I will not. It's a damnable business from beginning to end; and you deserve no better luck for helping in it. Ive seen it all among the out-patients at the hospital; and it used to make my blood boil to think that such things couldnt be prevented.

LICKCHEESE [*his suppressed spleen breaking out*] Oh indeed, sir. But I suppose youll take your share when you marry Miss Blanche, all the same. [*Furiously*] Which of us is the worse, I should like to know? me that wrings the money out to keep a home over my children, or you that spend it and try to shove the blame on to me?

COKANE. A most improper observation to address to a gentleman, Mr Lickcheese! A most revolutionary sentiment!

LICKCHEESE. Perhaps so. But then Robbins's Row aint a school for manners. You collect a week or two there – youre welcome to my place if I cant keep it for myself – and youll hear a little plain speaking, you will.

COCKANE [*with dignity*] Do you know to whom you are speaking, my good man?

LICKCHEESE [*recklessly*] I know well enough who I'm speaking to. What do I care for you, or a thousand such? I'm poor: thats enough to make a rascal of me. No consideration for me! nothing to be got by saying a word for me! [*Suddenly cringing to Trench*] Just a word, sir. It would cost you nothing. [*Sartorius appears at the door, unobserved*] Have some feeling for the poor.

TRENCH. I'm afraid you have shewn very little, by your own confession.

LICKCHEESE [*breaking out again*] More than your precious father-in-law, anyhow. I – [*Sartorius's voice, striking in with deadly coldness, paralyzes him*].

SARTORIUS. You will come here tomorrow not later than ten, Mr Lickcheese, to conclude our business. I shall trouble you no further today. [*Lickcheese, cowed, goes out amid dead silence. Sartorius continues, after an awkward pause*] He is one of my agents, or rather was; for I have unfortunately had to dismiss him for repeatedly disregarding my instructions. [*Trench says nothing. Sartorius throws off his embarrassment, and assumes a jocose, rallying air, unbecoming to him under any circumstances, and just now almost unbearably jarring*]. Blanche will be down presently, Harry [*Trench recoils*] – I suppose I must call you Harry now. What do you say to a stroll through the garden, Mr Cokane? We are celebrated here for our flowers.

COKANE. Charmed, my dear sir, charmed. Life here is an idyll – a perfect idyll. We were just dwelling on it.

SARTORIUS [*slyly*] Harry can follow with Blanche. She will
be down directly.

TRENCH [*hastily*] No. I cant face her just now.

SARTORIUS [*rallying him*] Indeed! Ha, ha!

*The laugh, the first they have heard from him, sets Trench's
teeth on edge. Cokane is taken aback, but instantly recovers himself.*

COKANE. Ha! ha! ha! Ho! ho!

TRENCH. But you dont understand.

SARTORIUS. Oh, I think we do, I think we do. Eh, Mr
Cokane? Ha! ha!

COKANE. I should think we do. Ha! ha! ha!

*They go out together, laughing at him. He collapses into a chair
shuddering in every nerve. Blanche appears at the door. Her face
lights up when she sees that he is alone. She trips noiselessly to the
back of his chair and clasps her hands over his eyes. With a convulsive
start and exclamation he springs up and breaks away from her.*

BLANCHE [*astonished*] Harry!

TRENCH [*with distracted politeness*] I beg your pardon. I was
thinking – wont you sit down?

BLANCHE [*looking suspiciously at him*] Is anything the matter?
[*She sits down slowly near the writing table. He takes Cokane's
chair*].

TRENCH. No. Oh no.

BLANCHE. Papa has not been disagreeable, I hope.

TRENCH. No: I have hardly spoken to him since I was with
you. [*He rises; takes up his chair; and plants it beside hers. This
pleases her better. She looks at him with her most winning smile.
A sort of sob breaks from him; and he catches her hands and kisses
them passionately. Then, looking into her eyes with intense
earnestness, he says*] Blanche: are you fond of money?

BLANCHE [*gaily*] Very. Are you going to give me any?

TRENCH [*wincing*] Dont make a joke of it: I'm serious. Do
you know that we shall be very poor?

BLANCHE. Is that what made you look as if you had
neuralgia?

TRENCH [*pleadingly*] My dear: it's no laughing matter. Do you know that I have a bare seven hundred a year to live on?

BLANCHE. How dreadful!

TRENCH. Blanche: it's very serious indeed: I assure you it is.

BLANCHE: It would keep me rather short in my house-keeping, dearest boy, if I had nothing of my own. But papa has promised me that I shall be richer than ever when we are married.

TRENCH. We must do the best we can with seven hundred. I think we ought to be self-supporting.

BLANCHE. Thats just what I mean to be, Harry. If I were to eat up half your seven hundred, I should be making you twice as poor; but I'm going to make you twice as rich instead. [*He shakes his head*]. Has papa made any difficulty?

TRENCH [*rising with a sigh and taking his chair back to its former place*] No. None at all. [*He sits down dejectedly. When Blanche speaks again her face and voice betray the beginning of a struggle with her temper*].

BLANCHE. Harry: are you too proud to take money from my father?

TRENCH. Yes, Blanche: I am too proud.

BLANCHE [*after a pause*] That is not nice to me, Harry.

TRENCH. You must bear with me, Blanche. I – I cant explain. After all, it's very natural.

BLANCHE. Has it occurred to you that I may be proud too?

TRENCH. Oh, thats nonsense. No one will accuse you of marrying for money.

BLANCHE. No one would think the worse of me if I did, or of you either. [*She rises and begins to walk restlessly about*]. We really cannot live on seven hundred a year, Harry; and I dont think it quite fair of you to ask me merely because you are afraid of people talking.

TRENCH. It's not that alone, Blanche.

BLANCHE. What else is it, then?

TRENCH. Nothing. I –

BLANCHE [*getting behind him, and speaking with forced playfulness as she bends over him, her hands on his shoulders*] Of course

64

it's nothing. Now dont be absurd, Harry: be good; and listen to me: I know how to settle it. You are too proud to owe anything to me; and I am too proud to owe anything to you. You have seven hundred a year. Well, I will take just seven hundred a year from papa at first; and then we shall be quits. Now, now, Harry, you know youve not a word to say against that.

TRENCH. It's impossible.

BLANCHE. Impossible!

TRENCH. Yes, impossible. I have resolved not to take any money from your father.

BLANCHE. But he'll give the money to me, not to you.

TRENCH. It's the same thing. [*With an effort to be sentimental*] I love you too well to see any distinction. [*He puts up his hand halfheartedly: she takes it over his shoulder with equal indecision. They are both trying hard to conciliate one another*].

BLANCHE. Thats a very nice way of putting it, Harry; but I'm sure theres something I ought to know. Has papa been disagreeable?

TRENCH. No: he has been very kind – to me, at least. It's not that. It's nothing you can guess, Blanche. It would only pain you – perhaps offend you. I dont mean, of course, that we shall live always on seven hundred a year. I intend to go at my profession in earnest, and work my fingers to the bone.

BLANCHE [*playing with his fingers, still over his shoulder*] But I shouldnt like you with your fingers worked to the bone, Harry. I must be told what the matter is. [*He takes his hand quickly away: she flushes angrily; and her voice is no longer even an imitation of the voice of a lady as she exclaims*] I hate secrets; and I dont like to be treated as if I were a child.

TRENCH [*annoyed by her tone*] Theres nothing to tell. I dont choose to trespass on your father's generosity: thats all.

BLANCHE. You had no objection half an hour ago, when you met me in the hall, and shewed me all the letters. Your family doesnt object. Do you object?

TRENCH [*earnestly*] I do not indeed. It's only a question of money.

BLANCHE [*imploringly, the voice softening and refining for the last time*] Harry: theres no use in our fencing in this way. Papa will never consent to my being absolutely dependent on you; and I dont like the idea of it myself. If you even mention such a thing to him you will break off the match: you will indeed.

TRENCH [*obstinately*] I cant help that.

BLANCHE [*white with rage*] You cant help –! Oh, I'm beginning to understand. I will save you the trouble. You can tell papa that *I* have broken off the match; and then there will be no further difficulty.

TRENCH [*taken aback*] What do you mean, Blanche? Are you offended?

BLANCHE. Offended! How dare you ask me?

TRENCH. Dare!

BLANCHE. How much more manly it would have been to confess that you were trifling with me that time on the Rhine! Why did you come here today? Why did you write to your people?

TRENCH. Well, Blanche, if you are going to lose your temper –

BLANCHE. Thats no answer. You depended on your family to get you out of your engagement; and they did not object: they were only too glad to be rid of you. You were not mean enough to stay away, and not manly enough to tell the truth. You thought you could provoke me to break the engagement: thats so like a man – to try to put the woman in the wrong. Well, you have your way: I release you. I wish youd opened my eyes by downright brutality; by striking me; by anything rather than shuffling as you have done.

TRENCH [*hotly*] Shuffling! If I'd thought you capable of turning on me like this, I'd never have spoken to you. Ive a good mind never to speak to you again.

BLANCHE. You shall not – not ever. I will take care of that [*going to the door*].

TRENCH [*alarmed*] What are you going to do?

BLANCHE. To get your letters: your false letters, and your presents: your hateful presents, to return them to you. I'm very glad it's all broken off; and if – [*as she puts her hand to the door it is opened from without by Sartorius, who enters and shuts it behind him*].

SARTORIUS [*interrupting her severely*] Hush, pray, Blanche: you are forgetting yourself: you can be heard all over the house. What is the matter?

BLANCHE [*too angry to care whether she is overheard or not*] You had better ask him. He has some excuse about money.

SARTORIUS. Excuse! Excuse for what?

BLANCHE. For throwing me over.

TRENCH [*vehemently*] I declare I never –

BLANCHE [*interrupting him still more vehemently*] You did. You did. You are doing nothing else –

TRENCH   } [*together: each trying to   { I am doing nothing
BLANCHE   }   shout down the other*]   { What else is it but

{ of the sort. You know very well that what you are saying
{ throwing me over? But I dont care for you. I hate you.
{ is disgracefully untrue. It's a damned lie. I wont stand –
{ I always hated you. Beastly – dirty – vile –

SARTORIUS [*in desperation at the noise*] Silence! [*Still more formidably*] Silence!! [*They obey. He proceeds firmly*] Blanche: you must control your temper: I will not have these repeated scenes within hearing of the servants. Dr Trench will answer for himself to me. You had better leave us. [*He opens the door, and calls*] Mr Cokane: will you kindly join us here?

COKANE [*in the conservatory*] Coming, my dear sir, coming. [*He appears at the door*].

BLANCHE. I'm sure I have no wish to stay. I hope I shall find you alone when I come back. [*An inarticulate exclamation bursts from Trench. She goes out, passing Cokane resentfully.*

67

*He looks after her in surprise ; then looks questioningly at the two men.
Sartorius shuts the door with an angry stroke, and turns to Trench].*

SARTORIUS [*aggressively*] Sir –

TRENCH [*interrupting him more aggressively*] Well, sir ?

COKANE [*getting between them*] Gently, dear boy, gently.
Suavity, Harry, suavity.

SARTORIUS [*mastering himself*] If you have anything to say
to me, Dr Trench, I will listen to you patiently. You will
then allow me to say what I have to say on my part.

TRENCH [*ashamed*] I beg your pardon. Of course, yes. Fire
away.

SARTORIUS. May I take it that you have refused to fulfil
your engagement with my daughter?

TRENCH. Certainly not: your daughter has refused to fulfil
her engagement with me. But the match is broken off, if
thats what you mean.

SARTORIUS. Dr Trench: I will be plain with you. I know
that Blanche has a quick temper. It is part of her strong
character and her physical courage, which is greater than
that of most men, I can assure you. You must be prepared
for that. If this quarrel is only Blanche's temper, you may
take my word for it that it will be over before tomorrow.
But I understood from what she said just now that you
have made some difficulty on the score of money.

TRENCH [*with renewed excitement*] It was Miss Sartorius who
made the difficulty. I shouldnt have minded that so much,
if it hadnt been for the things she said. She shewed that
she doesnt care that [*snapping his fingers*] for me.

COKANE [*soothingly*] Dear boy –

TRENCH. Hold your tongue, Billy: it's enough to make a
man wish he'd never seen a woman. Look here, Mr
Sartorius: I put the matter to her as delicately and con-
siderately as possible, never mentioning a word of my
reasons, but just asking her to be content to live on my
own little income; and yet she turned on me as if I'd
behaved like a savage.

SARTORIUS. Live on your income! Impossible: my daughter
is accustomed to a proper establishment. Did I not ex-
pressly undertake to provide for that? Did she not tell you
I promised her to do so?

TRENCH. Yes, I know all about that, Mr Sartorius; and
I'm greatly obliged to you; but I'd rather not take anything from you except Blanche herself.

SARTORIUS. And why did you not say so before?

TRENCH. No matter why. Let us drop the subject.

SARTORIUS. No matter! But it does matter, sir. I insist on
an answer. Why did you not say so before?

TRENCH. I didnt know before.

SARTORIUS [*provoked*] Then you ought to have known your
own mind on a point of such vital importance.

TRENCH [*much injured*] I ought to have known! Cokane:
is this reasonable? [*Cokane's features are contorted by an air of
judicial consideration; but he says nothing; and Trench again
addresses Sartorius, this time with a marked diminution of respect*].
How the deuce could I have known? You didnt tell me.

SARTORIUS. You are trifling with me, sir. You said that you
did not know your own mind before.

TRENCH. I said nothing of the sort. I say that I did not know
where your money came from before.

SARTORIUS. That is not true, sir. I –

COKANE. Gently, my dear sir. Gently, Harry, dear boy.
Suaviter in modo: fort –

TRENCH. Let him begin, then. What does he mean by
attacking me in this fashion?

SARTORIUS. Mr Cokane: you will bear me out. I was
explicit on the point. I said I was a self-made man; and I
am not ashamed of it.

TRENCH. You are nothing of the sort. I found out this
morning from your man – Lickcheese, or whatever his
confounded name is – that your fortune has been made
out of a parcel of unfortunate creatures that have hardly
enough to keep body and soul together – made by screw-

ing, and bullying, and threatening, and all sorts of petti-fogging tyranny.

SARTORIUS [*outraged*] Sir! [*They confront one another threateningly*].

COKANE [*softly*] Rent must be paid, dear boy. It is inevitable, Harry, inevitable. [*Trench turns away petulantly. Sartorius looks after him reflectively for a moment; then resumes his former deliberate and dignified manner, and addresses Trench with studied consideration, but with a perceptible condescension to his youth and folly*].

SARTORIUS. I am afraid, Dr Trench, that you are a very young hand at business; and I am sorry I forgot that for a moment or so. May I ask you to suspend your judgment until we have had a little quiet discussion of this senti-mental notion of yours? if you will excuse me for calling it so. [*He takes a chair, and motions Trench to another on his right*].

COKANE. Very nicely put, my dear sir. Come, Harry: sit down and listen; and consider the matter calmly and judicially. Dont be headstrong.

TRENCH. I have no objection to sit down and listen; but I dont see how that can make black white; and I am tired of being turned on as if I were in the wrong. [*He sits down*].

Cokane sits at Trench's elbow, on his right. They compose themselves for a conference.

SARTORIUS. I assume, to begin with, Dr Trench, that you are not a Socialist, or anything of that sort.

TRENCH. Certainly not. I'm a Conservative. At least, if I ever took the trouble to vote, I should vote for the Con-servative and against the other fellow.

COKANE. True blue, Harry, true blue!

SARTORIUS. I am glad to find that so far we are in perfect sympathy. I am, of course, a Conservative. Not a narrow or prejudiced one, I hope, not at all opposed to true progress. Still, a sound Conservative. As to Lickcheese, I need say no more about him than that I have dismissed him from my service this morning for a breach of trust;

and you will hardly accept his testimony as friendly or disinterested. As to my business, it is simply to provide homes suited to the small means of very poor people, who require roofs to shelter them just like other people. Do you suppose I can keep up those roofs for nothing?

TRENCH. Yes: thats all very fine; but the point is, what sort of homes do you give them for their money? People must live somewhere, or else go to jail. Advantage is taken of that to make them pay for houses that are not fit for dogs. Why dont you build proper dwellings, and give fair value for the money you take?

SARTORIUS [*pitying his innocence*] My young friend: these poor people do not know how to live in proper dwellings: they would wreck them in a week. You doubt me: try it for yourself. You are welcome to replace all the missing banisters, handrails, cistern lids and dusthole tops at your own expense; and you will find them missing again in less than three days: burnt, sir, every stick of them. I do not blame the poor creatures: they need fires, and often have no other way of getting them. But I really cannot spend pound after pound in repairs for them to pull down, when I can barely get them to pay me four and sixpence a week for a room, which is the recognized fair London rent. No, gentlemen: when people are very poor, you cannot help them, no matter how much you may sympathize with them. It does them more harm than good in the long run. I prefer to save my money in order to provide additional houses for the homeless, and to lay by a little for Blanche. [*He looks at them. They are silent: Trench unconvinced, but talked down; Cokane humanely perplexed. Sartorius bends his brows; comes forward in his chair as if gathering himself for a spring; and addresses himself, with impressive significance, to Trench*]. And now, Dr Trench, may I ask what your income is derived from?

TRENCH [*defiantly*] From interest: not from houses. My hands are clean as far as that goes. Interest on a mortgage.

SARTORIUS [*forcibly*] Yes: a mortgage on my property. When I, to use your own words, screw, and bully, and drive these people to pay what they have freely undertaken to pay me, I cannot touch one penny of the money they give me until I have first paid you your seven hundred a year out of it. What Lickcheese did for me, I do for you. He and I are alike intermediaries: you are the principal. It is because of the risks I run through the poverty of my tenants that you exact interest from me at the monstrous and exorbitant rate of seven per cent, forcing me to exact the uttermost farthing in my turn from the tenants. And yet, Dr Trench, you, who have never done a hand's turn of work in connection with the place, you have not hesitated to speak contemptuously of me because I have applied my industry and forethought to the management of our property, and am maintaining it by the same honorable means.

COKANE [*greatly relieved*] Admirable, my dear sir, excellent! I felt instinctively that Trench was talking unpractical nonsense. Let us drop the subject, my dear boy: you only make an ass of yourself when you meddle in business matters. I told you it was inevitable.

TRENCH [*dazed*] Do you mean to say that I am just as bad as you are?

COKANE. Shame, Harry, shame! Grossly bad taste! Be a gentleman. Apologize.

SARTORIUS. Allow me, Mr Cokane. [*To Trench*] If, when you say you are just as bad as I am, you mean that you are just as powerless to alter the state of society, then you are unfortunately quite right.

Trench does not at once reply. He stares at Sartorius, and then hangs his head and gazes stupidly at the floor, morally beggared, with his clasped knuckles between his knees, a living picture of disillusion. Cokane comes sympathetically to him and puts an encouraging hand on his shoulder.

COKANE [*gently*] Come, Harry, come! Pull yourself together.

You owe a word to Mr Sartorius.

TRENCH [*still stupefied, slowly unlaces his fingers; puts his hands on his knees, and lifts himself upright; pulls his waistcoat straight with a tug; and tries to take his disenchantment philosophically as he says, turning to Sartorius*] Well, people who live in glass houses have no right to throw stones. But, on my honor, I never knew that my house was a glass one until you pointed it out. I beg your pardon. [*He offers his hand*].

SARTORIUS. Say no more, Harry: your feelings do you credit: I assure you I feel exactly as you do, myself. Every man who has a heart must wish that a better state of things was practicable. But unhappily it is not.

TRENCH [*a little consoled*] I suppose not.

COKANE. Not a doubt of it, my dear sir: not a doubt of it. The increase of the population is at the bottom of it all.

SARTORIUS [*to Trench*] I trust I have convinced you that you need no more object to Blanche sharing my fortune than I need object to her sharing yours.

TRENCH [*with dull wistfulness*] It seems so. We're all in the same swim, it appears. I hope youll excuse my making such a fuss.

SARTORIUS. Not another word. In fact, I thank you for refraining from explaining the nature of your scruples to Blanche: I admire that in you, Harry. Perhaps it will be as well to leave her in ignorance.

TRENCH [*anxiously*] But I must explain now. You saw how angry she was.

SARTORIUS. You had better leave that to me. [*He looks at his watch, and rings the bell*]. Lunch is nearly due: while you are getting ready for it I can see Blanche; and I hope the result will be quite satisfactory to us all. [*The parlormaid answers the bell: he addresses her with his habitual peremptoriness*]. Tell Miss Blanche I want her.

THE PARLORMAID [*her face falling expressively*] Yes, sir. [*She turns reluctantly to go*].

SARTORIUS [*on second thoughts*] Stop. [*She stops*]. My love to

Miss Blanche; and I am alone here and would like to see her for a moment if she is not busy.

THE PARLORMAID [*relieved*] Yes sir. [*She goes out*].

SARTORIUS. I will shew you your room, Harry. I hope you will soon be perfectly at home in it. You also, Mr Cokane, must learn your way about here. Let us go before Blanche comes. [*He leads the way to the door*].

COKANE [*cheerily, following him*] Our little discussion has given me quite an appetite.

TRENCH [*moodily*] It's taken mine away.

The two friends go out, Sartorius holding the door for them. He is following when the parlormaid reappears. She is a snivelling sympathetic creature, and is on the verge of tears.

SARTORIUS. Well: is Miss Blanche coming?

THE PARLORMAID. Yes, sir. I think so, sir.

SARTORIUS. Wait here until she comes; and tell her that I will be back in a moment. I have to shew Dr Trench his room.

THE PARLORMAID. Yes, sir. [*She comes into the room. A sound between a sob and a sniff escapes her*].

Sartorius looks suspiciously at her. He half closes the door.

SARTORIUS [*lowering his voice*] Whats the matter with you?

THE PARLORMAID [*whimpering*] Nothing, sir.

SARTORIUS [*at the same pitch, more menacingly*] Take care how you behave yourself when there are visitors present. Do you hear.

THE PARLORMAID. Yes, sir. [*Sartorius goes out*].

SARTORIUS [*outside*] Excuse me: I had a word to say to the servant.

Trench is heard replying 'Not at all,' and Cokane 'Dont mention it, my dear sir.'

Their voices pass out of hearing. The parlormaid sniffs; dries her eyes; and takes some brown paper and a ball of string from a cupboard under the bookcase. She puts them on the table, and wrestles with another sob. Blanche comes in, with a jewel box in her hands. Her expression is that of a strong and determined woman in

74

an intense passion. The maid looks at her with abject wounded affection and bodily terror.

BLANCHE [*looking round*] Wheres my father?

THE PARLORMAID [*tremulously propitiatory*] He left word he'd be back directly, miss. I'm sure he wont be long. Heres the paper and string all ready, miss. [*She spreads the paper on the table*]. Can I do the parcel for you, miss?

BLANCHE. No. Mind your own business. [*She empties the box on the sheet of brown paper. It contains a packet of letters and some jewellery. She plucks a ring from her finger and throws it down on the heap so angrily that it rolls away and falls on the carpet. The maid submissively picks it up and puts it on the table, again sniffing and drying her eyes*]. What are you crying for?

THE PARLORMAID [*plaintively*] You speak so brutal to me, Miss Blanche; and I do love you so. I'm sure no one else would stay and put up with what I have to put up with.

BLANCHE. Then go. I dont want you. Do you hear? Go.

THE PARLORMAID [*piteously, falling on her knees*] Oh no, Miss Blanche. Dont send me away from you: dont —

BLANCHE [*with fierce disgust*] Agh! I hate the sight of you. [*The maid, wounded to the heart, cries bitterly*]. Hold your tongue. Are those two gentlemen gone?

THE PARLORMAID [*weeping*] Oh, how could you say such a thing to me, Miss Blanche: me that —

BLANCHE [*seizing her by the hair and throat*] Stop that noise, I tell you, unless you want me to kill you.

THE PARLORMAID [*protesting and imploring, but in a carefully subdued voice*] Let me go, Miss Blanche: you know youll be sorry: you always are. Remember how dreadfully my head was cut last time.

BLANCHE [*raging*] Answer me, will you. Have they gone?

THE PARLORMAID. Lickcheese has gone, looking dreadf — [*she breaks off with a stifled cry as Blanche's fingers tighten furiously on her*].

BLANCHE. Did I ask you about Lickcheese? You beast: you know who I mean: youre doing it on purpose.

THE PARLORMAID [*in a gasp*] Theyre staying to lunch.

BLANCHE [*looking intently into her face*] He?

THE PARLORMAID [*whispering with a sympathetic nod*] Yes, miss. [*Blanche lets her drop, and stands forlorn, with despair in her face. The parlormaid, recognizing the passing of the crisis of passion, and fearing no further violence, sits discomfitedly on her heels, and tries to arrange her hair and cap, whimpering a little with exhaustion and soreness*]. Now youve set my hands all trembling; and I shall jingle the things on the tray at lunch so that everybody will notice me. It's too bad of you, Miss Bl – [*Sartorius coughs outside*].

BLANCHE [*quickly*] Sh! Get up. [*The parlormaid hastily rises, and goes out as demurely as she can. Sartorius glances sternly at her and comes to Blanche*].

SARTORIUS [*mournfully*] My dear: can you not make a little better fight with your temper?

BLANCHE [*panting with the subsidence of her fit*] No I cant. I wont. I do my best. Nobody who really cares for me gives me up because of my temper. I never shew my temper to any of the servants but that girl; and she is the only one that will stay with us.

SARTORIUS. But, my dear, remember that we have to meet our visitors at luncheon presently. I have run down before them to say that I have arranged that little difficulty with Trench. It was only a piece of mischief made by Lickcheese. Trench is a young fool; but it is all right now.

BLANCHE. I dont want to marry a fool.

SARTORIUS. Then you will have to take a husband over thirty, Blanche. You must not expect too much, my child. You will be richer than your husband, and, I think, cleverer too. I am better pleased that it should be so.

BLANCHE [*seizing his arm*] Papa.

SARTORIUS. Yes, my dear.

BLANCHE. May I do as I like about this marriage; or must I do as you like?

SARTORIUS [*uneasily*] Blanche –

BLANCHE. No, papa: you must answer me.

SARTORIUS [*abandoning his self-control, and giving way recklessly to his affection for her*] You shall do as you like now and always, my beloved child. I only wish to do as my own darling pleases.

BLANCHE. Then I will not marry him. He has played fast and loose with me. He thinks us beneath him: he is ashamed of us: he dared to object to being benefited by you – as if it were not natural for him to owe you everything; and yet the money tempted him after all. [*She throws her arms hysterically about his neck*] Papa: I dont want to marry: I only want to stay with you and be happy as we have always been. I hate the thought of being married: I dont care for him: I dont want to leave you. [*Trench and Cokane come in; but she can hear nothing but her own voice and does not notice them*]. Only send him away: promise me that you will send him away and keep me here with you as we have always – [*seeing Trench*] Oh! [*She hides her face on her father's breast*].

TRENCH [*nervously*] I hope we are not intruding.

SARTORIUS [*formidably*] Dr Trench: my daughter has changed her mind.

TRENCH [*disconcerted*] Am I to understand –

COKANE [*striking in in his most vinegary manner*] I think, Harry, under the circumstances, we have no alternative but to seek luncheon elsewhere.

TRENCH. But, Mr Sartorius, have you explained?

SARTORIUS [*straight in Trench's face*] I have explained, sir. Good morning. [*Trench, outraged, advances a step. Blanche sinks away from her father into a chair. Sartorius stands his ground rigidly*].

TRENCH [*turning away indignantly*] Come on, Cokane.

COKANE. Certainly, Harry, certainly. [*Trench goes out, very angry. The parlormaid, with a tray jingling in her hands, passes outside*]. You have disappointed me, sir, very acutely. Good morning. [*He follows Trench*].

77

ACT III

The drawing room in Sartorius's house in Bedford Square, London. Winter evening: fire burning, curtains drawn, and lamps lighted. Sartorius and Blanche are sitting glumly near the fire. The parlormaid, who has just brought in coffee, is placing it on a small table between them. There is a large table in the middle of the room. Looking from it towards the two windows, the pianoforte, a grand, is on the right, with a photographic portrait of Blanche on a miniature easel on a sort of bedspread which covers the top, shewing that the instrument is seldom, if ever, opened. There are two doors: one on the left, further forward than the fireplace, leading to the study; the other by the corner nearest the right hand window, leading to the lobby. Blanche has her workbasket at hand, and is knitting. Sartorius, closer to the fire, has a newspaper. The parlormaid goes out.

SARTORIUS. Blanche, my love.

BLANCHE. Yes.

SARTORIUS. I had a long talk to the doctor today about our going abroad.

BLANCHE [*impatiently*] I am quite well; and I will not go abroad. I loathe the very thought of the Continent. Why will you bother me so about my health?

SARTORIUS. It was not about your health, Blanche, but about my own.

BLANCHE [*rising*] Yours! [*She goes anxiously to him*]. Oh, papa, theres nothing the matter with you, I hope?

SARTORIUS. There will be: there must be, Blanche, long before you begin to consider yourself an old woman.

BLANCHE. But theres nothing the matter now?

SARTORIUS. Well, my dear, the doctor says I need change, travel, excitement --

BLANCHE. Excitement! You need excitement! [*She laughs joyously, and sits down on the rug at his feet*]. How is it, papa, that you, who are so clever with everybody else, are not a bit clever with me? Do you think I cant see through your little plan to take me abroad? Since I will not be the invalid and allow you to be the nurse, you are to be the invalid and I am to be the nurse.

SARTORIUS. Well, Blanche, if you will have it that you are well and have nothing preying on your spirits, I must insist on being ill and have something preying on mine. And indeed, my girl, there is no use in our going on as we have for the last four months. You have not been happy; and I have been very far from comfortable. [*Blanche's face clouds: she turns away from him, and sits dumb and brooding. He waits in vain for some reply; then adds in a lower tone*] Need you be so inflexible, Blanche?

BLANCHE. I thought you admired inflexibility: you have always prided yourself on it.

SARTORIUS. Nonsense, my dear, nonsense! I have had to give in often enough. And I could shew you plenty of soft fellows who have done as well as I, and enjoyed themselves more, perhaps. If it is only for the sake of inflexibility that you are standing out –

BLANCHE. I am not standing out. I dont know what you mean. [*She tries to rise and go away*].

SARTORIUS [*catching her arm and arresting her on her knees*] Come, my child! you must not trifle with me as if I were a stranger. You are fretting because –

BLANCHE [*violently twisting herself free and speaking as she rises*] If you say it, papa, I will kill myself. It is not true. If he were here on his knees tonight, I would walk out of the house sooner than endure it. [*She goes out excitedly*].

Sartorius, greatly troubled, turns again to the fire with a heavy sigh.

SARTORIUS [*gazing gloomily into the glow*] Now if I fight it out with her, no more comfort for months! I might as well live with my clerk or my servant. And if I give in now, I shall have to give in always. Well! I cant help it. I have stuck to having my own way all my life; but there must be an end to that drudgery some day. She is young: let her have her turn at it.

The parlormaid comes in, evidently excited.

THE PARLORMAID. Please, sir, Mr Lickcheese wants to see you very particlar. On important business. Your business, he told me to say.

SARTORIUS. Mr Lickcheese! Do you mean Lickcheese who used to come here on my business?

THE PARLORMAID. Yes, sir. But indeed, sir, youd scarcely know him.

SARTORIUS [*frowning*] Hm! Starving, I suppose. Come to beg?

THE PARLORMAID [*intensely repudiating the idea*] O-o-o-o-h NO, sir. Quite the gentleman, sir! Sealskin overcoat, sir! Come in a hansom, all shaved and clean! I'm sure he's come into a fortune, sir.

SARTORIUS. Hm! Shew him up.

Lickcheese, who has been waiting at the door, instantly comes in. The change in his appearance is dazzling. He is in evening dress, with an overcoat lined throughout with furs presenting all the hues of the tiger. His shirt is fastened at the breast with a single diamond stud. His silk hat is of the glossiest black; a handsome gold watch-chain hangs like a garland on his filled-out waistcoat; he has shaved his whiskers and grown a moustache, the ends of which are waxed and pointed. As Sartorius stares speechless at him, he stands, smiling, to be admired, intensely enjoying the effect he is producing. The parlormaid, hardly less pleased with her own share in this coup-de-théâtre, goes out beaming, full of the news for the kitchen. Lickcheese clinches the situation by a triumphant nod at Sartorius.

SARTORIUS [*bracing himself: hostile*] Well?

LICKCHEESE. Quite well, Sartorius, thankee.

SARTORIUS. I was not asking after your health, sir, as you know, I think, as well as I do. What is your business?

LICKCHEESE. Business that I can take elsewhere if I meet with less civility than I please to put up with, Sartorius. You and me is man and man now. It was money that used to be my master, and not you: dont think it. Now that I'm independent in respect of money –

SARTORIUS [*crossing determinedly to the door, and holding it open*] You can take your independence out of my house, then. I wont have it here.

LICKCHEESE [*indulgently*] Come, Sartorius: dont be stiff-necked. I come here as a friend to put money in your pocket. No use your lettin on to me that youre above money. Eh?

SARTORIUS [*hesitates, and at last shuts the door saying guardedly*] How much money?

LICKCHEESE [*victorious, going to Blanche's chair and taking off his overcoat*] Ah! there you speak like yourself, Sartorius. Now suppose you ask me to sit down and make myself comfortable.

SARTORIUS [*coming from the door*] I have a mind to put you downstairs by the back of your neck, you infernal black-guard.

LICKCHEESE [*not a bit ruffled, hangs his overcoat on the back of Blanche's chair, pulling a cigar case out of one of the pockets as he does so*] You and me is too much of a pair for me to take anything you say in bad part, Sartorius. Ave a cigar?

SARTORIUS. No smoking here: this is my daughter's room. However, sit down, sit down. [*They sit*].

LICKCHEESE. I' bin gittin on a little since I saw you last.

SARTORIUS. So I see.

LICKCHEESE. I owe it partly to you, you know. Does that surprise you?

SARTORIUS. It doesnt concern me.

LICKCHEESE. So you think, Sartorius; because it never did concern you how *I* got on, so long as I got you on by bringin in the rents. But I picked up something for myself down at Robbins's Row.

SARTORIUS. I always thought so. Have you come to make restitution?

LICKCHEESE. You wouldnt take it if I offered it to you, Sartorius. It wasnt money: it was knowledge: knowledge

81

of the great public question of the Ousing of the Working Classes. You know theres a Royal Commission on it, dont you?

SARTORIUS. Oh, I see. Youve been giving evidence.

LICKCHEESE. Giving evidence! Not me. What good would that do me? Only my expenses; and that not on the professional scale, neither. No: I gev no evidence. But I'll tell you what I did. I kep it back, jast to oblige one or two people whose feelins would 'a bin urt by seeing their names in a bluebook as keepin a fever den. Their Agent got so friendly with me over it that he put his name on a bill of mine to the tune of – well, no matter: it gev me a start; and a start was all I ever wanted to get on my feet. Ive got a copy of the first report of the Commission in the pocket of my overcoat. [*He rises and gets at his overcoat, from a pocket of which he takes a bluebook*]. I turned down the page to shew you: I thought youd like to see it. [*He doubles the book back at the place indicated, and hands it to Sartorius*].

SARTORIUS. So blackmail is the game, eh? [*He puts the book on the table without looking at it, and strikes it emphatically with his fist*]. I dont care that for my name being in bluebooks. My friends dont read them; and I'm neither a Cabinet Minister nor a candidate for Parliament. Theres nothing to be got out of me on that lay.

LICKCHEESE [*shocked*] Blackmail! Oh, Mr Sartorius, do you think I would let out a word about your premises? Round on an old pal! no: that aint Lickcheese's way. Besides, they know all about you already. Them stairs that you and me quarrelled about, they was a whole arternoon examinin the clergyman that made such a fuss – you remember? – about the women that was urt on it. He made the worst he could of it, in an ungentlemanly, unchristian spirit. I wouldnt have that clergyman's disposition for worlds. Oh no: thats not what was in my thoughts.

SARTORIUS. Come, come, man! what was in your thoughts? Out with it.

LICKCHEESE [*with provoking deliberation, smiling and looking mysteriously at him*] You aint spent a few hundreds in repairs since we parted, ave you? [*Sartorius, losing patience, makes a threatening movement*]. Now dont fly out at me. I know a landlord that owned as beastly a slum as you could find in London, down there by the Tower. By my advice that man put half the houses into first-class repair, and let the other half to a new Company: the North Thames Iced Mutton Depot Company, of which I hold a few shares: promoter's shares. And what was the end of it, do you think?

SARTORIUS. Smash, I suppose.

LICKCHEESE. Smash! not a bit of it. Compensation, Mr Sartorius, compensation. Do you understand that?

SARTORIUS. Compensation for what?

LICKCHEESE. Why, the land was wanted for an extension of the Mint; and the Company had to be bought out, and the buildings compensated for. Somebody has to know these things beforehand, you know, no matter how dark theyre kept.

SARTORIUS [*interested, but cautious*] Well?

LICKCHEESE. Is that all you have to say to me, Mr Sartorius? Well! as if I was next door's dog! Suppose I'd got wind of a new street that would knock down Robbins's Row and turn Burke's Walk into a frontage worth thirty pound a foot! would you say no more to me than [*mimicking*] 'Well'? [*Sartorius hesitates, looking at him in great doubt. Lickcheese rises and exhibits himself*]. Come! look at my getup, Mr Sartorius. Look at this watch-chain! Look at the corporation Ive got on me! Do you think all that came from keeping my mouth shut? No: it came from keeping ears and eyes open.

Blanche comes in, followed by the parlormaid, who has a silver tray on which she collects the coffee cups. Sartorius, impatient at the interruption, rises and motions Lickcheese to the door of the study.

SARTORIUS. Sh! We must talk this over in the study. There
is a good fire there; and you can smoke. Blanche: an old
friend of ours.

LICKCHEESE. And a kind one to me. I hope I see you well,
Miss Blanche.

BLANCHE. Why, it's Mr Lickcheese! I hardly knew you.

LICKCHEESE. I find you a little changed yourself, miss.

BLANCHE [*hastily*] Oh, I am the same as ever. How are Mrs
Lickcheese and the chil –

SARTORIUS [*impatiently*] We have business to transact,
Blanche. You can talk to Mr Lickcheese afterwards. Come
on.

    *Sartorius and Lickcheese go into the study. Blanche, surprised
at her father's abruptness, looks after them for a moment. Then,
seeing Lickcheese's overcoat on her chair, she takes it up, amused,
and looks at the fur.*

THE PARLORMAID. Oh, we are fine, aint we, Miss Blanche?
I think Mr Lickcheese must have come into a legacy.
[*Confidentially*] I wonder what he can want with the master,
Miss Blanche! He brought him this big book. [*She shews
the bluebook to Blanche*].

BLANCHE [*her curiosity roused*] Let me see. [*She takes the book
and looks at it*]. Theres something about papa in it. [*She sits
down and begins to read*].

THE PARLORMAID [*folding the tea-table and putting it out of
the way*] He looks ever s'much younger, Miss Blanche,
dont he? I couldnt help laughing when I saw him with his
whiskers shaved off: it do look so silly when youre not accustomed to it. [*No answer from Blanche*]. You havnt
finished your coffee, miss: I suppose I may take it away?
[*No answer*]. Oh, you are interested in Mr Lickcheese's
book, miss.

    *Blanche springs up. The parlormaid looks at her face, and in-
stantly hurries out of the room on tiptoe with her tray.*

BLANCHE. So that was why he would not touch the money.
[*She tries to tear the book across. Finding this impossible she*

84

throws it violently into the fireplace. It falls into the fender]. Oh, if only a girl could have no father, no family, just as I have no mother! Clergyman! beast! 'The worst slum landlord in London.' 'Slum landlord.' Oh! [*She covers her face with her hands, and sinks shuddering into the chair on which the overcoat lies. The study door opens*].

LICKCHEESE [*in the study*] You just wait five minutes: I'll fetch him. [*Blanche snatches a piece of work from her basket, and sits erect and quiet, stitching at it. Lickcheese comes back, speaking to Sartorius, who follows him*]. He lodges round the corner in Gower Street; and my private ansom's at the door. By your leave, Miss Blanche [*pulling gently at his overcoat*].

BLANCHE [*rising*] I beg your pardon. I hope I havnt crushed it.

LICKCHEESE [*gallantly, as he gets into the coat*] Youre welcome to crush it again now, Miss Blanche. Dont say good evenin to me, miss: I'm comin back presently: me and a friend or two. Ta ta, Sartorius: I shant be long. [*He goes out*].

Sartorius looks about for the bluebook.

BLANCHE. I thought we were done with Lickcheese.

SARTORIUS. Not quite yet, I think. He left a book here for me to look over: a large book in a blue paper cover. Has the girl put it away? [*He sees it in the fender; looks at Blanche; and adds*] Have you seen it?

BLANCHE. No. Yes. [*Angrily*] No: I have not seen it. What have I to do with it?

Sartorius picks the book up and dusts it; then sits down quietly to read. After a glance up and down the columns, he nods assentingly, as if he found there exactly what he expected.

SARTORIUS. It's a curious thing, Blanche, that the Parliamentary gentlemen who write such books as these should be so ignorant of practical business. One would suppose, to read this, that we are the most grasping, grinding heartless pair in the world, you and I.

BLANCHE. Is it not true? About the state of the houses, I mean?

SARTORIUS [*calmly*] Oh, quite true.

BLANCHE. Then it is not our fault?

SARTORIUS. My dear: if we made the houses any better, the rents would have to be raised so much that the poor people would be unable to pay, and would be thrown homeless on the streets.

BLANCHE. Well, turn them out and get in a respectable class of people. Why should we have the disgrace of harboring such wretches?

SARTORIUS [*opening his eyes*] That sounds a little hard on them, doesnt it, my child?

BLANCHE. Oh, I hate the poor. At least, I hate those dirty, drunken, disreputable people who live like pigs. If they must be provided for, let other people look after them. How can you expect any one to think well of us when such things are written about us in that infamous book?

SARTORIUS [*coldly and a little wistfully*] I see I have made a real lady of you, Blanche.

BLANCHE [*defiantly*] Well? Are you sorry for that?

SARTORIUS. No, my dear: of course not. But do you know, Blanche, that my mother was a very poor woman, and that her poverty was not her fault?

BLANCHE. I suppose not; but the people we want to mix with now dont know that. And it was not my fault; so I dont see why *I* should be made to suffer for it.

SARTORIUS [*enraged*] Who makes you suffer for it, miss? What would you be now but for what your grandmother did for me when she stood at her wash-tub for thirteen hours a day and thought herself rich when she made fifteen shillings a week?

BLANCHE [*angrily*] I suppose I should have been down on her level instead of being raised above it, as I am now. Would you like us to go and live in that place in the book for the sake of grandmamma? I hate the idea of such

86

things. I dont want to know about them. I love you because you brought me up to something better. [*Half aside, as she turns away from him*] I should hate you if you had not.

SARTORIUS [*giving in*] Well, my child, I suppose it is natural for you to feel that way, after your bringing up. It is the ladylike view of the matter. So dont let us quarrel, my girl. You shall not be made to suffer any more. I have made up my mind to improve the property, and get in quite a new class of tenants. There! does that satisfy you? I am only waiting for the consent of the ground landlord, Lady Roxdale.

BLANCHE. Lady Roxdale!

SARTORIUS. Yes. But I shall expect the mortgagee to take his share of the risk.

BLANCHE. The mortgagee! Do you mean – [*She cannot finish the sentence: Sartorius does it for her*].

SARTORIUS. Harry Trench. Yes. And remember, Blanche: if he consents to join me in the scheme, I shall have to be friends with him.

BLANCHE. And to ask him to the house?

SARTORIUS. Only on business. You need not meet him unless you like.

BLANCHE [*overwhelmed*] When is he coming?

SARTORIUS. There is no time to be lost. Lickcheese has gone to ask him to come round.

BLANCHE [*in dismay*] Then he will be here in a few minutes! What shall I do?

SARTORIUS. I advise you to receive him as if nothing had happened, and then go out and leave us to our business. You are not afraid to meet him?

BLANCHE. Afraid! No: most certainly not. But –

LICKCHEESE'S VOICE [*without*] Straight in front of you, doctor. You never bin here before; but I know the house better than my own.

BLANCHE. Here they are. Dont say I'm here, papa. [*She rushes away into the study*].

87

Lickcheese comes in with Trench and Cokane. Both are in even-
ing dress. Cokane shakes hands effusively with Sartorius. Trench
who is coarsened and sullen, and has evidently not been making
the best of his disappointment, bows shortly and resentfully.
Lickcheese covers the general embarrassment by talking cheerfully
until they are all seated round the large table: Trench nearest the
fireplace; Cokane nearest the piano; and the other two between
them, with Lickcheese next Cokane].

LICKCHEESE. Here we are, all friends round St Paul's. You
remember Mr Cokane? he does a little business for me
now as a friend, and gives me a help with my correspondence: sekketerry we call it. Ive no litery style, and thats the
truth; so Mr Cokane kindly puts it into my letters and
draft prospectuses and advertisements and the like. Dont
you, Cokane? Of course you do: why shouldnt you? He's
been helping me to pursuade his old friend, Dr Trench,
about the matter we were speaking of.

COKANE [*austerely*] No, Mr Lickcheese, not trying to persuade him. No: this is a matter of principle with me. I say
it is your duty, Henry – your duty – to put those abominable buildings into proper and habitable repair. As a man
of science you owe it to the community to perfect the
sanitary arrangements. In questions of duty there is no
room for persuasion, even from the oldest friend.

SARTORIUS [*to Trench*] I certainly feel, as Mr Cokane puts
it, that it is our duty: one which I have perhaps too long
neglected out of regard for the poorest class of tenants.

LICKCHEESE. Not a doubt of it, gents: a dooty. I can be
as sharp as any man when it's a question of business; but
dooty's another pair o' shoes.

TRENCH. Well, I dont see that it's any more my duty now
than it was four months ago. I look at it simply as a
question of so much money.

COKANE. Shame, Harry, shame! Shame!

TRENCH. Oh, shut up, you fool. [*Cokane springs up*].

LICKCHEESE [*catching his coat and holding him*] Steady! steady!

88

Mr Sekketerry. Dr Trench is only joking.

COKANE. I insist on the withdrawal of that expression. I have been called a fool.

TRENCH [*morosely*] So you are a fool.

COKANE. Then you are a damned fool. Now, sir!

TRENCH. All right. Now weve settled that. [*Cokane, with a snort, sits down*]. What I mean is this. Dont lets have any nonsense about this job. As I understand it, Robbins's Row is to be pulled down to make way for the new street into the Strand; and the straight tip now is to go for compensation.

LICKCHEESE [*chuckling*] That'so, Dr Trench. Thats it.

TRENCH [*continuing*] Well, it appears that the dirtier a place is the more rent you get; and the decenter it is, the more compensation you get. So we're to give up dirt and go in for decency.

SARTORIUS. I should not put it exactly in that way; but –

COKANE. Quite right, Mr Sartorius, quite right. The case could not have been stated in worse taste or with less tact.

LICKCHEESE. Sh-sh-sh-sh!

SARTORIUS. I do not quite go with you there, Mr Cokane. Dr Trench puts the case frankly as a man of business. I take the wider view of a public man. We live in a progressive age; and humanitarian ideas are advancing and must be taken into account. But my practical conclusion is the same as his. I should hardly feel justified in making a large claim for compensation under existing circumstances.

LICKCHEESE. Of course not; and you wouldnt get it if you did. You see, it's like this, Dr Trench. Theres no doubt that the Vestries has legal powers to play old Harry with slum properties, and spoil the houseknacking game if they please. That didnt matter in the good old times, because the Vestries used to be us ourselves. Nobody ever knew a word about the election; and we used to get ten of us into a room and elect one another, and do what we liked. Well, that cock wont fight any longer; and, to put it short, the game is up for men in the position of you and Mr Sartorius. My advice to you is, take the present chance of getting out of it. Spend a little money on the block at the Cribbs Market end: enough to make it look like a model dwelling, you know; and let the other block to me on fair terms for a depot of the North Thames Iced Mutton Company. Theyll be knocked down inside of two years to make room for the new north and south main thoroughfare; and youll be compensated to the tune of double the present valuation, with the cost of the improvements thrown in. Leave things as they are; and you stand a good chance of being fined, or condemned, or pulled down before long. Now's your time.

COKANE. Hear, hear! Hear, hear! Hear, hear! Admirably put from the business point of view! I recognize the uselessness of putting the moral point of view to you, Trench; but even you must feel the cogency of Mr Lickcheese's business statement.

TRENCH. But why cant you act without me? What have I got to do with it? I'm only a mortgagee.

SARTORIUS. There is a certain risk in this compensation investment, Dr Trench. The County Council may alter the line of the new street. If that happens, the money spent in improving the houses will be thrown away: simply thrown away. Worse than thrown away, in fact; for the new buildings may stand unlet or half let for years. But you will expect your seven per cent as usual.

TRENCH. A man must live.

COKANE. Je n'en vois pas la nécessité.

TRENCH. Shut up, Billy; or else speak some language you understand. No, Mr Sartorius: I should be very glad to stand in with you if I could afford it; but I cant; so you may leave me out of it.

LICKCHEESE. Well, all I can say is that youre a very foolish young man.

COKANE. What did I tell you, Harry?

TRENCH. I dont see that it's any business of yours, Mr Lickcheese.

LICKCHEESE. It's a free country: every man has a right to his opinion.

COKANE. Hear, hear!

LICKCHEESE. Come! wheres your feelins for them poor people, Dr Trench? Remember how it went to your heart when I first told you about them. What! are you going to turn hard?

TRENCH. No: it wont do: you cant get over me that way. You proved to me before that there was no use in being sentimental over that slum shop of ours; and it's no good your turning round on the philanthropic tack now that you want me to put my capital into your speculation. Ive had my lesson; and I'm going to stick to my present income. It's little enough for me as it is.

SARTORIUS. It really matters nothing to me, Dr Trench, how you decide. I can easily raise the money elsewhere and pay you off. Then since you are resolved to run no risks, you can invest your ten thousand pounds in Consols and get two hundred and fifty pounds a year for it instead of seven hundred.

Trench, completely outwitted, stares at them in consternation. Cokane breaks the silence.

COKANE. This is what comes of being avaricious, Harry. Two thirds of your income gone at one blow. And I must say it serves you right.

TRENCH. Thats all very fine; but I dont understand it. If you can do this to me, why didnt you do it long ago?

SARTORIUS. Because, as I should probably have had to borrow at the same rate, I should have saved nothing; whereas you would have lost over four hundred a year: a very serious matter for you. I had no desire to be unfriendly; and even now I should be glad to let the mortgage stand, were it not that the circumstances mentioned by Mr Lickcheese force my hand. Besides, Dr Trench, I hoped for some time that our interests might be joined by closer ties than those of friendship.

LICKCHEESE [*jumping up, relieved*] There! Now the murder's out. Excuse me, Dr Trench. Ex – cuse me, Mr Sartorius: excuse my freedom. Why not Dr Trench marry Miss Blanche, and settle the whole affair that way?

Sensation. Lickcheese sits down triumphant.

COKANE. You forget, Mr Lickcheese, that the young lady, whose taste has to be considered, decisively objected to him.

TRENCH. Oh! Perhaps you think she was struck with you.

COKANE. I do not say so, Trench. No man of any delicacy would suggest such a thing. You have an untutored mind, Trench, an untutored mind.

TRENCH. Well, Cokane: Ive told you my opinion of you already.

COKANE [*rising wildly*] And I have told you my opinion of you. I will repeat it if you wish. I am ready to repeat it.

LICKCHEESE. Come, Mr Sekketerry: you and me, as married men, is out of the unt as far as young ladies is concerned. I know Miss Blanche: she has her father's eye for business. Explain this job to her; and she'll make it up with Dr Trench. Why not have a bit of romance in business when it costs nothing? We all have our feelins: we aint mere calculatin machines.

SARTORIUS [*revolted*] Do you think, Lickcheese, that my daughter is to be made part of a money bargain between you and these gentlemen?

LICKCHEESE. Oh come, Sartorius! dont talk as if you was the only father in the world. I have a daughter too; and my feelins in that matter is just as fine as yours. I propose nothing but what is for Miss Blanche's advantage and Dr Trench's.

COKANE. Lickcheese expresses himself roughly, Mr Sartorius; but his is a sterling nature; and what he says is to the point. If Miss Sartorius can really bring herself to care for Harry, I am far from desiring to stand in the way of such an arrangement.

TRENCH. Why, what have you got to do with it?

LICKCHEESE. Easy, Dr Trench, easy. We want your opinion. Are you still on for marrying Miss Blanche if she's agreeable?

TRENCH [*shortly*] I dont know that I am. [*Sartorius rises indignantly*].

LICKCHEESE. Easy one moment, Mr Sartorius. [*To Trench*] Come now, Dr Trench! you say you dont know that you are. But do you know that you aint? thats what we want to know.

TRENCH [*sulkily*] I wont have the relations between Miss Sartorius and myself made part of a bargain. [*He rises to leave the table*].

LICKCHEESE [*rising*] Thats enough: a gentleman could say no less. [*Insinuatingly*] Now, would you mind me and Cokane and the guvnor steppin into the study to arrange about the lease to the North Thames Iced Mutton Company?

TRENCH. Oh, *I* dont mind. I'm going home. Theres nothing more to say.

LICKCHEESE. No: dont go. Only just a minute: me and Cokane will be back in no time to see you home. Youll wait for us, wont you?

TRENCH. Oh well, if you wish, yes.

LICKCHEESE [*cheerily*] Didnt I know you would!

SARTORIUS [*at the study door, to Cokane*] After you, sir.

Cokane bows formally and goes into the study.

LICKCHEESE [*at the door, aside to Sartorius*] You never ad such a managin man as me, Sartorius. [*He goes into the study chuckling, followed by Sartorius*].

Trench, left alone, looks round carefully and listens a moment. Then he goes on tiptoe to the piano and leans upon it with folded arms, gazing at Blanche's portrait. Blanche herself appears presently at the study door. When she sees how he is occupied, she closes it softly and steals over to him, watching him intently. He rises from his leaning attitude, and takes the portrait from the easel, and is about to kiss it when, taking a second look round to reassure himself that nobody is watching him, he finds Blanche close upon him. He drops the portrait, and stares at her without the least presence of mind.

BLANCHE [*shrewishly*] Well? So you have come back here. You have had the meanness to come into this house again. [*He flushes and retreats a step. She follows him up remorselessly*]. What a poor spirited creature you must be! Why dont you go? [*Red and wincing, he starts huffily to get his hat from the table; but when he turns to the door with it she deliberately stands in his way; so that he has to stop*]. I dont want you to stay. [*For a moment they stand face to face, quite close to one another, she provocative, taunting, half defying, half inviting him to advance, in a flush of undisguised animal excitement. It suddenly flashes on him that all this ferocity is erotic: that she is making love to him. His eye lights up: a cunning expression comes into the corners of his mouth: with a heavy assumption of indifference he walks straight back to his chair, and plants himself in it with his arms folded. She comes down the room after him*]. But I forgot: you have found that there is some money to be made here. Lickcheese told you. You, who were so disinterested, so independent, that you could not accept anything from my father! [*At the end of every sentence she waits to see what execution she has done*]. I suppose you will try to persuade me that you have come down here on a great philanthropic enterprise – to befriend the poor by having those houses rebuilt, eh? [*Trench maintains his attitude and makes no sign*]. Yes: when my father makes you do it. And when Lickcheese has discovered some way of making it profitable. Oh, I know papa; and I know you. And for the sake of that, you come back here – into the house where you were refused – ordered out. [*Trench's face darkens: her eyes gleam as she sees it*]. Aha! you remember that. You know it's true: you cant deny it. [*She sits down, and softens her tone a little as she affects to pity him*]. Well, let me tell you that you cut a poor figure, a very, very poor figure, Harry. [*At the word Harry he relaxes the fold of his arms; and a faint grin of anticipated victory appears on his face*]. And you, too, a gentleman! so highly connected! with such distinguished relations! so particular as to where your money comes from! I wonder at you. I really wonder at you. I should have thought that if your fine family gave you nothing else, it might at least have given you some sense of personal dignity. Perhaps you think you look dignified at present: eh? [*No reply*]. Well, I can assure you that you dont: you look most ridiculous – as foolish as a man could look – you dont know what to say; and you dont know what to do. But after all, I really dont see what any one could say in defence of such conduct. [*He looks straight in front of him, and purses up his lips as if whistling. This annoys her; and she becomes affectedly polite*]. I am afraid I am in your way, Dr Trench. [*She rises*]. I shall not intrude on you any longer. You seem so perfectly at home that I need make no apology for leaving you to yourself. [*She makes a feint of going to the door; but he does not budge; and she returns and comes behind his chair*]. Harry. [*He does not turn. She comes a step nearer*]. Harry: I want you to answer me a question. [*Earnestly, stooping over him*] Look me in the face. [*No reply*]. Do you hear? [*Seizing his cheeks and twisting his head round*] Look – me – in – the – face. [*He shuts his eyes tight and grins. She suddenly kneels down beside him with her breast against his shoulder*]. Harry: what were you doing with my photograph just now, when you thought you were alone? [*He opens his eyes: they are full of delight. She flings her arms around him, and crushes him in an ecstatic embrace as she adds, with furious tenderness*] How dare you touch anything belonging to me?

The study door opens and voices are heard.

TRENCH. I hear some one coming.

She regains her chair with a bound, and pushes it back as far as

95

possible. Cokane, Lickcheese, and Sartorius come from the study.
Sartorius and Lickcheese come to Trench. Cokane crosses to
Blanche in his most killing manner.

COKANE. How do you do, Miss Sartorius? Nice weather for
the return of l'enfant prodigue, eh?

BLANCHE. Capital, Mr Cokane. So glad to see you. [*She*
gives him her hand, which he kisses with gallantry].

LICKCHEESE [*on Trench's left, in a low voice*] Any noos for us,
Dr Trench?

TRENCH [*to Sartorius, on his right*] I'll stand in, compensation
or no compensation. [*He shakes Sartorius's hand*].

The parlormaid has just appeared at the door.

THE PARLORMAID. Supper is ready, miss.

COKANE. Allow me.

Exeunt omnes: Blanche on Cokane's arm; Lickcheese jocosely
taking Sartorius on one arm, and Trench on the other.

THE PHILANDERER
A Topical Comedy

PREFATORY NOTE

THERE is a disease to which plays as well as men become liable with advancing years. In men it is called doting, in plays dating. The more topical the play the more it dates. The Philanderer suffers from this complaint. In the eighteen-nineties, when it was written, not only dramatic literature but life itself was staggering from the impact of Ibsen's plays, which reached us in 1889. The state of mind represented by the Ibsen Club in this play was familiar then to our Intelligentsia. That far more numerous body which may be called the Unintelligentsia was as unconscious of Ibsen as of any other political influence: quarter of a century elapsed before an impatient heaven rained German bombs down on them to wake them from their apathy. That accustomed them to much more startling departures from Victorian routine than those that shock the elderly colonel and the sentimental theatre critic in The Philanderer; but they do not associate their advance in liberal morals with the great Norwegian. Even the Intelligentsia have forgotten that the lesson that might have saved the lives of ten million persons hideously slaughtered was offered to them by Ibsen.

I make no attempt to bring the play up to date. I should as soon think of bringing Ben Jonson's Bartholomew Fair up to date by changing the fair into a Woolworth store. The human nature in it is still in the latest fashion: indeed I am far from sure that its ideas, instead of being 36 years behind the times, are not for a considerable section of the community 36 years ahead of them. My picture of the past may be for many people a picture of the future. At all events I shall leave the play as it is; for all the attempts within my experience to modernize ancient plays have only produced worse anachronisms than those they aimed at remedying.

1930

THE PHILANDERER

ACT I

A lady and gentleman are making love to one another in the drawing room of a flat in Ashley Gardens in the Victoria district of London. It is past ten at night. The walls are hung with theatrical engravings and photographs: Kemble as Hamlet, Mrs Siddons as Queen Katharine pleading in court, Macready as Werner (after Maclise), Sir Henry Irving as Richard III (after Long), Ellen Terry, Mrs Kendal, Ada Rehan, Sarah Bernhardt, Henry Arthur Jones, Sir Arthur Pinero, Sydney Grundy, and so on, but not Eleonora Duse nor anyone connected with Ibsen. The room is not rectangular, one corner being cut off diagonally by the doorway, and the opposite one rounded by a turret window filled up with a stand of flowers surrounding a statuet of Shakespear. The fireplace is on the doorway side, with an armchair near it. A small round table, further from the door on the same side, with a chair beside it, has a yellow backed French novel lying open on it. The piano, a grand, is on the Shakespear side, open, with the keyboard at right angles to the wall. The piece of music on the desk is When Other Lips. Incandescent lights, well shaded, are on the piano and mantelpiece. Near the piano is a sofa, on which the lady and gentleman are seated affectionately side by side, in one another's arms.

The lady, Grace Tranfield, is about 32, slight of build, delicate of feature, and sensitive in expression. She is just now given up to the emotion of the moment; but her well closed mouth, proudly set brows, firm chin, and elegant carriage shew plenty of determination and self-respect. She is in evening dress.

The gentleman, Leonard Charteris, a few years older, is unconventionally but smartly dressed in a velvet jacket and cashmere trousers. His collar, dyed Wotan blue, is part of his shirt, and turns over a garnet colored scarf of Indian silk, secured by a turquoise ring. He wears socks and leather sandals. The arrangement of his tawny hair, and of his moustaches and short beard, is apparently left to Nature; but he has taken care that Nature shall do him the fullest justice. His amative enthusiasm, at which he is himself laughing, and

*his clever, imaginative, humorous ways, contrast strongly with the
sincere tenderness and dignified quietness of the woman.*

CHARTERIS [*impulsively clasping Grace*] My dearest love.

GRACE [*responding affectionately*] My darling. Are you happy?

CHARTERIS. In Heaven.

GRACE. My own.

CHARTERIS. My heart's love. [*He sighs happily, and takes her
hands in his, looking quaintly at her*]. That must positively be
my last kiss, Grace; or I shall become downright silly. Let
us talk. [*He releases her and sits a little apart*]. Grace: is this
your first love affair?

GRACE. Have you forgotten that I am a widow? Do you
think I married Tranfield for money?

CHARTERIS. How do I know? Besides, you might have
married him not because you loved him, but because you
didnt love anybody else. When one is young, one marries
out of mere curiosity, just to see what it's like.

GRACE. Well, since you ask me, I never was in love with
Tranfield, though I only found that out when I fell in love
with you. But I used to like him for being in love with me.
It brought out all the good in him so much that I have
wanted to be in love with someone ever since. I hope, now
that I am in love with you, you will like me for it just as I
liked Tranfield.

CHARTERIS. My dear: it is because I like you that I want to
marry you. I could love anybody—any pretty woman, that is.

GRACE. Do you really mean that, Leonard?

CHARTERIS. Of course. Why not?

GRACE [*reflecting*] Never mind. Now tell me, is this your
first love affair?

CHARTERIS [*amazed at the simplicity of the question*] No, bless
my soul, no; nor my second, nor my third.

GRACE. But I mean your first serious one?

CHARTERIS [*with a certain hesitation*] Yes. [*There is a pause.
She is not convinced. He adds, with a very perceptible load on his*

conscience] It is the first in which *I* have been serious.

GRACE [*searchingly*] I see. The other parties were always serious.

CHARTERIS. Not always. Heaven forbid!

GRACE. How often?

CHARTERIS. Well, once.

GRACE. Julia Craven?

CHARTERIS [*recoiling*] Who told you that? [*She shakes her head mysteriously. He turns away from her moodily and adds*] You had much better not have asked.

GRACE [*gently*] I'm sorry, dear. [*She puts out her hand and pulls softly at him to bring him near her again*].

CHARTERIS [*yielding mechanically to the pull, and allowing her hand to rest on his arm, but sitting squarely without the least attempt to return the caress*] Do I feel harder to the touch than I did five minutes ago?

GRACE. What nonsense!

CHARTERIS. I feel as if my body had turned into the toughest hickory. That is what comes of reminding me of Julia Craven. [*Brooding, with his chin on his right hand and his elbow on his knee*] I have sat alone with her just as I am sitting with you –

GRACE [*shrinking from him*] Just!

CHARTERIS [*sitting upright and facing her steadily*] Just exactly. She has put her hands in mine, and laid her cheek against mine, and listened to me saying all sorts of silly things. [*Grace, chilled to the soul, rises from the sofa and sits down on the piano stool, with her back to the keyboard*]. Ah, you dont want to hear any more of the story. So much the better.

GRACE [*deeply hurt, but controlling herself*] When did you break it off?

CHARTERIS [*guiltily*] Break it off?

GRACE [*firmly*] Yes: break it off.

CHARTERIS. Well: let me see. When did I fall in love with you?

GRACE. Did you break it off then?

CHARTERIS [*making it plainer and plainer that it has not been broken off*] It was clear then, of course, that it must be broken off.

GRACE. And did you break it off?

CHARTERIS. Oh, yes: *I* broke it off.

GRACE. But did she break it off?

CHARTERIS [*rising*] As a favor to me, dearest, change the subject. Come away from the piano: I want you to sit here with me. [*He takes a step towards her*].

GRACE. No. I also have grown hard to the touch: much harder than hickory for the present. Did she break it off?

CHARTERIS. My dear, be reasonable. It was fully explained to her that it was to be broken off.

GRACE. Did she accept the explanation?

CHARTERIS. She did what a woman like Julia always does. When I explained personally, she said it was not my better self that was speaking, and that she knew I still really loved her. When I wrote it to her with brutal explicitness, she read the letter carefully and then sent it back to me with a note to say that she had not had the courage to open it, and that I ought to be ashamed of having written it. [*He comes beside Grace, and puts his left hand caressingly round her neck*]. You see, dearie, she wont look the situation in the face.

GRACE [*shaking off his hand and turning a little away on the stool*] I am afraid, from the light way you speak of it, you did not sound the right chord.

CHARTERIS. My dear: when you are doing what a woman calls breaking her heart, you may sound the very prettiest chords you can find on the piano; but to her ears it is just like this. [*He sits down on the bass end of the keyboard. Grace puts her fingers in her ears. He rises and moves away from the piano, saying*] No, my dear: Ive been kind; Ive been frank; Ive been everything that a good-natured man can be; but she only takes it as the making up of a lovers' quarrel. [*Grace winces*]. Frankness and kindness: one is as bad as the other. Especially frankness. Ive tried both. [*He crosses to the fire-*

place, and stands facing the fire, looking at the ornaments on the mantelpiece, and warming his hands].

GRACE [*her voice a little strained*] What are you going to try now?

CHARTERIS [*on the hearthrug, turning to face her*] Action, my dear. Marriage. In that she must believe. She wont be convinced by anything short of it; because, you see, Ive had some tremendous philanderings before, and have gone back to her after them.

GRACE. And so that is why you want to marry me?

CHARTERIS. I cannot deny it, my love. Yes: it is your mission to rescue me from Julia.

GRACE [*rising*] Then, if you please, I decline to be made use of for any such purpose. I will not steal you from another woman. [*She walks up and down the room with ominous disquiet*].

CHARTERIS. Steal me! [*He comes towards her*]. Grace: I have a question to put to you as an advanced woman. Mind! as an advanced woman. Does Julia belong to me? Am I her owner – her master?

GRACE. Certainly not. No woman is the property of a man. A woman belongs to herself and to nobody else.

CHARTERIS. Quite right. Ibsen for ever! Thats exactly my opinion. Now tell me, do I belong to Julia; or have I a right to belong to myself?

GRACE [*puzzled*] Of course you have; but –

CHARTERIS [*interrupting her triumphantly*] Then how can you steal me from Julia if I dont belong to her? [*He catches her by the shoulders and holds her out at arm's length in front of him*]. Eh, little philosopher? No, my dear: if Ibsen sauce is good for the goose, it's good for the gander as well. Besides [*coaxing her*] it was nothing but a philander with Julia. Nothing else in the world, I assure you.

GRACE [*breaking away from him*] So much the worse! I hate your philanderings: they make me ashamed of you and of myself. [*She goes to the sofa and sits in the corner furthest from the piano, leaning gloomily on her elbow with her face averted*].

103

CHARTERIS. Grace: you utterly misunderstand the origin of my philanderings. [*He sits down beside her*]. Listen to me. Am I a particularly handsome man?

GRACE [*astonished at his conceit*] No.

CHARTERIS [*triumphantly*] You admit it. Am I a well dressed man?

GRACE. Not particularly.

CHARTERIS. Of course not. Have I a romantic mysterious charm about me? do I look as if a secret sorrow preyed on me? am I gallant to women?

GRACE. Not in the least.

CHARTERIS. Certainly not. No one can accuse me of it. Then whose fault is it that half the women I speak to fall in love with me? Not mine: I hate it: it bores me to distraction. At first it flattered me – delighted me – that was how Julia got me, because she was the first woman who had the pluck to make me a declaration. But I soon had enough of it; and at no time have I taken the initiative and persecuted women with my advances as women have persecuted me. Never. Except, of course, in your case.

GRACE. Oh, you need not make any exception. I had a good deal of trouble to induce you to come and see us. You were very coy.

CHARTERIS [*fondly, taking her hand*] With you, dearest, the coyness was sheer coquetry. I loved you from the first, and fled only that you might pursue. But come! let us talk about something really interesting. [*He takes her in his arms*]. Do you love me better than anyone else in the world?

GRACE. I dont think you like to be loved too much.

CHARTERIS. That depends on who the person is. You [*pressing her to his heart*] cannot love me too much: you cannot love me half enough. I reproach you every day for your coldness, your – [*A violent double knock without. They start and listen, still in one another's arms, hardly daring to breathe*]. Who the deuce is calling at this hour?

GRACE. I cant imagine. [*They listen guiltily. The door of the flat is opened without. They hastily get away from one another*].

A WOMAN'S VOICE OUTSIDE. Is Mr Charteris here?

CHARTERIS [*springing up*] Julia! The devil! [*He stands at the end of the sofa with his eyes fixed on the door and his heart beating very unpleasantly*].

GRACE [*rising also*] What can she want?

THE VOICE. Never mind: I will announce myself. [*A beautiful, dark, tragic looking woman, in mantle and toque, appears at the door, raging*]. Oh, this is charming. I have interrupted a pretty tête-à-tête. Oh, you villain! [*She comes straight at Grace. Charteris runs across behind the sofa, and stops her. She struggles furiously with him. Grace preserves her self-possession, but retreats quietly to the piano. Julia, finding Charteris too strong for her, gives up her attempt to get at Grace, but strikes him in the face as she frees herself*].

CHARTERIS [*shocked*] Oh, Julia, Julia! This is too bad.

JULIA. Is it, indeed, too bad? What are you doing up here with that woman? You scoundrel! But now listen to me, Leonard: you have driven me to desperation; and I dont care what I do, or who hears me. I'll not bear it. She shall not have my place with you –

CHARTERIS. Sh-sh!

JULIA. No, no: I dont care: I will expose her true character before everybody. You belong to me; you have no right to be here; and she knows it.

CHARTERIS. I think you had better let me take you home, Julia.

JULIA. I will not. I am not going home: I am going to stay here – h e r e – until I have made you give her up.

CHARTERIS. My dear: you must be reasonable. You really cannot stay in Mrs Tranfield's house if she objects. She can ring the bell and have us both put out.

JULIA. Let her do it then. Let her ring the bell if she dares. Let us see how this pure virtuous creature will face the scandal of what I will declare about her. Let us see how you will face it. I have nothing to lose. Everybody knows how you have treated me: you have boasted of your conquests, you poor pitiful vain creature: I am the common talk of your acquaintances and hers. Oh, I have calculated my advantage [*she tears off her mantle*]: I am a most unhappy and injured woman; but I am not the fool you take me to be. I am going to stay: see! [*She flings the mantle on the round table; puts her toque on it; and sits down*]. Now, Mrs Tranfield: theres the bell [*pointing to the button beside the fireplace*]: why dont you ring? [*Grace, looking attentively at Charteris, does not move*]. Ha! ha! I thought so.

CHARTERIS [*quietly, without relaxing his watch on Julia*] Mrs Tranfield: I think you had better go into another room. [*Grace makes a movement towards the door, but stops and looks inquiringly at Charteris as Julia springs up to intercept her. He advances a step to guard the way to the door*].

JULIA. She shall not. She shall stay here. She shall know what you are, and how you have been in love with me: how it is not two days since you kissed me and told me that the future would be as happy as the past. [*Screaming at him*] You did: deny it if you dare.

CHARTERIS [*to Grace in a low voice*] Go.

GRACE [*with nonchalant disgust, going*] Get her away as soon as you can, Leonard.

Julia, with a stifled cry of rage, rushes at Grace, who is crossing behind the sofa towards the door. Charteris seizes Julia, and prevents her from getting past the sofa. Grace goes out. Charteris, holding Julia fast, looks around to the door to see whether Grace is safely out of the room.

JULIA [*suddenly ceasing to struggle, and speaking with the most pathetic dignity*] Oh, there is no need to be violent. [*He passes her across to the sofa, and leans against the end of it, panting and mopping his forehead*]. That is worthy of you! to use brute force! to humiliate me before her! [*She bursts into tears*].

CHARTERIS [*to himself, with melancholy conviction*] This is going to be a cheerful evening. Now patience! patience! patience! [*He sits down on a chair near the round table*].

JULIA [*in anguish*] Leonard: have you no feeling for me?

CHARTERIS. Only an intense desire to get you safely out of this.

JULIA [*fiercely*] I am not going to stir.

CHARTERIS [*wearily*] Well, well. [*He heaves a long sigh*].

> *They sit silent for a while : Julia striving, not to regain her self-control, but to maintain her rage at boiling point.*

JULIA [*rising suddenly*] I am going to speak to that woman.

CHARTERIS [*jumping up*] No, no. Hang it, Julia, dont lets have another wrestling match. Remember: I'm getting on for forty: youre too young for me. Sit down; or else let me take you home. Suppose her father comes in!

JULIA. I dont care. It rests with you. I am ready to go if she will give you up: until then I stay. Those are my terms: you owe me that. [*She sits down determinedly*].

> *Charteris looks at her for a moment; then, making up his mind, goes resolutely to the sofa; sits down near the end of it, she being at the opposite end; and speaks with biting emphasis.*

CHARTERIS. I owe you just exactly nothing.

JULIA [*reproachfully*] Nothing! You can look me in the face and say that? Oh, Leonard!

CHARTERIS. Let me remind you, Julia, that when first we became acquainted, the position you took up was that of a woman of advanced views.

JULIA. That should have made you respect me the more.

CHARTERIS [*placably*] So it did, my dear. But that is not the point. As a woman of advanced views, you were determined to be free. You regarded marriage as a degrading bargain, by which a woman sells herself to a man for the social status of a wife and the right to be supported and pensioned in old age out of his income. Thats the advanced view: our view. Besides, if you had married me, I might have turned out a drunkard, a criminal, an imbecile, a horror to you; and you couldnt have released yourself. Too big a risk, you see. Thats the rational view: our view. Accordingly, you reserved the right to leave me at any time if you found our companionship incompatible with – what was the expression you used? – with your full development as a human being. I think that was how you put the Ibsenist view: our view. So I had to be content with a charming philander, which taught me a great deal, and brought some hours of exquisite happiness.

JULIA. Leonard: you confess, then, that you owe me something?

CHARTERIS [*haughtily*] No: what I received, I paid. Did you learn nothing from me? was there no delight for you in our friendship?

JULIA [*vehemently and movingly; for she is now sincere*] No. You made me pay dearly for every moment of happiness. You revenged yourself on me for the humiliation of being the slave of your passion for me. I was never sure of you for a moment. I trembled whenever a letter came from you, lest it should contain some stab for me. I dreaded your visits almost as much as I longed for them. I was your plaything, not your companion. [*She rises, exclaiming*] Oh, there was such suffering in my happinesss that I hardly knew joy from pain. [*She sinks on the piano stool, and adds, as she buries her face in her hands and turns away from him*] Better for me if I had never met you!

CHARTERIS [*rising indignantly*] You ungenerous wretch! Is this your gratitude for the way I have just been flattering you? What have I not endured from you? endured with angelic patience? Did I not find out, before our friendship was a fortnight old, that all your advanced views were merely a fashion picked up and followed like any other fashion, without understanding or meaning a word of them? Did you not, in spite of your care for your own liberty, set up claims on me compared to which the claims of the most jealous wife would have been trifles? Have I a single woman friend whom you have not abused as old, ugly, vicious –

JULIA [*quickly looking up*] So they are.

CHARTERIS. Well, then I'll come to grievances that even you can understand. I accuse you of habitual and intolerable jealousy and ill temper; of insulting me on imaginary provocation; of positively beating me; of stealing letters of mine —

JULIA. Yes, nice letters!

CHARTERIS. — of breaking your solemn promises not to do it again; of spending hours — aye, days! piecing together the contents of my waste paper basket in your search for more letters; and then representing yourself as an ill used saint and martyr wantonly betrayed and deserted by a selfish monster of a man.

JULIA [*rising*] I was justified in reading your letters. Our perfect confidence in one another gave me the right to do it.

CHARTERIS. Thank you. Then I hasten to break off a confidence which gives such rights. [*He sits down sulkily on the sofa*].

JULIA [*bending over him threateningly*] You have no right to break it off.

CHARTERIS. I have. You refused to marry me because —

JULIA. I did not. You never asked me. If we were married, you would never dare treat me as you are doing now.

CHARTERIS [*laboriously going back to his argument*] It was understood between us as people of advanced views that we were not to marry; because, as the law stands, I might have become a drunkard, a —

JULIA. — a criminal, an imbecile, or a horror. You said that before. [*She sits down beside him with a fling*].

CHARTERIS [*politely*] I beg your pardon, my dear. I know I have a habit of repeating myself. The point is that you reserved your freedom to give me up when you pleased.

JULIA. Well, what of that? I do not please to give you up; and I will not. You have not become a drunkard or a criminal.

CHARTERIS. You dont see the point yet, Julia. You seem to forget that in reserving your freedom to leave me in case

109

I should turn out badly, you also reserved my freedom to leave you in case you should turn out badly.

JULIA. Very ingenious. And pray, have *I* become a drunkard, or a criminal, or an imbecile?

CHARTERIS. You have become what is infinitely worse than all three together: a jealous termagant.

JULIA [*shaking her head bitterly*] Yes: abuse me: call me names.

CHARTERIS. I now assert the right I reserved: the right of breaking with you when I please. Advanced views, Julia, involve advanced duties: you cannot be an advanced woman when you want to bring a man to your feet, and a conventional woman when you want to hold him there against his will. Advanced people form charming friendships: conventional people marry. Marriage suits a good many people; and its first duty is fidelity. Friendship suits some people; and its first duty is unhesitating uncomplaining acceptance of a notice of change of feeling from either side. You chose friendship instead of marriage. Now do your duty, and accept your notice.

JULIA. Never. We are engaged in the eye of – the eye of –

CHARTERIS. Yes, Julia? Cant you get it out? In the eye of something that advanced women dont believe in, eh?

JULIA [*throwing herself at his feet*] Oh, Leonard, dont be cruel. I'm too miserable to argue – to think. I only know I love you. You reproach me with not wanting to marry you. I would have married you at any time after I came to love you, if you had asked me. I will marry you now if you will.

CHARTERIS. I wont, my dear. Thats flat. We're intellectually incompatible.

JULIA. But why? We could be so happy. You love me: I know you love me. I feel it. You say 'My dear' to me: you have said it several times this evening. I know I have been wicked, odious, bad: I say nothing in defence of myself. But dont be hard on me. I was distracted by the thought of losing you. I cant face life without you, Leonard. I was happy when I met you: I had never loved

any one; and if you had only let me alone, I could have
gone on contentedly by myself. But I cant now. I must
have you with me. Dont cast me off without a thought of
all I have at stake. I could be a friend to you if you would
only let me; if you would only tell me your plans; give me
a share in your work; treat me as something more than
the amusement of an idle hour. Oh, Leonard, Leonard,
youve never given me a chance: indeed you havnt. I'll take
pains; I'll read; I'll try to think; I'll conquer my jealousy;
I'll – [*she breaks down, rocking her head desperately on his knees
and writhing*]. Oh, I'm mad: I'm mad: youll kill me if you
desert me.

CHARTERIS [*petting her*] My dear love, dont cry: dont go
on in this way. You know I cant help it.

JULIA [*sobbing as he rises and tenderly lifts her with him*] Oh,
you can, you can. One word from you will make us happy
for ever.

CHARTERIS [*diplomatically*] Come, my dear: we really must
go. We cant stay until Cuthbertson comes. [*He releases
her gently, and takes her mantle from the table*]. Here is your
mantle: put it on and be good. You have given me a
terrible evening: you must have some consideration for me.

JULIA [*dangerous again*] Then I am to be cast off?

CHARTERIS [*coaxingly*] You are to put on your bonnet,
dearest. [*He puts the mantle on her shoulders*].

JULIA [*with a bitter half laugh, half sob*] Well, I suppose I must
do what I am told. [*She goes to the table, and looks for her
toque. She sees the yellow backed French novel*]. Ah, look at that
[*holding it out to him*]! Look at what the creature reads!
filthy, vile French stuff that no decent woman would
touch. And you – you have been reading it with her.

CHARTERIS. You recommended that book to me yourself.

JULIA. Faugh! [*She dashes it on the floor*].

CHARTERIS [*running anxiously to the book*] Dont damage
property, Julia. [*He picks it up and dusts it*]. Making scenes
is an affair of sentiment: damaging property is serious,

[*He replaces it on the table*]. And now do pray come along.

JULIA [*implacably*] You can go: there is nothing to prevent you. I will not stir. [*She sits down stubbornly on the sofa*].

CHARTERIS [*losing patience*] Oh come! I am not going to begin all this over again. There are limits even to my forbearance. Come on.

JULIA. I will not. I tell you.

CHARTERIS. Then goodnight. [*He makes resolutely for the door. With a rush, she gets there before him and bars his way*]. I thought you wanted me to go.

JULIA [*at the door*] You shall not leave me here alone.

CHARTERIS. Then come with me.

JULIA. Not until you have sworn to me to give up that woman.

CHARTERIS. My dear: I will swear anything if youll only come away and put an end to this.

JULIA [*perplexed, doubting him*] You will swear?

CHARTERIS. Solemnly. Propose the oath. I have been on the point of swearing for the last half hour.

JULIA [*despairingly*] You are only making fun of me. I want no oaths. I want your promise: your sacred word of honor.

CHARTERIS. Certainly: anything you demand, on condition that you come away immediately. On my sacred word of honor as a gentleman – as an Englishman – as anything you like – I will never see her again, never speak to her, never think of her. Now come.

JULIA. But are you in earnest? Will you keep your word?

CHARTERIS [*smiling subtly*] Now you are getting unreasonable. Do come along without any more nonsense. At any rate, I am going. I am not strong enough to carry you home; but I am strong enough to make my way through that door in spite of you. You will then have a new grievance against me for my brutal violence. [*He takes a step towards the door*].

JULIA [*solemnly*] If you do, I swear I will throw myself from that window, Leonard, as you pass out.

CHARTERIS [*unimpressed*] That window is at the back of the building. I shall pass out at the front: so you will not hurt me. Goodnight. [*He approaches the door*].

JULIA. Leonard: have you no pity?

CHARTERIS. Not the least. When you condescend to these antics you force me to despise you. How can a woman who behaves like a spoiled child and talks like a sentimental novel have the audacity to dream of being a companion for a man of any sort of sense or character? [*She gives an inarticulate cry, and throws herself sobbing on his breast*]. Come! dont cry, my dear Julia: you dont look half so beautiful as when youre happy: and it makes me all damp. Come along.

JULIA [*affectionately*] I'll come, dear, if you wish it. Give me one kiss.

CHARTERIS [*exasperated*] This is too much. No: I'm dashed if I will. Here: let me go, Julia [*She clings to him*]. Will you come without another word if I give you a kiss?

JULIA. I will do anything you wish, darling.

CHARTERIS. Well here. [*He takes her in his arms and gives her an unceremonious kiss*]. Now remember your promise. Come along.

JULIA. That was not a nice kiss, dearest. I want one of our old real kisses.

CHARTERIS [*furious*] Oh, go to the deuce. [*He disengages himself impulsively; and she, as if he had flung her down, falls pathetically with a stifled moan. With an angry look at her, he strides out and slams the door. She raises herself on one hand, listening to his retreating footsteps. They stop. Her face lights up with eager, triumphant cunning. The steps return hastily. She throws herself down again as before. Charteris reappears, in the utmost dismay, exclaiming*] Julia: we're done. Cuthbertson's coming upstairs with your father [*she sits up quickly*]. Do you hear? the two fathers!

JULIA [*sitting on the floor*] Impossible. They dont know one another.

CHARTERIS [*desperately*] I tell you theyre coming up together like twins. What on earth are we to do?

JULIA [*scrambling up with the help of his hand*] Quick: the lift: we can go down in that. [*She rushes to the table for her toque*].

CHARTERIS. No: the man's gone home; and the lift's locked.

JULIA [*putting on her toque at express speed*] Lets go up to the next floor.

CHARTERIS. There's no next floor. We're at the top of the house. No, no: you must invent some thumping lie. I cant think of one: you can, Julia. Exercise all your genius. I'll back you up.

JULIA. But –

CHARTERIS. Sh-sh! Here they are. Sit down and look at home. [*Julia tears off her toque and mantle; throws them on the table; and darts to the piano, at which she seats herself*].

JULIA. Come and sing.

She plays the symphony to When Other Lips. *Charteris stands at the piano, as if about to sing. Two elderly gentlemen enter. Julia stops playing.*

The elder of the two newcomers, Colonel Daniel Craven, affects the bluff simple veteran, and carries it off pleasantly and well, having a fine upright figure, and being, in fact, a goodnaturedly impulsive credulous person who, after an entirely thoughtless career as an officer and a gentleman, is now being startled into some sort of self-education by the surprising proceedings of his children.

His companion, Mr Joseph Cuthbertson, Grace's father, has none of the Colonel's boyishness. He is a man of fervent idealistic sentiment, so frequently outraged by the facts of life that he has acquired an habitually indignant manner, which unexpectedly becomes enthusiastic or affectionate when he speaks.

The two men differ greatly in expression. The Colonel's face is lined with weather, with age, with eating and drinking, and with the cumulative effect of many petty vexations, but not with thought: he is still fresh, still full of expectations of pleasure and novelty.

THE PHILANDERER

Cuthbertson has the lines of sedentary London brain work, with its chronic fatigue and longing for rest and recreative emotion, and its disillusioned indifference to adventure and enjoyment, except as a means of recuperation. His vigilant, irascible eye, piled-up hair, and the honorable seriousness with which he takes himself, give him an air of considerable consequence.

They are both in evening dress. Cuthbertson has not taken off his fur-collared overcoat.

CUTHBERTSON [*with a hospitable show of delight at finding visitors*] Dont stop, Miss Craven. Go on, Charteris.

He comes behind the sofa, and hangs his overcoat on it, after taking an opera glass and a theatre program from the pockets, and putting them down on the piano. Craven meanwhile goes to the fireplace, and plants himself on the hearthrug.

CHARTERIS. No, thank you. Miss Craven has just been taking me through an old song; and Ive had enough of it. [*He takes the song off the piano desk and lays it aside; then closes the lid over the keyboard*].

JULIA [*passing between the sofa and piano to shake hands with Cuthbertson*] Why, youve brought Daddy! What a surprise! [*Looking across to Craven*] So glad youve come, Dad. [*She takes a chair near the window, and sits there*].

CUTHBERTSON. Craven: let me introduce you to Mr Leonard Charteris, the famous Ibsenist philosopher.

CRAVEN. Oh, we know one another already. Charteris is quite at home in our house, Jo.

CUTHBERTSON. I beg both your pardons. He's quite at home here too. [*Charteris sits down on the piano stool*] By the bye, wheres Grace?

JULIA AND CHARTERIS. Er – [*They stop and look at one another*].

JULIA [*politely*] I beg your pardon, Mr Charteris: I interrupted you.

CHARTERIS. Not at all, Miss Craven. [*An awkward pause*].

CUTHBERTSON [*to help them out*] You were going to tell us about Grace, Charteris.

115

CHARTERIS. I was only going to say that I didnt know that you and Craven were acquainted.

CRAVEN. Why, *I* didnt know it until tonight. It's a most extraordinary thing. We met by chance at the theatre; and he turns out to be my oldest friend.

CUTHBERTSON [*energetically*] Yes, Craven; and do you see how this proves what I was saying to you about the break-up of family life? Here are all our young people bosom friends, inseparables; and yet they never said a word of it to us. We two, who knew each other before they were born, might never have met again if you hadnt popped into the stall next mine tonight by pure chance. Come: sit down [*bustling over to him affectionately, and pushing him into the armchair above the fire*]: theres your place, by my fireside, whenever you choose to fill it. [*He posts himself at the end of the sofa, leaning against it and admiring Craven*]. Just imagine you being Dan Craven!

CRAVEN. Just imagine you being Jo Cuthbertson, though! Thats a far more extraordinary coincidence; because I'd got it into my head that your name was Tranfield.

CUTHBERTSON. Oh, thats my daughter's name. She's a widow, you know. How uncommonly well you look, Dan! The years havnt hurt you much.

CRAVEN [*suddenly becoming unnaturally gloomy*] I look well. I even feel well. But my days are numbered.

CUTHBERTSON [*alarmed*] Oh, dont say that, my dear fellow. I hope not.

JULIA [*with anguish in her voice*] Daddy! [*Cuthbertson looks inquiringly round at her*].

CRAVEN. There, there, my dear: I was wrong to talk of it. It's a sad subject. But it's better that Cuthbertson should know. We used to be very close friends, and are so still, I hope. [*Cuthbertson goes to Craven and presses his hand silently; then returns to the sofa and sits down, pulling out his handkerchief, and displaying some emotion*].

CHARTERIS [*a little impatiently*] The fact is, Cuthbertson,

Craven's a devout believer in the department of witch-craft called medical science. He's celebrated in all the medical schools as an example of the newest sort of liver complaint. The doctors say he cant last another year: and he has fully made up his mind not to survive next Easter, just to oblige them.

CRAVEN [*with military affectation*] It's very kind of you to try to keep up my spirits by making light of it, Charteris. But I shall be ready when my time comes. I'm a soldier. [*A sob from Julia*]. Dont cry, Julia.

CUTHBERTSON [*huskily*] I hope you may long be spared, Dan.

CRAVEN. To oblige me, Jo, change the subject. [*He gets up, and again posts himself on the hearthrug with his back to the fire*].

CHARTERIS. Persuade him to join our club, Cuthbertson. He mopes.

JULIA. It's no use. Sylvia and I are always at him to join; but he wont.

CRAVEN. My child: I have my own club.

CHARTERIS [*contemptuously*] Yes: the Junior Army and Navy! Do you call that a club? Why, they darent let a woman cross the doorstep!

CRAVEN [*a little ruffled*] Clubs are a matter of taste, Charteris. You like a cock-and-hen club: I dont. It's bad enough to have Julia and her sister – a girl under twenty! – spending half their time at such a place. Besides, now really, such a name for a club! The Ibsen club! I should be laughed out of London. The Ibsen club! Come, Cuthbertson! back me up. I'm sure you agree with me.

CHARTERIS. Cuthbertson's a member.

CRAVEN [*amazed*] No! Why, he's been talking to me all the evening about the way in which everything is going to the dogs through advanced ideas in the younger genera-tion.

CHARTERIS. Of course. He's been studying it in the club. He's always there.

CUTHBERTSON [*warmly*] Not always. Dont exaggerate, Charteris. You know very well that though I joined the club on Grace's account, thinking that her father's presence there would be a protection and a – a sort of sanction, as it were, I never approved of it.

CRAVEN [*tactlessly harping on Cuthbertson's inconsistency*] Well, you know, this is unexpected: now it's really very unexpected. I should never have thought it from hearing you talk, Jo. Why, you said the whole modern movement was abhorrent to you because your life had been passed in witnessing scenes of suffering nobly endured and sacrifice willingly rendered by womanly women and manly men and deuce knows what else. Is it at the Ibsen club that you see all this manliness and womanliness?

CHARTERIS. Certainly not: the rules of the club forbid anything of the sort. Every candidate for membership must be nominated by a man and a woman, who both guarantee that the candidate, if female, is not womanly, and if male, not manly.

CRAVEN [*chuckling cunningly as he stoops to press his heated trousers againts his legs, which are chilly*] Wont do, Charteris. Cant take me in with so thin a story as that.

CUTHBERTSON [*vehemently*] It's true. It's monstrous: but it's true.

CRAVEN [*with rising indignation, as he begins to draw the inevitable inferences*] Do you mean to say that somebody had the audacity to guarantee that my Julia is not a womanly woman?

CHARTERIS [*darkly*] It sounds incredible; but a man was found ready to take that inconceivable lie on his conscience.

JULIA [*firing up*] If he has nothing worse than that on his conscience, he may sleep pretty well. In what way am I more womanly than any of the rest of them, I should like to know? They are always saying things like that behind my back: I hear of them from Sylvia. Only the other day

a member of the committee said I ought never to have
been elected – that you [*to Charteris*] had smuggled me in.
I should like to see her say it to my face: thats all.

CRAVEN. But, my precious, I most sincerely hope she was
right. She paid you the highest compliment. Why, the
place must be a den of infamy.

CUTHBERTSON [*emphatically*] So it is, Craven: so it is.

CHARTERIS. Exactly. Thats what keeps it so select: nobody
but people whose reputations are above suspicion dare
belong to it. If we once got a good name, we should
become a mere whitewashing shop for all the shady characters in London. Better join us, Craven. Let me put
you up.

CRAVEN. What! Join a club where theres some scoundrel
who guaranteed my daughter to be an unwomanly
woman! If I werent an invalid, I'd kick him.

CHARTERIS. Oh dont say that. It was I.

CRAVEN [*reproachfully*] You! Now upon my soul, Charteris,
this is very vexing. Now how could you bring yourself to
do such a thing?

CHARTERIS. She made me. Why, I had to guarantee
Cuthbertson as unmanly; and he's the leading representative of manly sentiment in London.

CRAVEN. That didnt do Jo any harm; but it took away my
Julia's character.

JULIA [*outraged*] Daddy!

CHARTERIS. Not at the Ibsen club: quite the contrary.
After all, what can we do? You know what breaks up most
clubs for men and women. Theres a quarrel – a scandal –
cherchez la femme – always a woman at the bottom of it.
Well, we knew this when we founded the club; but we
noticed that the woman at the bottom of it was always a
womanly woman. The unwomanly women who work for
their living, and know how to take care of themselves,
never give any trouble. So we simply said we wouldnt
have any womanly women; and when one gets smuggled in

she has to take care not to behave in a womanly way. We get on all right. [*He rises*]. Come to lunch with me there tomorrow and see the place.

CUTHBERTSON [*rising*] No: he's engaged to me. But you can join us.

CHARTERIS. What hour?

CUTHBERTSON. Any time after twelve. [*To Craven*] It's at 90 Cork Street, at the other end of the Burlington Arcade.

CRAVEN [*making a note on his cuff*] 90, you say. After twelve. [*Suddenly relapsing into gloom*] By the bye, dont order anything special for me. I'm not allowed wine: only Apollinaris. No meat either: only a scrap of fish occasionally. I'm to have a short life, but not a merry one. [*Sighing*] Well, well! [*Bracing himself up*] Now Julia: it's time for us to be off [*Julia rises*].

CUTHBERTSON. But where on earth is Grace? I must go and look for her. [*He turns to the door*].

JULIA [*stopping him*] Oh pray dont disturb her, Mr Cuthbertson. She's so tired.

CUTHBERTSON. But just for a moment, to say goodnight. *Julia and Charteris look at one another in dismay. Cuthbertson looks quickly at them, perceiving that something is wrong*].

CHARTERIS. We must make a clean breast of it, I see.

CUTHBERTSON. Of what?

CHARTERIS. The truth is, Cuthbertson, Mrs Tranfield, who is, as you know, the most thoughtful of women, took it into her head that I – well, that I particularly wanted to speak to Miss Craven alone. So she said she was tired, and went to bed.

CRAVEN [*scandalized*] Tut! tut!

CUTHBERTSON. Oho! is that it? Then it's all right: she never goes to bed as early as this. I'll fetch her in a moment. [*He goes out confidently, leaving Charteris aghast*].

JULIA. Now youve done it. [*She rushes to the round table, and snatches up her mantle and toque*]. I'm off. [*She makes for the door*].

CRAVEN [*horrified*] What are you doing, Julia? You cant go until youve said goodnight to Mrs Tranfield. It'd be horribly rude.

JULIA. You can stay if you like, Daddy: I cant. I'll wait for you in the hall. [*She hurries out*].

CRAVEN [*following her*] But what on earth am I to say? [*She disappears, shutting the door behind her in his face. He turns to Charteris, grumbling*]. Now really you know, Charteris, this is devilish awkward: upon my life it is. That was a most indelicate thing of you to say plump out before us all: that about you and Julia.

CHARTERIS. I'll explain it all tomorrow. Just at present we'd really better follow Julia's example and bolt. [*He starts for the door.*]

CRAVEN [*intercepting him*] Stop! dont leave me like this: I shall look like a fool. Now I shall really take it in bad part if you run away, Charteris.

CHARTERIS. All right. I'll stay. [*He lifts himself on to the shoulder of the grand piano and sits there swinging his legs and contemplating Craven resignedly*].

CRAVEN [*pacing up and down*] I'm excessively vexed about Julia's conduct: I am indeed. She cant bear to be crossed in the slightest thing, poor child. I'll have to apologize for her, you know: her going away is a downright slap in the face for these people here. Cuthbertson may be offended already for all I know.

CHARTERIS. Oh, never mind about him. Mrs Tranfield bosses this establishment.

CRAVEN [*cunningly*] Ah, thats it, is it? He's just the sort of fellow that would have no control over his daughter. [*He goes back to his former place on the hearthrug with his back to the fire*]. By the bye, what the dickens did he mean by all that about passing his life amid – what was it? – 'scenes of suffering nobly endured and sacrifice willingly rendered by womanly women and manly men' and a lot more of the same sort? I suppose he's something in a hospital.

CHARTERIS. Hospital! Nonsense! he's a dramatic critic. Didnt you hear me say he was the leading representative of manly sentiment in London?

CRAVEN. You dont say so! Now really, who'd have thought it! How jolly it must be to be able to go to the theatre for nothing! I must ask him to get me a few tickets occasionally. But isnt it ridiculous for a man to talk like that? I'm hanged if he dont take what he sees on the stage quite seriously.

CHARTERIS. Of course: thats why he's a good critic. Besides, if you take people seriously off the stage, why shouldnt you take them seriously on it, where theyre under some sort of decent restraint? [*He jumps down from the piano, and goes to the window*].

Cuthbertson comes back.

CUTHBERTSON [*to Craven, rather sheepishly*] The fact is, Grace has gone to bed. I must apologize to you and Miss – [*He turns to Julia's seat, and stops on seeing it vacant*].

CRAVEN [*embarrassed*] It is I who have to apologize for Julia, Jo. She –

CHARTERIS [*interrupting*] She said she was quite sure that if we didnt go, youd persuade Mrs Tranfield to get up to say goodnight for the sake of politeness; so she went straight off.

CUTHBERTSON. Very kind of her indeed. I'm really ashamed –

CRAVEN. Dont mention it, Jo: dont mention it. She's waiting for me below. [*Going*] Goodnight. Goodnight, Charteris.

CHARTERIS. Goodnight.

CUTHBERTSON [*seeing Craven out*] Goodnight. Say goodnight and thanks to Miss Craven for me. Tomorrow any time after twelve, remember. [*They go out*].

Charteris, with a long sigh, crosses to the fireplace, thoroughly tired out.

CRAVEN [*outside*] All right.

CUTHBERTSON [*outside*] Take care of the stairs: theyre rather steep. Goodnight. [*The outside door shuts*].

    Cuthbertson returns. Instead of entering, he stands impressively in the doorway with one hand in the breast of his waistcoat, eyeing Charteris sternly.

CHARTERIS. Whats the matter?

CUTHBERTSON [*sternly*] Charteris: what has been going on here? I insist on knowing. Grace has not gone to bed: I have seen and spoken with her. What is it all about?

CHARTERIS. Ask your theatrical experience, Cuthbertson. A man, of course.

CUTHBERTSON [*coming forward and confronting him*] Dont play the fool with me, Charteris: I'm too old a hand to be amused by it. I ask you, seriously, what is the matter?

CHARTERIS. I tell you, seriously, I'm the matter. Julia wants to marry me: I want to marry Grace. I came here tonight to sweetheart Grace. Enter Julia. Alarums and excursions. Exit Grace. Enter you and Craven. Subterfuges and excuses. Exeunt Craven and Julia. And here we are. Thats the whole story. Sleep over it. Goodnight. [*He leaves*].

CUTHBERTSON [*staring after him*] Well I'll be –

ACT II

Next day at noon, in the library of the Ibsen club. A long room, with glass doors half-way down on both sides, leading respectively to the dining room corridor and the main staircase. At the end, in the middle, is the fireplace, surmounted by a handsome mantelpiece, with a bust of Ibsen, and decorative inscriptions of the titles of his plays. There are circular recesses at each side of the fireplace, with divan seats running round them, the space above the divans lined with books. A long settee faces the fire. Along the back of the settee, and touching it, is a green table, littered with journals. Ibsen, looking down the room, has the dining door on his left, and further on, nearly in the middle of the library, a revolving bookcase, with an easy chair close to it. On his right, between the door and the recess, is a light library step-ladder. Further on, past the door an easy chair, and a smaller one between it and the middle of the room. Placards inscribed SILENCE *are conspicuously exhibited here and there.*

Cuthbertson is seated in the easy chair at the revolving bookstand, reading The Daily Graphic. *Dr Paramore is on the divan in the recess on Ibsen's right, reading* The British Medical Journal. *He is young as age is counted in the professions: barely forty. His hair is wearing bald on his forehead; and his dark arched eyebrows, coming rather close together, give him a conscientiously sinister appearance. He wears the frock coat of the fashionable physician, and cultivates the professional bedside manner with scrupulous conventionality. Not at all a happy or frank man, but not consciously unhappy nor intentionally insincere, and highly self-satisfied intellectually.*

Sylvia Craven is sitting in the middle of the settee before the fire, reading a volume of Ibsen, only the back of her head being visible from the middle of the room. She is a pretty girl of eighteen, small and trim, wearing a mountaineering suit of Norfolk jacket and breeches with neat town stockings and shoes. A detachable cloth skirt lies ready to her hand across the end of the settee.

A page boy's voice, monotonously calling for Dr Paramore, is heard approaching outside on the right.

THE PAGE [*outside*] Dr Paramore, Dr Paramore, Dr Para-more [*he enters, carrying a salver with a card on it*] Dr Par –

PARAMORE [*sharply sitting up*] Here, boy. [*The boy presents the salver. Paramore takes the card and looks at it*]. All right: I'll come down to him. [*The boy goes. Paramore rises, and comes from the recess, throwing his paper on the table*] Good morning, Mr Cuthbertson [*stopping to pull out his cuffs, and shake his coat straight*]. Mrs Tranfield quite well, I hope?

SYLVIA [*turning her head indignantly*] Sh – sh – sh!
Paramore turns, surprised. Cuthbertson rises energetically and looks across the bookstand to see who is the author of this impertinence.

PARAMORE [*to Sylvia stiffly*] I beg your pardon, Miss Craven; I did not mean to disturb you.

SYLVIA [*flustered and self-assertive*] You may talk as much as you like if you will have the common consideration to ask first whether the other people object. What I protest against is your assumption that my presence doesnt matter because I'm only a female member. Thats all. Now go on, pray: you dont disturb me in the least. [*She turns to the fire, and again buries herself in Ibsen*].

CUTHBERTSON [*with emphatic dignity*] No gentleman would have dreamt of objecting to our exchanging a few words, madam. [*She takes no notice. He resumes angrily*] As a matter of fact I was about to say to Dr Paramore that if he would care to bring his visitor up here, *I* should not object. The impudence! [*He dashes his paper down on the chair*].

PARAMORE. Oh, many thanks; but it's only an instrument maker.

CUTHBERTSON. Any new medical discoveries, doctor?

PARAMORE. Well, since you ask me, yes; perhaps a most important one. I have discovered something that has hitherto been overlooked; a minute duct in the liver of the guinea pig. Miss Craven will forgive my mentioning it when I say that it may throw an important light on her father's case. The first thing, of course, is to find out what the duct is there for.

CUTHBERTSON [*reverently, feeling that he is in the presence of Science*] Indeed? How will you do that?

PARAMORE. Oh, easily enough, by simply cutting the duct, and seeing what will happen to the guinea pig. [*Sylvia rises, horrified*]. I shall require a knife specially made to get at it. The man who is waiting for me downstairs has brought me a few handles to try before fitting it and sending it to the laboratory. I am afraid it would not do to bring such weapons up here.

SYLVIA. If you attempt such a thing, Dr Paramore, I will complain to the committee. A majority of the members are anti-vivisectionists. You ought to be ashamed of yourself. [*She snatches up the detachable skirt, and begins buttoning it on as she flounces out at the staircase door.*]

PARAMORE [*with patient contempt*] Thats the sort of thing we scientific men have to put up with nowadays, Mr Cuthbertson. Ignorance, superstition, sentimentality: they are all one. A guinea pig's convenience is set above the health and lives of the entire human race.

CUTHBERTSON [*vehemently*] It's not ignorance nor superstition, Paramore; it's sheer downright Ibsenism; thats what it is. Ive been wanting to sit comfortably at that fire the whole morning; but Ive never had a chance with that girl there. I couldnt go and plump myself down on a seat beside her: goodness knows what she'd think I wanted! Thats one of the delights of having women in the club: when they come in here they all want to sit at the fire and adore that bust. I sometimes feel that I should like to take the poker, and fetch it a wipe across the nose. Ugh!

PARAMORE. I must say I prefer the elder Miss Craven to her sister.

CUTHBERTSON [*his eye lighting up*] Ah, Julia! I believe you. A splendid fine creature: every inch a woman. No Ibsenism about her!

PARAMORE. I quite agree with you there, Mr Cuthbertson.

Er – by the way, do you think is Miss Craven attached to Charteris at all?

CUTHBERTSON. What! that fellow! Not he. He hangs about after her; but he's not man enough for her. A woman of that sort likes a strong, manly, deep throated, broad chested man.

PARAMORE [*anxiously*] Hm! a sort of sporting character, you think?

CUTHBERTSON. Oh, no, no. A scientific man, perhaps, like yourself. But you know what I mean: a MAN. [*He strikes himself a sounding blow on the chest*].

PARAMORE. Of course; but Charteris is a man.

CUTHBERTSON. Pah! You dont see what I mean.

The page boy returns with his salver.

THE PAGE [*calling monotonously as before*] Mr Cuthbertson, Mr Cuthbertson, Mr Cuth –

CUTHBERTSON. Here, boy. [*He takes a card from the salver*]. Bring the gentleman up here. [*The boy goes out*]. It's Craven. He's coming to lunch with me and Charteris. You might join us if youve nothing better to do, when youve finished with the instrument man. If Julia turns up I'll ask her too.

PARAMORE [*flushing with pleasure*] I shall be very pleased. Thank you. [*He is going out at the staircase door when Craven enters*]. Good morning, Colonel Craven.

CRAVEN [*at the door*] Good morning: glad to see you. I'm looking for Cuthbertson.

PARAMORE [*smiling*] There he is. [*He goes out*].

CUTHBERTSON [*greeting Craven effusively*] Delighted to see you. Now will you come to the smoking room; or will you sit down here, and have a chat while we're waiting for Charteris? If you like company, the smoking room's always full of women. Here in the library we shall have it pretty well all to ourselves until about three o'clock.

CRAVEN. I dont like to see women smoking. I'll make myself comfortable here. [*He sits in the easy chair on the staircase side*].

127

CUTHBERTSON [*taking the smaller chair on his left*] Neither do I. Theres not a room in this club where I can enjoy a pipe quietly without a woman coming in and beginning to roll a cigaret. It's a disgusting habit in a woman: it's not natural to her sex.

CRAVEN [*sighing*] Ah, Jo, times have changed since we both courted Molly Ebden all those years ago. I took my defeat well, old chap, didnt I?

CUTHBERTSON [*with earnest approval*] You did, Dan. The thought of it has often helped me to behave well myself: it has, on my honor.

CRAVEN. Yes: you always believed in hearth and home, Jo: in a true English wife, and a happy wholesome fireside. How did Molly turn out?

CUTHBERTSON [*trying to be fair to Molly*] Well, not bad. She might have been worse. You see, I couldnt stand her relations: all the men were roaring cads; and she couldnt get on with my mother. And then she hated being in town; and of course I couldnt live in the country on account of my work. But we hit it off as well as most people until we separated.

CRAVEN [*taken aback*] Separated! [*He is irresistibly amused*]. Oh! that was the end of the hearth and home, Jo, was it?

CUTHBERTSON [*warmly*] It was not my fault, Dan. [*Sentimentally*] Some day the world will know how I loved that woman. But she was incapble of valuing a true man's affection. Do you know, she often said she wished she'd married you instead.

CRAVEN [*sobered by the suggestion*] Dear me! dear me! Well, perhaps it was better as it was. You heard about my marriage, I suppose.

CUTHBERTSON. Oh yes: we all heard of it.

CRAVEN. Well, Jo, I may as well make a clean breast of it: everybody knew it. *I* married for money.

CUTHBERTSON [*encouragingly*] And why not, Dan? Why not? We cant get on without it, you know.

128

CRAVEN [*with sincere feeling*] I got to be very fond of her, Jo. I had a home until she died. Now everything's changed. Julia's always here. Sylvia's of a different nature; but she's always here too.

CUTHBERTSON [*sympathetically*] I know. It's the same with Grace. She's always here.

CRAVEN. And now they want me to be always here. Theyre at me every day to join the club. To stop my grumbling, I suppose. Thats what I want to consult you about. Do you think I ought to join?

CUTHBERTSON. Well, if you have no conscientious objection –

CRAVEN [*testily interrupting him*] I object to the existence of the place on principle; but whats the use of that? Here it is in spite of my objection; and I may as well have the benefit of any good that may be in it.

CUTHBERTSON [*soothing him*] Of course: thats the only reasonable view of the matter. Well, the fact is, it's not so inconvenient as you might think. When youre at home, you have the house more to yourself; and when you want to have your family about you, you can dine with them at the club.

CRAVEN [*not much attracted by this*] True.

CUTHBERTSON. Besides, if you dont want to dine with them, you neednt.

CRAVEN [*convinced*] True, very true. But dont they carry on here, rather?

CUTHBERTSON. Oh no: they dont exactly carry on. Of course the usual tone of the club is low, because the women smoke, and earn their own living, and all that; but still theres nothing actually to complain of. And it's convenient, certainly.

Charteris comes in, looking round for them.

CRAVEN [*rising*] Do you know, Ive a great mind to join, just to see what it's like.

CHARTERIS [*coming between them*] Do so by all means. I hope

I havnt disturbed your chat by coming too soon.

CRAVEN. Not at all. [*He shakes his hand cordially*].

CHARTERIS. Thats right. I'm earlier than I intended. The fact is, I have something rather pressing to say to Cuthbertson.

CRAVEN. Private?

CHARTERIS. Not particularly. [*To Cuthbertson*] Only what we were speaking of last night.

CUTHBERTSON. Well, Charteris, I think that is private, or ought to be.

CRAVEN [*retiring discreetly towards the table*] I'll just take a look at The Times –

CHARTERIS [*stopping him*] Oh, it's no secret: everybody in the club guesses it. [*To Cuthbertson*] Has Grace never mentioned to you that she wants to marry me?

CUTHBERTSON [*indignantly*] She has mentioned that you want to marry her.

CHARTERIS. Ah; but then it's not what I want, but what Grace wants, that will weigh with you.

CRAVEN [*a little shocked*] Excuse me, Charteris: this is private. I'll leave you to yourselves [*again moving towards the table*].

CHARTERIS. Wait a bit, Craven: youre concerned in this. Julia wants to marry me too.

CRAVEN [*in the tone of the strongest remonstrance*] Now really! Now upon my life and soul!

CHARTERIS. It's a fact, I assure you. Didnt it strike you as rather odd, our being up there last night, and Mrs Tranfield not with us?

CRAVEN. Well, yes it did. But you explained it. And now really, Charteris, I must say your explanation was in shocking bad taste before Julia.

CHARTERIS. Never mind. It was a good, fat, healthy, bouncing lie.

CRAVEN AND CUTHBERTSON. Lie!

CHARTERIS. Didnt you suspect that?

CRAVEN. Certainly not. Did you, Jo?

CUTHBERTSON. Not at the moment.

CRAVEN. Whats more, I dont believe you. I'm sorry to have to say such a thing; but you forget that Julia was present, and didnt contradict you.

CHARTERIS. She didnt want to.

CRAVEN. Do you mean to say that my daughter deceived me?

CHARTERIS. Delicacy towards me compelled her to, Craven.

CRAVEN [*taking a very serious tone*] Now look here, Charteris; have you any proper sense of the fact that youre standing between two fathers?

CUTHBERTSON. Quite right, Dan, quite right. I repeat the question on my own account.

CHARTERIS. Well, I'm a little dazed still by standing for so long between two daughters; but I think I grasp the situation. [*Cuthbertson flings away with an exclamation of disgust*].

CRAVEN. Then I'm sorry for your manners, Charteris: thats all. [*He turns away sulkily; then suddenly flares up and comes back to Charteris*]. How dare you tell me my daughter wants to marry you? Who are you, pray, that she should have any such ambition?

CHARTERIS. Just so: youre quite right: she couldnt have made a worse choice. But she wont listen to reason. I assure you, my dear Craven, Ive said everything that fifty fathers could have said; but it's no use: she wont give me up. And if she wont listen to me, what likelihood is there of her listening to you?

CRAVEN [*in angry bewilderment*] Cuthbertson: did you ever hear anything like this?

CUTHBERTSON. Never! Never!

CHARTERIS. Oh, bother! Come! dont behave like a couple of conventional old fathers; this is a serious affair. Look at these letters [*producing a letter and a letter-card*]! This [*shewing the card*] is from Grace – by the way, Cuthbertson, I wish youd ask her not to write on letter-cards: the blue colour makes it so easy for Julia to pick the bits out of my waste paper basket and piece them together. Now listen. 'My dear Leonard: Nothing could make it worth my while to be exposed to such scenes as last night's. You had much better go back to Julia, and forget me. Yours sincerely, Grace Tranfield.'

CUTHBERTSON. I approve of every word of that letter.

CHARTERIS [*turning to Craven and preparing to read the letter*] Now for Julia. [*The Colonel turns away to hide his face from Charteris, anticipating a shock, and puts his hand on a chair to steady himself*]. 'My dearest boy: Nothing will make me believe that this odious woman can take my place in your heart. I send some of the letters you wrote me when we first met; and I ask you to read them. They will recall what you felt when you wrote them. You cannot have changed so much as to be indifferent to me: whoever may have struck your fancy for the moment, your heart is still mine' – and so on: you know the sort of thing – 'Ever and always your loving Julia.' [*The Colonel sinks on the chair, and covers his face with his hand*]. You dont suppose she's serious, do you? thats the sort of thing she writes me three times a day. [*To Cuthbertson*] Grace is in earnest though, confound it. [*He holds out Grace's letter*] A blue card as usual! This time I shall not trust the waste paper basket. [*He goes to the fire, and throws the letters into it*].

CUTHBERTSON [*facing him with folded arms as he comes back to them*] May I ask, Mr Charteris, is this the New Humor?

CHARTERIS [*still too preoccupied with his own affairs to have any sense of the effect he is producing on the others*] Oh, stuff! Do you suppose it's a joke to be situated as I am? Youve got your head so stuffed with the New Humor and the New Woman and the New This, That, and The Other, all mixed up with your own old Adam, that youve lost your senses.

CUTHBERTSON [*strenuously*] Do you see that old man, grown grey in the honored service of his country, whose last days you have blighted?

CHARTERIS [*surprised, looking at Craven and realizing his distress with genuine concern*] I'm very sorry. Come, Craven: dont take it to heart. [*Craven shakes his head*]. I assure you it means nothing: it happens to me constantly.

CUTHBERTSON. There is only one excuse for you. You are not fully responsible for your actions. Like all advanced people, you have got neurasthenia.

CHARTERIS [*appalled*] Great Heavens! whats that?

CUTHBERTSON. I decline to explain. You know as well as I do. I'm going downstairs now to order lunch. I shall order it for three; but the third place is for Paramore, whom I have invited, not for you. [*He goes out through the dining room door*].

CHARTERIS [*putting his hand on Craven's shoulder*] Come, Craven: advise me. Youve been in this sort of fix yourself probably.

CRAVEN. Charteris: no woman writes such a letter to a man unless he has made advances to her.

CHARTERIS [*mournfully*] How little you know the world, Colonel! The New Woman is not like that.

CRAVEN. I can only give you very oldfashioned advice, my boy; and that is that it's well to be off with the Old Woman before youre on with the New. I'm sorry you told me. You might have waited for my death: it's not far off now. [*His head droops again*].

  Julia and Paramore come in from the staircase. Julia stops as she catches sight of Charteris, her face clouding, and her breast heaving. Paramore, seeing the Colonel apparently ill, hurries down to him with his bedside manner in full play.

CHARTERIS [*seeing Julia*] Oh, Lord! [*He retreats under the lee of the revolving bookstand*].

PARAMORE [*sympathetically to the Colonel, taking his wrist, and beginning to count his pulse*] Allow me.

CRAVEN [*looking up*] Eh? [*He withdraws his hand and rises rather crossly*]. No, Paramore: it's not my liver now: it's private business.

*A chase begins between Julia and Charteris, all the more excit-
ing to them because the huntress and her prey alike must conceal the
real object of their movements from the others. Charteris first makes
for the staircase door. Julia immediately retreats to it, barring his
path. He doubles back round the bookstand, setting it whirling as
he makes for the other door, Julia crossing in pursuit of him. He is
about to escape when he is cut off by the return of Cuthbertson.
Turning back, he sees Julia close upon him. There being nothing
else for it, he bolts into the recess on Ibsen's left.*

CUTHBERTSON. Good morning, Miss Craven. [*They shake
hands*]. Wont you join us at lunch? Paramore's coming
too.

JULIA. Thanks: I shall be very pleased. [*She strolls with
affected purposelessness towards the recess. Charteris, almost
trapped in it, crosses to the opposite recess by way of the fender,
knocking down the fireirons with a crash as he does so*].

CRAVEN [*who has crossed to the whirling bookcase and stopped it*]
What the dickens are you doing there, Charteris?

CHARTERIS. Nothing. It's such a confounded room to get
about in.

JULIA [*maliciously*] Yes: isnt it? [*She is about to move to guard
the staircase door when Cuthbertson offers her his arm*].

CUTHBERTSON. May I take you down?

JULIA. No, really: you know it's against the rules of the
club to coddle women in any way. Whoever is nearest the
door goes first.

CUTHBERTSON. Oh, well, if you insist. Come, gentlemen:
let us go to lunch in the Ibsen fashion: the unsexed
fashion. [*He turns and goes out, followed by Paramore, who
raises his politest consulting-room laugh. Craven goes last*].

CRAVEN [*at the door, gravely*] Come, Julia.

JULIA [*with patronizing affection*] Yes, Daddy dear, presently.
Dont wait for me: I'll come in a moment. [*The Colonel
hesitates*]. It's all right, Daddy.

CRAVEN [*very gravely*] Dont be long, my dear. [*He goes out*].

CHARTERIS. I'm off. [*He makes a dash for the staircase door*].

JULIA [*darting at him and seizing his wrists*] Arnt you coming?

CHARTERIS. No. Unhand me, Julia. [*He tries to get away: she holds him*]. If you dont let me go, I'll scream for help.

JULIA [*reproachfully*] Leonard! [*He breaks away from her*]. Oh, how can you be so rough with me, dear! Did you get my letter?

CHARTERIS. Burnt it –

Julia turns away, struck to the heart, and buries her face in her hands.

CHARTERIS [*continuing*] – along with hers.

JULIA [*quickly turning again*] Hers! Has she written to you?

CHARTERIS. Yes: to break off with me on your account!

JULIA [*her eyes gleaming*] Ah!

CHARTERIS. You are pleased. Wretch! Now you have lost the last scrap of my regard. [*He turns to go, but is stopped by the return of Sylvia. Julia turns away and stands pretending to read a paper which she picks up from the table*].

SYLVIA [*offhandedly*] Hallo Charteris! how are you getting on? [*She takes his arm familiarly, and walks down the room with him*] Have you seen Grace Tranfield this morning? [*Julia drops the paper, and comes a step nearer to listen*]. You generally know where she's to be found.

CHARTERIS. I shall never know any more, Sylvia. She's quarrelled with me.

SYLVIA. Sylvia! How often am I to tell you that I am not Sylvia at the club?

CHARTERIS. I forgot. I beg your pardon, Craven, old chap [*slapping her on the shoulder*].

SYLVIA. Thats better. A little overdone, but better.

JULIA. Dont be a fool, Silly.

SYLVIA. Remember, Julia, if you please, that here we are members of the club, not sisters. I dont take liberties with you here on family grounds: dont you take any with me. [*She goes to the settee, and resumes her former place*].

CHARTERIS. Quite right, Craven. Down with the tyranny of the elder sister!

JULIA. You ought to know better than to encourage a child to make herself ridiculous, Leonard, even at my expense.

CHARTERIS [*seating himself on the edge of the table*] Your lunch will be cold, Julia.

Julia is about to retort furiously when she is checked by the reappearance of Cuthbertson at the dining room door.

CUTHBERTSON. What has become of you, Miss Craven? Your father is getting quite uneasy. We're all waiting for you.

JULIA. So I have just been reminded, thank you. [*She goes out angrily past him, Sylvia looking round to see*].

CUTHBERTSON [*looking first after her, then at Charteris*] More neurasthenia! [*He follows her*].

SYLVIA [*jumping up on her knees on the settee, and speaking over the back of it*] Whats up, Charteris? Julia been making love to you?

CHARTERIS [*speaking to her over his shoulder*] No. Jealous of Grace.

SYLVIA. Serve you right. You are an awful devil for phil-andering.

CHARTERIS [*calmly*] Do you consider it good club form to talk that way to a man who might nearly be your father?

SYLVIA [*knowingly*] Oh, I know you, my lad.

CHARTERIS. Then you know that I never pay any special attention to any woman.

SYLVIA [*thoughtfully*] Do you know, Leonard, I really be-lieve you. I dont think you care a bit more for one woman than for another.

CHARTERIS. You mean I dont care a bit less for one woman than another.

SYLVIA. That makes it worse. But what I mean is that you never bother about their being only women: you talk to them just as you do to me or any other fellow. Thats the secret of your success. You cant think how sick they get of being treated with the respect due to their sex.

CHARTERIS. Ah, if Julia only had your wisdom, Craven! [*He gets off the table with a sigh, and perches himself reflectively on the step-ladder*].

SYLVIA. She cant take things easy: can she, old man? But dont you be afraid of breaking her heart: she gets over her little tragedies. We found that out at home when our great sorrow came.

CHARTERIS. What was that?

SYLVIA. I mean when we learned that poor papa had Paramore's disease.

CHARTERIS. Paramore's disease! Why, whats the matter with Paramore?

SYLVIA. Oh, not a disease that he suffers from, but one that he discovered.

CHARTERIS. The liver business?

SYLVIA. Yes: thats what made Paramore's reputation, you know. Papa used to get bad occasionally; but we always thought that it was partly his Indian service, and partly his eating and drinking too much. He used to wolf down a lot in those days, did Dad. The doctor never knew what was wrong with him until Paramore discovered a dreadful little microbe in his liver. There are forty millions of them to every square inch of liver. Paramore discovered them first; and now he declares that everybody should be inoculated against them as well as vaccinated. But it was too late to inoculate poor papa. All they could do was to prolong his life for two years more by putting him on a strict diet. Poor old boy! they cut off his liquor; and he's not allowed to eat meat.

CHARTERIS. Your father appears to me to be uncommonly well.

SYLVIA. Yes: you would think he was a great deal better. But the microbe is at work, slowly but surely. In another year it will be all over. Poor old Dad! it's unfeeling to talk about him in this attitude: I must sit down properly. [*She comes down from the settee, and takes the chair near the bookstand*].

137

I should like papa to live for ever just to take the conceit
out of Paramore. I believe he's in love with Julia.

CHARTERIS [*starting up excitedly*] In love with Julia? A ray of
hope on the horizon! Do you really mean it?

SYLVIA. I should think I do. Why do you suppose he's
hanging about the club today in a beautiful new coat and
tie instead of attending to his patients? That lunch with
Julia will finish him. He'll ask Daddy's consent before
they come back: I'll bet you three to one he will, in anything you please.

CHARTERIS. Gloves?

SYLVIA. No: cigarets.

CHARTERIS. Done! But what does she think about it? Does
she give him any encouragement?

SYLVIA. Oh, the usual thing. Enough to keep any other
woman from getting him.

CHARTERIS. Just so. I understand. Now listen to me: I am
going to speak as a philosopher. Julia is jealous of everybody: everybody. If she saw you flirting with Paramore
she'd begin to value him directly. You might play up a
little, Craven, for my sake: eh?

SYLVIA [*rising*] Youre too awful, Leonard. For shame! However, anything to oblige a fellow Ibsenite. I'll bear your
affair in mind. But I think it would be more effective if
you got Grace to do it.

CHARTERIS. Think so? Hm! perhaps youre right.

THE PAGE [*outside as before*] Dr Paramore, Dr Paramore, Dr
Paramore –

SYLVIA. They ought to get that boy's voice properly culti-
vated: it's a disgrace to the club. [*She goes into the recess on
Ibsen's left*].

The page enters, carrying the British Medical Journal.

CHARTERIS [*calling to the page*] Dr Paramore is in the dining
room.

THE PAGE. Thank you, sir. [*He is about to go into the dining
room when Sylvia swoops on him*].

SYLVIA. Here: where are you taking that paper? It belongs to this room.

THE PAGE. It's Dr Paramore's particular orders, miss. The British Medical Journal has always to be brought to him dreckly it comes.

SYLVIA. What cheek! Charteris: oughtnt we to stop this on principle?

CHARTERIS. Certainly not. Principle's the poorest reason I know for making yourself nasty.

SYLVIA. Bosh! Ibsen!

CHARTERIS [to the page] Off with you, my boy: Dr Paramore's waiting breathless with expectation.

THE PAGE [seriously] Indeed, sir? [He hurries off].

CHARTERIS. That boy will make his way in this country. He has no sense of humor.

Grace comes in. Her dress, very convenient and businesslike, is made to please herself and serve her own purposes without the slightest regard to fashion, though by no means without a careful concern for her personal elegance. She enters briskly, like an habitually busy woman.

SYLVIA [running to her] Here you are at last, Tranfield, old girl. Ive been waiting for you this last hour. I'm starving.

GRACE. All right, dear. [To Charteris] Did you get my letter?

CHARTERIS. Yes. I wish you wouldnt write on those confounded blue letter-cards.

SYLVIA [to Grace] Shall I go down first, and secure a table?

CHARTERIS [taking the reply out of Grace's mouth] Do, old boy.

SYLVIA. Dont be too long. [She goes into the dining room]

GRACE. Well?

CHARTERIS. I'm afraid to face you after last night. Can you imagine a more horrible scene? Dont you hate the very sight of me after it?

GRACE. Oh no.

CHARTERIS. Then you ought to. Ugh! it was hideous: an insult: an outrage. A nice end to all my plans for making

you happy: for making you an exception to all the women
who swear I have made them miserable!

GRACE [*sitting down placidly*] I am not at all miserable. I'm
sorry; but I shant break my heart.

CHARTERIS. No; yours is a thoroughbred heart: you dont
scream and cry every time it's pinched. Thats why you
are the only possible woman for me.

GRACE [*shaking her head*] Not now. Never any more.

CHARTERIS. Never! What do you mean?

GRACE. What I say, Leonard.

CHARTERIS. Jilted again! The fickleness of the women I
love is only equalled by the infernal constancy of the
women who love me. Well, well! I see how it is, Grace:
you cant forget that horrible scene last night. Imagine her
saying I had kissed her within the last two days!

GRACE [*rising eagerly*] Was that not true?

CHARTERIS. True! No: a thumping lie.

GRACE. Oh, I'm so glad. That was the only thing that
really hurt me.

CHARTERIS. Just why she said it. How adorable of you to
care! My darling. [*He seizes her hands, and presses them to his
breast*].

GRACE. Remember! it's all broken off.

CHARTERIS. Ah yes: you have my heart in your hands.
Break it. Throw my happiness out of the window.

GRACE. Oh, Leonard, does your happiness really depend
on me?

CHARTERIS [*tenderly*] Absolutely. [*She beams with delight. A
sudden revulsion comes to him at the sight: he recoils, dropping her
hands and crying*] Ah no: why should I lie to you? [*He folds
his arms and adds firmly*] My happiness depends on nobody
but myself. I can do without you.

GRACE [*nerving herself*] So you shall. Thank you for the
truth. Now *I* will tell you the truth.

CHARTERIS [*unfolding his arms in terror*] No, please. Dont.
As a philosopher, it's my business to tell other people the

truth; but it's not their business to tell it to me. I dont like it: it hurts.

GRACE [*quietly*] It's only that I love you.

CHARTERIS. Ah! thats not a philosophic truth. You may tell me that as often as you like. [*He takes her in his arms*].

GRACE. Yes, Leonard; but I'm an advanced woman. [*He checks himself, and looks at her in some consternation*]. I'm what my father calls the New Woman. [*He lets her go, and stares at her*]. I quite agree with all your ideas.

CHARTERIS [*scandalized*] Thats a nice thing for a respectable woman to say! You ought to be ashamed of yourself.

GRACE. I am quite in earnest about them too, though you are not. That is why I will never marry a man I love too much. It would give him a terrible advantage over me: I should be utterly in his power. Thats what the New Woman is like. Isnt she right, Mr Philosopher?

CHARTERIS. The struggle between the Philosopher and the Man is fearful, Grace. But the Philosopher says you are right.

GRACE. I know I am right. And so we must part.

CHARTERIS. Not at all. You must marry some one else; and then I'll come and philander with you.

Sylvia comes back.

SYLVIA [*holding the door open*] Oh, I say: come along. I'm starving.

CHARTERIS. So am I. I'll lunch with you if I may.

SYLVIA. I thought you would. Ive ordered soup for thrce. [*Grace passes out. Sylvia continues, to Charteris*] You can watch Paramore from our table: he's pretending to read the British Medical Journal; but he must be making up his mind for the plunge: he looks green with nervousness. [*She goes out*].

CHARTERIS. Good luck to him! [*He follows her*].

The library remains unoccupied for ten minutes.

Then Julia, angry and miserable, comes in from the dining

room, followed by Craven. She crosses the room tormentedly, and throws herself into a chair.

CRAVEN [*impatiently*] What is the matter? Has every one gone mad today? What do you mean by suddenly getting up from the table and tearing away like that? What does Paramore mean by reading his paper, and not answering when he's spoken to? [*Julia writhes impatiently*]. Come, come [*tenderly*]: wont my pet tell her own Daddy what – [*irritably*] what the devil is wrong with everybody. Do pull yourself together, Julia, before Cuthbertson comes. He's only paying the bill: he'll be here in a moment.

JULIA. I couldnt bear it any longer. Oh, to see them sitting there at lunch together, laughing, chatting, making game of me! I should have screamed out in another moment. I should have taken a knife and killed her. I should have –

Cuthbertson appears, stuffing the luncheon bill into his waistcoat pocket as he comes to them. He begins speaking the moment he enters.

CUTHBERTSON. I'm afraid youve had a very poor lunch, Dan. It's disheartening to see you picking at a few beans, and drinking soda water. I wonder how you live!

JULIA. Thats all he ever takes, Mr Cuthbertson, I assure you. He hates to be bothered about it.

CRAVEN. Wheres Paramore?

CUTHBERTSON. Reading his paper. I asked him wasnt he coming; but he didnt hear me. It's amazing how anything scientific absorbs him. Clever man! Monstrously clever man!

CRAVEN [*pettishly*] Oh yes, thats all very well, Jo; but it's not good manners at table: he should shut up the shop sometimes. Heaven knows I am only too anxious to forget his science, since it has pronounced my doom. [*He sits down with a melancholy air*].

CUTHBERTSON [*compassionately*] You mustnt think about that, Craven: perhaps he was mistaken. [*He sighs deeply and sits down*]. But he certainly is a very clever fellow. He thinks twice before he commits himself.

142

They sit in silence, full of gloom. Suddenly Paramore enters, pale and in the utmost disorder, with The British Medical Journal in his clenched hand. They rise in alarm. He tries to speak, but chokes, clutching at his throat, and staggers. Cuthbertson quickly takes his chair and places it behind Paramore, who sinks into it as they crowd about him, Craven at his right shoulder, Cuthbertson on his left, and Julia behind.

CRAVEN. Whats the matter, Paramore?

JULIA. Are you ill?

CUTHBERTSON. No bad news, I hope?

PARAMORE [*despairingly*] The worst of news! Terrible news! Fatal news! My disease –

CRAVEN [*quickly*] Do you mean my disease?

PARAMORE [*fiercely*] I mean my disease: Paramore's disease: the disease I discovered: the work of my life! Look here [*he points to the journal with a ghastly expression of horror*]! If this is true, it was all a mistake: there is no such disease.

Cuthbertson and Julia look at one another, hardly daring to believe the good news.

CRAVEN [*in strong remonstrance*] And you call this bad news! Now really, Paramore –

PARAMORE [*cutting him short hoarsely*] It's natural for you to think only of yourself. I dont blame you: all invalids are selfish. Only a scientific man can feel what I feel now. [*Writhing under a sense of intolerable injustice*] It's the fault of the wickedly sentimental laws of this country. I was not able to make experiments enough: only three dogs and a monkey. Think of that, with all Europe full of my professional rivals! men burning to prove me wrong! There is freedom in France: enlightened republican France! One Frenchman experiments on two hundred monkeys to disprove my theory. Another sacrifices £36 – three hundred dogs at three francs apiece – to upset the monkey experiments. A third proves them both wrong by a single experiment in which he gets the temperature of a camel's liver sixty degrees below zero. And now comes this cursed

Italian who has ruined me. He has a government grant to buy animals with, besides having the run of the largest hospital in Italy. [*With desperate resolution*] But I wont be beaten by any Italian. I'll go to Italy myself. I'll rediscover my disease: I know it exists; I feel it; and I'll prove it if I have to experiment on every mortal animal thats got a liver at all. [*He folds his arms and breathes hard at them*].

CRAVEN [*his sense of injury growing on him*] Am I to understand, Paramore, that you took it on yourself to pass sentence of death on me: yes, of Death! on the strength of three dogs and an infernal monkey?

PARAMORE [*utterly contemptuous of Craven's narrow personal view of the matter*] Yes. That was all I could get a license for.

CRAVEN. Now upon my soul, Paramore, I'm vexed at this. I dont wish to be unfriendly; but I'm extremely vexed, really. Why, confound it, do you realize what youve done? Youve cut off my meat and drink for a year! made me an object of public scorn! a miserable vegetarian and teetotaller.

PARAMORE [*rising*] Well, you can make up for lost time now. [*Bitterly, shewing Craven the journal*] There! you can read for yourself. The camel was fed on beef dissolved in alcohol; and he gained half a ton on it. Eat and drink as much as you please. [*Still unable to stand without support, he makes his way past Cuthbertson to the revolving bookcase, and stands there with his back to them, leaning on it with his head in his hands*].

CRAVEN [*grumbling*] Oh yes: it's very easy for you to talk, Paramore. But what am I to say to the Humanitarian societies and the Vegetarian societies that have made me Vice President?

CUTHBERTSON [*chuckling*] Aha! You made a virtue of it, did you, Dan?

CRAVEN [*warmly*] I made a virtue of necessity, Jo. No one can blame me.

JULIA [*soothing him*] Well, never mind, Daddy. Come back

to the dining room, and have a good beefsteak.

CRAVEN [*shuddering*] Ugh! [*Plaintively*] No: Ive lost my old manly taste for it. My very nature's been corrupted by living on pap. [*To Paramore*] Thats what comes of all this vivisection. You go experimenting on horses; and of course the result is that you try to get me into condition by feeding me on beans.

PARAMORE [*curtly, without changing his position*] Well, if theyve done you good, so much the better for you.

CRAVEN [*querulously*] Thats all very well: but it's very vexing. You dont half see how serious it is to make a man believe that he has only another year to live: you really dont, Paramore: I cant help saying it. Ive made my will, which was altogether unnecessary; and Ive been reconciled to a lot of people I'd quarrelled with: people I cant stand under ordinary circumstances. Then Ive let the girls get round me at home to an extent I should never have done if I'd had my life before me. Ive done a lot of serious thinking and reading and extra church going. And now it turns out simple waste of time. On my soul, it's too disgusting: I'd far rather die like a man when I said I would.

PARAMORE [*as before*] Perhaps you may. Your heart's shaky, if thats any satisfaction to you.

CRAVEN [*offended*] You must excuse me, Paramore, if I say that I no longer feel any confidence in your opinion as a medical man. [*Paramore's eye flashes: he straightens himself and listens*]. I paid you a pretty stiff fee for that consultation when you condemned me; and I cant say I think you gave me value for it.

PARAMORE [*turning and facing Craven with dignity*] Thats unanswerable, Colonel Craven. I shall return the fee.

CRAVEN. Oh, it's not the money; but I think you ought to realize your position. [*Paramore turns stiffly away. Craven follows him impulsively, exclaiming remorsefully*] Well, perhaps it was a nasty thing of me to allude to it. [*He offers Paramore his hand*].

PARAMORE [*conscientiously taking it*] Not at all. You are quite in the right, Colonel Craven: my diagnosis was wrong; and I must take the consequences.

CRAVEN [*holding his hand*] No, dont say that. It was natural enough: my liver is enough to set any man's diagnosis wrong. [*A long handshake, very trying to Paramore's nerves. Paramore then retires to the recess on Ibsen's left, and throws himself on the divan with a half suppressed sob, bending over The British Medical Journal with his head on his hands and his elbows on his knees*].

CUTHBERTSON [*who has been rejoicing with Julia at the other side of the room*] Well, lets say no more about it. I congratulate you, Craven, and hope you may long be spared. [*Craven offers his hand*]. No, Dan: your daughter first. [*He takes Julia's hand gently and hands her across to Craven, into whose arms she flies with a gush of feeling*].

JULIA. Dear old Daddy!

CRAVEN. Ah, is Julia glad that the old Dad is let off for a few years more?

JULIA [*almost crying*] Oh, so glad! so glad!

    Cuthbertson sobs audibly. The Colonel is affected. Sylvia, entering from the dining room, stops abruptly at the door on seeing the three. Paramore, in the recess, escapes her notice.

SYLVIA. Hallo!

CRAVEN. Tell her the news, Julia: it would sound ridiculous from me. [*He goes to the weeping Cuthbertson, and pats him consolingly on the shoulder*].

JULIA. Silly: only think! Dad's not ill at all. It was only a mistake of Dr Paramore's. Oh, dear! [*She catches Craven's left hand and stoops to kiss it, his right hand being still on Cuthbertson's shoulder*].

SYLVIA [*contemptuously*] I knew it. Of course it was nothing but eating too much. I always said Paramore was an ass. [*Sensation. The group of Cuthbertson, Craven, and Julia breaks up as they turn in dismay*].

PARAMORE [*without malice*] Never mind, Miss Craven. That

is what is being said all over Europe now. Never mind.

SYLVIA [*a little abashed*] I'm so sorry, Dr Paramore. You must excuse a daughter's feelings.

CRAVEN [*huffed*] It evidently doesnt make much difference to you, Sylvia.

SYLVIA. I'm not going to be sentimental over it, Dad, you may bet. [*Coming to Craven*] Besides, I knew it was nonsense all along. [*Petting him*] Poor old Dad! why should your days be numbered any more than any one else's? [*He pats her cheek, mollified. Julia impatiently turns away from them*]. Come to the smoking room; and lets see what you can do after teetotalling for a year.

CRAVEN [*playfully*] Vulgar little girl! [*He pinches her ear*]. Shall we come, Jo! Youll be the better for a pick-me-up after all this emotion.

CUTHBERTSON. I'm not ashamed of it, Dan. It has done me good. [*He goes up to the table and shakes his fist at the bust over the mantelpiece*]. It would do you good too, if you had eyes and ears to take it in.

CRAVEN [*astonished*] Who?

SYLVIA. Why, good old Henrik, of course.

CRAVEN [*puzzled*] Henrik?

CUTHBERTSON [*impatiently*] Ibsen, man: Ibsen. [*He goes out by the staircase door, followed by Sylvia, who kisses her hand to the bust as she passes. Craven stares blankly after her, and then at the bust. Giving the problem up as insoluble, he shakes his head and follows them. Near the door, he checks himself, and comes back*].

CRAVEN [*softly*] By the way, Paramore?

PARAMORE [*rousing himself with an effort*] Yes?

CRAVEN. You werent in earnest that time about my heart, were you?

PARAMORE. Oh nothing, nothing. Theres a slight murmur: mitral valves a little worn perhaps: but theyll last your time if youre careful. Dont smoke too much.

CRAVEN. What! More privations! Now really, Paramore, really –

147

PARAMORE [*rising distractedly*] Excuse me: I cant pursue the subject. I – I –

JULIA. Dont worry him now, Daddy.

CRAVEN. Well, well: I wont. [*He comes to Paramore, who is pacing restlessly up and down the middle of the room*] Come, Paramore! I'm not selfish, believe me: I can feel for your disappointment. But you must face it like a man. And after all, now really, doesnt this shew that theres a lot of rot about modern science? Between ourselves, you know, it's horribly cruel: you must admit that it's a deuced nasty thing to go ripping up and crucifying camels and monkeys. It must blunt all the finer feelings sooner or later.

PARAMORE [*turning to him*] How many camels and horses and men were ripped up in that Soudan campaign where you won your Victoria Cross, Colonel Craven?

CRAVEN [*firing up*] That was fair fighting: a very different thing, Paramore.

PARAMORE. Yes: Martinis and machine guns against naked spearman.

CRAVEN [*hotly*] Naked spearman can kill, Paramore. I risked my life: dont forget that.

PARAMORE [*with equal spirit*] And I have risked mine, as all doctors do, oftener than any soldier.

CRAVEN [*handsomely*] Thats true. I didnt think of that. I beg your pardon, Paramore: I'll never say another word against your profession. But I hope youll let me stick to the good oldfashioned shaking-up treatment for my liver: a clinking run across country with the hounds.

PARAMORE [*with bitter irony*] Isnt that rather cruel? a pack of dogs ripping up a fox?

JULIA [*coming coaxingly between them*] Oh please dont begin arguing again. Do go to the smoking room, Daddy: Mr Cuthbertson will wonder what has become of you.

CRAVEN. Very well, very well: I'll go. But youre really not reasonable today, Paramore, to talk that way of fair sport –

JULIA. Sh – sh [*coaxing him towards the door*].

CRAVEN. Well, well, I'm off. [*He goes goodhumoredly, pushed out by Julia*].

JULIA [*turning at the door with her utmost witchery of manner*] Dont look so disappointed, Dr Paramore. Cheer up. Youve been most kind to us; and youve done papa a lot of good.

PARAMORE [*delighted, rushing over to her*] How beautiful it is of you to say that to me, Miss Craven!

JULIA. I hate to see any one unhappy. I cant bear unhappiness. [*She runs out, casting a Parthian glance at him as she flies*].

> Paramore stands enraptured, gazing after her through the glass door. Whilst he is thus absorbed, Charteris comes in from the dining room and touches him on the arm.

PARAMORE [*starting*] Eh? Whats the matter?

CHARTERIS [*significantly*] Charming woman, isnt she, Paramore? [*Looking admiringly at him*] How have you managed to fascinate her?

PARAMORE. I! Do you really mean – [*He looks at him; then recovers himself, and adds coldly*] Excuse me: this is a subject I do not care to jest about. [*He walks away from Charteris, and sits down in the nearest easy chair, reading his journal to intimate that he does not wish to pursue the conversation*].

CHARTERIS [*ignoring the hint, and coolly sitting down beside him*] Why dont you get married, Paramore? You know it's a scandalous thing for a man in your profession to be single.

PARAMORE [*shortly, still pretending to read*] Thats my own business: not yours.

CHARTERIS. Not at all: it's pre-eminently a social question. Youre going to get married, arnt you?

PARAMORE. Not that I am aware of.

CHARTERIS [*alarmed*] No! Dont say that. Why?

PARAMORE [*rising angrily and rapping one of the SILENCE placards*] Allow me to call your attention to that. [*He crosses the room to the easy chair near the revolving bookstand, and flings himself into it with determined hostility*].

CHARTERIS [*following him, too deeply concerned to mind the rebuff*] Paramore: you alarm me more than I can say. Youve muffed this business somehow. I fully expected to find you a joyful accepted suitor.

PARAMORE [*angrily*] Yes, you have been watching me because you admire Miss Craven yourself. Well, you may go in and win now. You will be pleased to hear that I am a ruined man.

CHARTERIS. You! Ruined! How? The turf?

PARAMORE [*contemptuously*] The turf! ! Certainly not.

CHARTERIS. Paramore: if the loan of all I possess will help you over this difficulty, you have only to ask.

PARAMORE [*rising in surprise*] Charteris! I – [*Suspiciously*] Are you joking?

CHARTERIS. Why on earth do you always suspect me of joking? I never was more serious in my life.

PARAMORE [*shamed by Charteris's generosity*] Then I beg your pardon. I thought the news would please you.

CHARTERIS [*deprecating this injustice to his good feeling*] My dear fellow!

PARAMORE. I see I was wrong. I am really very sorry. [*They shake hands*]. And now you may as well learn the truth. I had rather you heard it from me than from the gossip of the club. My liver discovery has been – er – er – [*he cannot bring himself to say it*].

CHARTERIS [*helping him out*] Confirmed? [*Sadly*] I see: the poor Colonel's doomed.

PARAMORE. No: on the contrary, it has been – er – called in question. The Colonel now believes himself to be in perfectly good health; and my friendly relations with the Cravens are entirely spoilt.

CHARTERIS. Who told him about it?

PARAMORE. I did, of course, the moment I read the news in this. [*He shews the journal, and puts it down on the bookstand*].

CHARTERIS. Why, man, you've been a messenger of glad tidings! Didnt you congratulate him?

PARAMORE [*scandalized*] Congratulate him! Congratulate a
man on the worst blow pathological science has received
for the last three hundred years!

CHARTERIS. No, no, no. Congratulate him on having his
life saved. Congratulate Julia on having her father spared.
Swear that your discovery and your reputation are as
nothing to you compared with the pleasure of restoring
happiness to the household in which the best hopes of
your life are centred. Confound it, man, youll never get
married if you cant turn things to account with a woman
in these little ways.

PARAMORE [*gravely*] Excuse me; but my self-respect is
dearer to me even than Miss Craven. I cannot trifle with
scientific questions for the sake of a personal advantage.
[*He turns away coldly, and goes towards the table*].

CHARTERIS. Well, this beats me! The Nonconformist conscience is bad enough; but the scientific conscience is the
very devil. [*He follows Paramore, and puts his arm familiarly
round his shoulder, bringing him back again whilst he speaks*].
Now look here, Paramore: I have no conscience in that
sense at all: I loathe it as I loathe all the snares of idealism;
but I have some common humanity and common sense.
[*He replaces him in an easy chair, and sits down opposite him*].
Come! what is a really scientific theory? A true theory,
isnt it?

PARAMORE. No doubt.

CHARTERIS. For instance, you have a theory about
Craven's liver, eh?

PARAMORE. I still believe that to be a true theory, though
it has been upset for the moment.

CHARTERIS. And you have a theory that it would be
pleasant to be married to Julia?

PARAMORE. I suppose so. In a sense.

CHARTERIS. That theory also will be upset, probably
before youre a year older.

PARAMORE. Always cynical, Charteris.

CHARTERIS. Never mind that. Now it's a perfectly damnable thing for you to hope that your liver theory is true, because it amounts to hoping that Craven will die an agonizing death.

PARAMORE. And always paradoxical, Charteris.

CHARTERIS. Well, at least youll admit that it's amiable and human to hope that your theory about Julia is right, because it amounts to hoping that she may live happily ever after.

PARAMORE. I do hope that with all my soul – [*correcting himself*] I mean with all my function of hoping.

CHARTERIS. Then, since both theories are equally scientific, why not devote yourself, as a humane man, to proving the amiable theory rather than the damnable one?

PARAMORE. But how?

CHARTERIS. I'll tell you. You think I'm fond of Julia myself. So I am; but then I'm fond of everybody; so I dont count. Besides, if you try the scientific experiment of asking her whether she loves me, she'll tell you that she hates and despises me. So I'm out of the running. Nevertheless, like you, I hope that she may be happy with all my – what did you call your soul?

PARAMORE [*impatiently*] Oh, go on, go on: finish what you were going to say.

CHARTERIS [*suddenly affecting complete indifference, and rising carelessly*] I dont know that I was going to say anything more. If I were you I should invite the Cravens to tea in honor of the Colonel's escape from a horrible doom. By the way, if youve done with that British Medical Journal, I should like to see how theyve smashed your theory up.

PARAMORE [*wincing as he also rises*] Oh, certainly, if you wish it. I have no objection. [*He takes the journal from the bookstand*]. I admit that the Italian experiments apparently upset my theory. But please remember that it is doubtful – extremely doubtful – whether anything can be proved by experiments on animals. [*He hands Charteris the journal*].

CHARTERIS [*taking it*] It doesnt matter: I dont intend to make any. [*He retires to the recess on Ibsen's right, picking up the step-ladder as he passes and placing it so that he is able to use it for a leg rest as he settles himself to read on the divan with his back to the corner of the mantelpiece*].

 Paramore goes to the dining room door, and is about to leave the library when he meets Grace entering.

GRACE. How do you do, Dr Paramore? So glad to see you. [*They shake hands*].

PARAMORE. Thanks. Quite well, I hope?

GRACE. Quite, thank you. Youre looking overworked. We must take more care of you, Doctor.

PARAMORE. You are too kind.

GRACE. It is you who are too kind – to your patients. You sacrifice yourself. Have a little rest. Come and talk to me. Tell me all about the latest scientific discoveries, and what I ought to read to keep myself up to date. But perhaps youre busy.

PARAMORE. No, not at all. Only too delighted. [*They go into the recess on Ibsen's left, and sit there chatting in whispers, very confidentially*].

CHARTERIS. How they all love a doctor! They can say what they like to him. [*Julia returns, but does not look his way. He takes his feet from the ladder and sits up*] Whew! [*Julia wanders along his side of the room, apparently looking for someone. Charteris steals after her*].

CHARTERIS [*in a low voice*] Looking for me, Julia?

JULIA [*starting violently*] Oh! how you startled me!

CHARTERIS. Sh! I want to shew you something. Look! [*He points to the pair in the recess*].

JULIA [*jealously*] That woman!

CHARTERIS. My young woman, carrying off your young man.

JULIA. What do you mean? Do you dare insinuate –

CHARTERIS. Sh – sh – sh! Dont disturb them.

Paramore rises; takes down a book; and sits on a foot-stool at Grace's feet.

JULIA. Why are they whispering like that?

CHARTERIS. Because they dont want any one to hear what they are saying to one another.

Paramore shews Grace a picture in the book. They both laugh heartily over it.

JULIA. What is he shewing her?

CHARTERIS. Probably a diagram of the liver. [*Julia, with an exclamation of disgust, makes for the recess. Charteris catches her sleeve*]. Stop. Be careful, Julia [*She frees herself by giving him a push which upsets him into the easy chair; then crosses to the recess, and stands looking down at Grace and Paramore from the corner next the fireplace*].

JULIA [*with suppressed fury*] You seem to have found a very interesting book, Dr Paramore. [*They look up, astonished*]. May I ask what it is? [*She stoops swiftly; snatches the book from Paramore; and comes down to the table quickly to look at it whilst they rise in amazement*]. Good Words! [*She flings it on the table, and sweeps back past Charteris, exclaiming contemptuously*] You fool! [*Paramore and Grace, meanwhile, come from the recess: Paramore bewildered; Grace very determined*].

CHARTERIS [*aside to Julia as he gets out of the easy chair*] Idiot! She'll have you turned out of the club for this.

JULIA [*terrified*] She cant: can she?

PARAMORE. What is the matter, Miss Craven?

CHARTERIS [*hastily*] Nothing. My fault: a stupid practical joke. I beg your pardon and Mrs Tranfield's.

GRACE [*firmly*] It is not your fault in the least, Mr Charteris. Dr Paramore: will you oblige me by finding Sylvia Craven for me, if you can?

PARAMORE [*hesitating*] But –

GRACE. I want you to go now, if you please.

PARAMORE [*succumbing*] Certainly. [*He bows and goes out by the staircase door*].

GRACE. You are going with him, Charteris.

JULIA. You will not leave me here to be insulted by this woman, Mr Charteris. [*She takes his arm as if to go with him*].

GRACE. When two ladies quarrel in this club, it is against the rules to settle it when there are gentlemen present: especially the gentlemen they are quarrelling about. I presume you do not wish to break that rule, Miss Craven. [*Julia sullenly drops Charteris's arm. Grace turns to Charteris, and adds*] Now! Trot off.

CHARTERIS. Certainly. Certainly. [*He follows Paramore ignominiously*].

GRACE [*to Julia, with quiet peremptoriness*] Now: what have you to say to me?

JULIA [*suddenly throwing herself tragically on her knees at Grace's feet*] Dont take him from me. Oh dont – dont be so cruel. Give him back to me. You dont know what youre doing – what our past has been – how I love him. You dont know –

GRACE. Get up; and dont be a fool. Suppose any one comes in and sees you in that ridiculous attitude!

JULIA. I hardly know what I'm doing. I dont care what I'm doing: I'm too miserable. Oh, wont you listen to me?

GRACE. Do you suppose I am a man, to be imposed on by this sort of rubbish?

JULIA [*getting up and looking darkly at her*] You intend to take him from me then?

GRACE. Do you expect me to help you to keep him after the way you have behaved?

JULIA [*trying her theatrical method in a milder form: reasonable and impulsively goodnatured instead of tragic*] I know I was wrong to act as I did last night. I beg your pardon. I am sorry I was mad.

GRACE. Not a bit mad. You calculated to an inch how far you could go. When he is present to stand between us and play out the scene with you, I count for nothing. When we are alone, you fall back on your natural way of getting anything you want: crying for it like a baby until it is given to you.

JULIA [*with unconcealed hatred*] You learnt this from him.

GRACE. I learnt it from yourself, last night and now. How I hate to be a woman when I see, by you, what wretched childish creatures we are! Those two men would cut you dead and have you turned out of the club if you were a man, and had behaved in such a way before them. But because you are only a woman, they are forbearing! sympathetic! gallant! Oh, if you had a scrap of self-respect, their indulgence would make you creep all over. I understand now why Charteris has no respect for women.

JULIA. How dare you say that?

GRACE. Dare! I love him. And I have refused his offer to marry me.

JULIA [*incredulous, but hopeful*] You have refused!

GRACE. Yes; because I will not give myself to any man who has learnt how to treat women from you and your like. I can do without his love, but not without his respect; and it is your fault that I cannot have both. Take his love then; and much good may it do you! Run to him, and beg him to take you back.

JULIA. Oh, what a liar you are! He loved me before he ever saw you – before he ever dreamt of you, you pitiful thing. Do you think *I* need go down on my knees to men to make them come to me? That may be your experience, you creature with no figure: it is not mine. There are dozens of men who would give their souls for a look from me. I have only to lift my finger.

GRACE. Lift it then; and see whether he will come.

JULIA. How I should like to kill you! I dont know why I dont.

GRACE. Yes: you like to get out of your difficulties at other people's expense. It is something to boast of, isnt it, that dozens of men would make love to you if you invited them?

JULIA [*sullenly*] I suppose it's better to be like you, with a cold heart and a serpent's tongue. Thank Heaven, I have

a heart: that is why you can hurt me as I cannot hurt you.
And you are a coward. You are giving him up to me without a struggle.

GRACE. Yes: it is for you to struggle. I wish you success.
[*She turns away contemptuously, and is going to the dining room door when Sylvia enters on the opposite side, followed by Cuthbertson and Craven, who come to Julia, whilst Sylvia crosses to Grace*].

SYLVIA. Here I am, sent by the faithful Paramore. He hinted that I'd better bring the elder members of the family too: here they are. Whats the row?

GRACE [*quietly*] Nothing, dear. Theres no row.

JULIA [*hysterically, tottering and stretching out her arms to Craven*] Daddy!

CRAVEN [*taking her in his arms*] My precious! Whats the matter?

JULIA [*through her tears*] She's going to have me expelled from the club; and we shall all be disgraced. Can she do it, Daddy?

CRAVEN. Well, really, the rules of this club are so extraordinary that I dont know. [*To Grace*] May I ask, madam, whether you have any complaint to make of my daughter's conduct?

GRACE. Yes, sir. I am going to complain to the committee.

SYLVIA. I knew youd overdo it some day, Julia.

CRAVEN. Do you know this lady, Jo?

CUTHBERTSON. This is my daughter, Mrs Tranfield, Dan. Grace: this is my old friend Colonel Craven.

Grace and Craven bow to one another constrainedly.

CRAVEN. May I ask the ground of complaint, Mrs Tranfield?

GRACE. Simply that Miss Craven is essentially a womanly woman, and, as such, not eligible for membership.

JULIA. It's false. I'm not a womanly woman. I was guaranteed when I joined just as you were.

GRACE. By Mr Charteris, I think, at your own request. I shall call him as a witness to your thoroughly womanly conduct just now in his presence and Dr Paramore's.

CRAVEN. Cuthbertson: are they joking? or am I dreaming?

CUTHBERTSON [*grimly*] It's real, Dan: youre awake.

SYLVIA [*taking Craven's left arm, and hugging it affectionately*] Dear old Rip Van Winkle!

CRAVEN. Well, Mrs Tranfield, all I can say is that I hope you will succeed in establishing your complaint, and that Julia may soon see the last of this most outrageous institution.
Charteris returns.

CHARTERIS [*at the door*] May I come in?

SYLVIA. Yes: youre wanted here as a witness. [*Charteris comes in, and places himself with evident misgiving between Julia and Grace*]. It's a bad case of womanliness.

GRACE [*Half aside to him, significantly*] You understand? [*Julia watching them jealously, leaves her father and gets close to Charteris. Grace adds aloud*] I shall expect your support before the committee.

JULIA. If you have a scrap of manhood in you you will take my part.

CHARTERIS. But then I shall be expelled for being a manly man. Besides, I'm on the committee myself; I cant act as judge and witness too. You must apply to Paramore: he saw it all.

GRACE. Where is Dr Paramore?

CHARTERIS. Just gone home.

JULIA [*with sudden resolution*] What is Dr Paramore's number in Savile Row?

CHARTERIS. Seventynine.

Julia goes out quickly by the staircase door; to their astonishment Charteris follows her to the door, which swings back in his face, leaving him staring after her through the glass.

SYLVIA [*running to Grace*] Grace: go after her. Dont let her get beforehand with Paramore. She'll tell him the most heartbreaking stories about how she's been treated, and get round him completely.

CRAVEN [*thundering*] Sylvia! is that the way to speak of your sister, miss? [*Grace squeezes Sylvia's hand to console her; takes a magazine from the table; and sits down calmly. Sylvia posts her-self behind Grace's chair, leaning over the back to watch the en-suing colloquy between the three men].* I assure you, Mrs Tran-field, Dr Paramore has just invited us all to take afternoon tea with him; and if my daughter has gone to his house, she is simply taking advantage of his invitation to extricate herself from a very embarrassing scene here. We're all going there. Come, Sylvia. [*He turns to go, followed by Cuthbertson*].

CHARTERIS [*in consternation*] Stop! [*He gets between Craven and Cuthbertson*]. What hurry is there? Cant you give the man time?

CRAVEN. Time! What for?

CHARTERIS [*talking foolishly in his agitation*] Well, to get a little rest, you know: a busy professional man like that! He's not had a moment to himself all day.

CRAVEN. But Julia's with him.

CHARTERIS. Well, no matter: she's only one person. And she ought to have an opportunity of laying her case before him. As a member of the committee, I think thats only just. Be reasonable, Craven: give him half an hour.

CUTHBERTSON [*sternly*] What do you mean by this, Charteris?

CHARTERIS. Nothing, I assure you. Only common con-sideration for poor Paramore.

CUTHBERTSON. Youve some motive. Craven: I strongly advise that we go at once. [*He grasps the door handle*].

CHARTERIS [*coaxingly*] No, no. [*He puts his hand persuasively on Craven's arm, adding*] It's not good for your liver, Craven, to rush about immediately after lunch.

CUTHBERTSON. His liver's cured. Come on, Craven. [*He opens the door*].

CHARTERIS [*catching Cuthbertson by the sleeve*] Cuthbertson: youre mad. Paramore's going to propose to Julia. We must give him time: he's not the man to come to the point in three seconds as you or I would. [*Turning to*

Craven] Dont you see? that will get me out of the difficulty we were speaking of this morning: you and I and Cuthbertson. You remember?

CRAVEN. Now is this a thing to say plump out before everybody, Charteris? Confound it, have you no decency?

CUTHBERTSON [*severely*] None whatever.

CHARTERIS [*turning to Cuthbertson*] No: dont be unkind, Cuthbertson. Back me up. My future, her future, Mrs Tranfield's future, Craven's future, everybody's future depends on Julia being Paramore's affianced bride when we arrive. He's certain to propose if youll only give him time. You know youre a kindly and sensible man as well as a deucedly clever one, Cuthbertson, in spite of all the nonsense you pick up in the theatre. Say a word for me.

CRAVEN. I'm quite willing to leave the decision to Cuthbertson: and I have no doubt whatever as to what that decision will be.

Cuthbertson carefully shuts the door, and comes back into the room with an air of weighty reflection.

CUTHBERTSON. I am now going to speak as a man of the world: that is, without moral responsibility.

CRAVEN. Quite so, Jo. Of course.

CUTHBERTSON. Therefore, though I have no sympathy whatever with Charteris's views, I think we can do no harm by waiting – say ten minutes or so. [*He sits down*].

CHARTERIS [*delighted*] Ah, theres nobody like you after all, Cuthbertson, when theres a difficult situation to be judged. [*He sits down on the settee back*].

CRAVEN [*deeply disappointed*] Oh well, Jo, if that is your decision, I must keep my word and abide by it. Better sit down and make ourselves comfortable, I suppose. [*He sits also, under protest*].

A pause, very trying for the three men.

GRACE [*looking up from her magazine*] Dont fidget, Leonard.

CHARTERIS [*slipping off the settee back*] I cant help it: I'm too restless. The fact is, Julia has made me so nervous that I cant answer for myself until I know her decision. Mrs Tranfield will tell you what a time Ive had lately. Julia's really a most determined woman, you know.

CRAVEN [*starting up*] Well, upon my life! Upon my honour and conscience!! Now really!!! I shall go this instant. Come on, Sylvia, Cuthbertson: I hope youll mark your sense of this sort of thing by coming on to Paramore's with us at once. [*He marches to the door*].

CHARTERIS [*desperately*] Craven; youre trifling with your daughter's happiness. I ask only five minutes more.

CRAVEN. Not five seconds, sir. Fie for shame. Charteris! [*He goes out*].

CUTHBERTSON [*to Charteris, as he passes him on his way to the door*] Bungler! [*He follows Craven*].

SYLVIA. Serve you right, you duffer! [*She follows Cuthbertson*].

CHARTERIS. Oh, these headstrong old men! [*To Grace*] Nothing to be done now but to go with them, and delay the Colonel as much as possible. So I'm afraid I must leave you.

GRACE [*rising*] Not at all. Paramore invited me, too.

CHARTERIS [*aghast*] You dont meant to say youre coming!

GRACE. Most certainly. Do you suppose I will let that woman think I am afraid to meet her? [*Charteris sinks on a chair with a prolonged groan*]. Come: dont be silly: youll not overtake the Colonel if you delay any longer.

CHARTERIS. Why was I ever born, child of misfortune that I am! [*He rises despairingly*]. Well, if you must come, you must. [*He offers his arm, which she takes*]. By the way, what happened after I left you?

GRACE. I gave her a lecture on her behavior which she will remember to the last day of her life.

CHARTERIS [*approvingly*] That was right, darling. [*He slips his arm round her waist*] Just one kiss. To soothe me.

GRACE [*complacently offering her cheek*] Foolish boy! [*He kisses her*]. Now come along. [*They go out together*].

ACT III

Paramore's reception room in Savile Row. Viewing the room from the front windows, the door is seen in the opposite wall near the left hand corner. Another door, a light noiseless one covered with green baize, leading to the consulting room, is in the right hand wall towards the back. The fireplace is on the left. At the nearer corner of it a couch is placed at right angles to the wall, settlewise. At the other corner, an easy chair. On the right the wall is occupied by a bookcase, further orward than the green baize door. Beyond the door is a cabinet of anatomical preparations, with a framed photograph of Rembrandt's School of Anatomy hanging on the wall above it. In front, a little to the right, a teatable.

Paramore is seated in a round-backed chair, on castors, pouring out tea. Julia sits opposite him, with her back to the fire. He is in high spirits: she very downcast.

PARAMORE [*handing her the cup he has just filled*] There! Making tea is one of the few things I consider myself able to do thoroughly well. Cake?

JULIA. No, thank you. I dont like sweet things. [*She sets down the cup untasted*].

PARAMORE. Anything wrong with the tea?

JULIA. No. It's very nice.

PARAMORE. I'm afraid I'm a bad entertainer. The fact is, I am too professional. I shine only in consultation. I almost wish you had something serious the matter with you; so that you might call out my knowledge and sympathy. As it is, I can only admire you, and feel how pleasant it is to have you here.

JULIA [*bitterly*] And pet me, and say pretty things to me. I wonder you dont offer me a saucer of milk at once.

PARAMORE [*astonished*] Why?

JULIA. Because you seem to regard me very much as if I were a Persian cat.

PARAMORE [*in strong remonstrance*] Miss Cra –

JULIA [*cutting him short*] Oh, you neednt protest. I'm used to it: it's the sort of attachment I seem always to inspire. [*Ironically*] You cant think how flattering it is.

PARAMORE. My dear Miss Craven, what a cynical thing to say! You! who are loved at first sight by the people in the street as you pass. Why, in the club I can tell by the faces of the men whether you have been lately in the room or not.

JULIA [*shrinking fiercely*] Oh, I hate that look in their faces. Do you know that I have never had one human being care for me since I was born?

PARAMORE. Thats not true, Miss Craven. Even if it were true of your father, and of Charteris, who loves you madly in spite of your dislike for him, it is not true of me.

JULIA [*startled*] Who told you that about Charteris?

PARAMORE. Why, he himself.

JULIA [*with deep, poignant conviction*] He cares for only one person in the world; and that is himself. There is not in his whole nature one unselfish spot. He would not spend one hour of his real life with – [*a sob chokes her: she rises passionately, crying*] You are all alike, every one of you. Even my father only makes a pet of me. [*She goes away to the fireplace, and stands with her back to him to hide her face*].

PARAMORE [*following her humbly*] I dont deserve this from you: indeed I do not.

JULIA [*rating him*] Then why do you gossip about me behind my back with Charteris?

PARAMORE. We said nothing disparaging of you. Nobody shall ever do that in my presence. We spoke of the subject nearest our hearts.

JULIA. His heart! Oh God, his heart! [*She sits down on the couch, and covers her face*].

PARAMORE [*sadly*] I am afraid you love him, for all that, Miss Craven.

JULIA [*raising her head instantly*] If he says that, he lies. If ever you hear it said that I cared for him, contradict it: it is false.

PARAMORE [*quickly advancing to her*] Miss Craven: is the way clear for me then?

JULIA [*losing interest in the conversation, and looking crossly away from him*] What do you mean?

PARAMORE [*impetuously*] You must see what I mean. Contradict the rumor of your attachment to Charteris, not by words – it has gone too far for that – but by becoming my wife. [*Earnestly*] Believe me: it is not merely your beauty that attracts me [*Julia, interested, looks up at him quickly*]: I know other beautiful women. It is your heart, your sincerity, your sterling reality, [*Julia rises and gazes at him, breathless with a new hope*] your great gifts of character that are only half developed because you have never been understood by those about you.

JULIA [*looking intently at him, and yet beginning to be derisively sceptical in spite of herself*] Have you really seen all that in me?

PARAMORE. I have felt it. I have been alone in the world; and I need you, Julia. That is how I have divined that you, also, are alone in the world.

JULIA [*with theatrical pathos*] You are right there. I am indeed alone in the world.

PARAMORE [*timidly approaching her*] With you I should not be alone. And you? with me?

JULIA. You! [*She gets quickly out of his reach, taking refuge at the teatable*]. No, no. I cant bring myself – [*She breaks off, perplexed, and looks uneasily about her*]. Oh, I dont know what to do. You will expect too much from me. [*She sits down*].

PARAMORE. I have more faith in you than you have in yourself. Your nature is richer than you think.

JULIA [*doubtfully*] Do you really believe that I am not the shallow, jealous, devilish tempered creature they all pretend I am!

PARAMORE. I am ready to place my happiness in your hands. Does that prove what I think of you?

JULIA. Yes: I believe you really care for me. [*He approaches her eagerly: she has a violent revulsion, and rises with her hand up as if to beat him off, crying*] No, no, no, no. I cannot. It's impossible. [*She goes towards the door*].

PARAMORE [*looking wistfully after her*] Is it Charteris?

JULIA [*stopping and turning*] Ah, you think that! [*She comes back*]. Listen to me. If I say yes, will you promise not to touch me? Will you give me time to accustom myself to our new relations?

PARAMORE. I promise most faithfully. I would not press you for the world.

JULIA. Then – then – Yes: I promise.

PARAMORE. Oh, how unspeakably hap –

JULIA [*stopping his raptures*] No: not another word. Let us forget it. [*She resumes her seat at the table*]. I havnt touched my tea. [*He hastens to his former seat. As he passes, she puts her left hand on his arm and says*] Be good to me, Percy: I need it sorely.

PARAMORE [*transported*] You have called me Percy! Hurrah!
    Charteris and Craven come in. Paramore hastens to meet them, beaming.

PARAMORE. Delighted to see you here with me, Colonel Craven. And you too, Charteris. Sit down. [*The Colonel sits down on the end of the couch*]. Where are the others?

CHARTERIS. Sylvia has dragged Cuthbertson off into the Burlington Arcade to buy some caramels. He likes to encourage her in eating caramels: he thinks it's a womanly taste. Besides, he likes them himself. Theyll be here presently. [*He strolls across to the cabinet, and pretends to study the Rembrandt photograph, so as to be as far out of Julia's reach as possible*].

CRAVEN. Yes; and Charteris has been trying to persuade me that theres a short cut between Cork Street and Savile Row somewhere in Conduit Street. Now did you ever hear such nonsense? Then he said my coat was getting shabby, and wanted me to go into Poole's and order a new one. Paramore: is my coat shabby?

PARAMORE. Not that I can see.

CRAVEN. I should think not. Then he wanted to draw me into an argument about the Egyptian war. We should have been here quarter of an hour ago only for his nonsense.

CHARTERIS [*still contemplating Rembrandt*] I did my best to keep him from disturbing you, Paramore.

PARAMORE [*gratefully*] You kept him exactly the right time, to a second. [*Formally*] Colonel Craven: I have something very particular to say to you.

CRAVEN [*springing up in alarm*] In private, Paramore: now really it must be in private.

PARAMORE [*surprised*] Of course. I was about to suggest my consulting room: theres nobody there. Miss Craven: will you excuse me: Charteris will entertain you until I return. [*He leads the way to the green baize door*].

CHARTERIS [*aghast*] Oh, I say, hadnt you better wait until the others come?

PARAMORE [*exultant*] No need for further delay now, my best friend. [*He wrings Charteris's hand*]. Will you come, Colonel?

CRAVEN. At your service, Paramore: at your service.

Craven and Paramore go into the consulting room. Julia turns her head, and stares insolently at Charteris. His nerves play him false: he is completely out of countenance in a moment. She rises suddenly. He starts, and comes hastily forward between the table and the bookcase. She crosses to that side behind the table; and he immediately crosses to the opposite side in front of it, dodging her.

CHARTERIS [*nervously*] Dont, Julia. Now dont abuse your advantage. Youve got me here at your mercy. Be good for once; and dont make a scene.

JULIA [*contemptuously*] Do you suppose I am going to touch you?

CHARTERIS. No. Of course not.

She comes forward on her side of the table. He retreats on his side of it. She looks at him with utter scorn; sweeps across to the

*couch; and sits down imperially. With a great sigh of relief he
drops into Paramore's chair.*

JULIA. Come here. I have something to say to you.

CHARTERIS. Yes? [*He rolls the chair a few inches towards her*].

JULIA. Come here, I say. I am not going to shout across the
room at you. Are you afraid of me?

CHARTERIS. Horribly. [*He moves the chair slowly, with great
misgivings, to the end of the couch*].

JULIA [*with studied insolence*] Has that woman told you that
she has given you up to me without an attempt to defend
her conquest?

CHARTERIS [*whispering persuasively*] Shew that you are
capable of the same sacrifice. Give me up too.

JULIA. Sacrifice! And so you think I'm dying to marry you,
do you?

CHARTERIS. I am afraid your intentions have been honorable, Julia.

JULIA. You cad!

CHARTERIS [*with a sigh*] I confess I am something either
more or less than a gentleman, Julia. You once gave me
the benefit of the doubt.

JULIA. Indeed! I never told you so. If you cannot behave
like a gentleman, you had better go back to the society of
the woman who has given you up: if such a coldblooded,
cowardly creature can be called a woman. [*She rises
majestically: he makes his chair fly back to the table*]. I know
you now, Leonard Charteris, through and through, in all
your falseness, your petty spite, your cruelty and your
vanity. The place you coveted has been won by a man
more worthy of it.

CHARTERIS [*springing up, and coming close to her, gasping with
eagerness*] What do you mean? Out with it. Have you
accep –

JULIA. I am engaged to Dr Paramore.

CHARTERIS [*enraptured*] My own Julia! [*He attempts to embrace her*].

JULIA [*recoiling: he catching her hands and holding them*] How dare you! Are you mad! Do you wish me to call Dr Paramore?

CHARTERIS. Call everybody, my darling – everybody in London. Now I shall no longer have to be brutal; to defend myself; to go in fear of you. How I have looked forward to this day! You know now that I dont want you to marry me or to love me: Paramore can have all that. I only want to look on and rejoice disinterestedly in the happiness of [*kissing her hand*] my dear Julia, [*kissing the other*] my beautiful Julia. [*She tears her hands away and raises them as if to strike him, as she did the night before at Cuthbertson's: he faces them with joyous recklessness*]. No use to threaten me now: I am not afraid of those hands: the loveliest hands in the world.

JULIA. How have you the face to turn round like this after insulting and torturing me?

CHARTERIS. Never mind, dearest: you never did understand me; and you never will. Our vivisecting friend has made a successful experiment at last.

JULIA [*earnestly*] It is you who are the vivisector: a far crueller, more wanton vivisector than he.

CHARTERIS. Yes; but then I learn so much more from my experiments than he does! and the victims learn as much as I do. Thats where my moral superiority comes in.

JULIA [*sitting down again on the couch with rueful humor*] Well, you shall not experiment on me any more. Go to your Grace if you want a victim. She'll be a tough one.

CHARTERIS [*reproachfully, sitting down beside her*] And you drove me to propose to her to escape from you! Suppose she had accepted me, where should I be now?

JULIA. Where *I* am, I suppose, now that I have accepted Paramore.

CHARTERIS. But I should have made Grace unhappy. [*Julia sneers*]. However, now I come to think of it, youll make Paramore unhappy. And yet if you refuse him he would be in despair. Poor devil!

JULIA [*her temper flashing up for a moment again*] He is a better man than you.

CHARTERIS [*humbly*] I grant you that, my dear.

JULIA [*impetuously*] Dont call me your dear. And what do you mean by saying that I shall make him unhappy? Am I not good enough for him?

CHARTERIS [*dubiously*] Well, that depends on what you mean by good enough.

JULIA [*earnestly*] You might have made me good if you had chosen to. You had a great power over me. I was like a child in your hands; and you knew it.

CHARTERIS. Yes, my dear. That means that whenever you got jealous and flew into a tearing rage, I could always depend on its ending happily if I only waited long enough, and petted you very hard all the time. When you had had your fling, and called the object of your jealousy every name you could lay your tongue to, and abused me to your heart's content for a couple of hours, then the reaction could come; and you would at last subside into a soothing rapture of affection which gave you a sensation of being angelically good and forgiving. Oh, I know that sort of goodness! You may have thought on these occasions that I was bringing out your latent amiability; but I thought you were bringing out mine, and using up rather more than your fair share of it.

JULIA. According to you, then, I have no good in me. I am an utterly vile worthless woman. Is that it?

CHARTERIS. Yes, if you are to be judged as you judge others. From the conventional point of view, theres nothing to be said for you, Julia: nothing. Thats why I have to find some other point of view to save my self-respect when I remember how I have loved you. Oh, what I have learnt from you! from you! who could learn nothing from me! I made a fool of you; and you brought me wisdom: I broke your heart; and you brought me joy: I made you curse your womanhood; and you revealed my manhood to me.

Blessings for ever and ever on my Julia's name! [*With genuine emotion, he takes her hand to kiss it again*].

JULIA [*snatching her hand away in disgust*] Oh, stop talking that nasty sneering stuff.

CHARTERIS [*laughingly appealing to the heavens*] She calls it nasty sneering stuff! Well, well: I'll never talk like that to you again, dearest. It only means that you are a beautiful woman, and that we all love you.

JULIA. Dont say that: I hate it. It sounds as if I were a mere animal.

CHARTERIS. Hm! A fine animal is a very wonderful thing. Dont let us disparage animals, Julia.

JULIA. That is what you really think me.

CHARTERIS. Come, Julia! you dont expect me to admire you for your moral qualities, do you?

Julia turns and looks hard at him. He starts up apprehensively, and backs away from her. She rises and follows him up slowly and intently.

JULIA [*deliberately*] I have seen you very much infatuated with this depraved creature who has no moral qualities.

CHARTERIS [*retreating*] Keep off, Julia. Remember your new obligations to Paramore.

JULIA [*overtaking him in the middle of the room*] Never mind Paramore: that is my business. [*She grasps the lapels of his coat in her hands, and looks fixedly at him*]. Oh, if the people you talk so cleverly to could only know you as I know you! Sometimes I wonder at myself for ever caring for you.

CHARTERIS [*beaming at her*] Only sometimes?

JULIA. You fraud! You humbug! You miserable little plaster saint! [*He looks delighted*]. Oh! [*In a paroxysm half of rage, half of tenderness, she shakes him, growling over him like a tigress over her cub*].

Paramore and Craven return from the consulting room, and are thunderstruck at the spectacle.

CRAVEN [*shouting, utterly scandalized*] Julia!!

Julia releases Charteris, but stands her ground disdainfully as they come forward, Craven on her left, Paramore on her right.

PARAMORE. Whats the matter?

CHARTERIS. Nothing, nothing. Youll soon get used to this, Paramore.

CRAVEN. Now really, Julia, this is a very extraordinary way to behave. It's not fair to Paramore.

JULIA [*coldly*] If Dr Paramore objects, he can break off our engagement. [*To Paramore*] Pray dont hesitate.

PARAMORE [*looking doubtfully and anxiously at her*] Do you wish me to break it off?

CHARTERIS [*alarmed*] Nonsense! dont act so hastily. It was my fault. I annoyed Miss Craven – insulted her. Hang it all, dont go and spoil everything like this.

CRAVEN. This is most infernally perplexing. I cant believe that you insulted Julia, Charteris. Ive no doubt you annoyed her: youd annoy anybody: upon my soul you would; but insult! now what do you mean by that?

PARAMORE [*very earnestly*] Miss Craven: in all delicacy and sincerity I ask you to be frank with me. What are the relations between you and Charteris?

JULIA [*enigmatically*] Ask him. [*She goes to the fireplace, turning her back on them*].

CHARTERIS. Certainly: I'll confess. I'm in love with Miss Craven. Ive persecuted her with my addresses ever since I knew her. It's been no use: she utterly despises me. A moment ago the spectacle of a rival's happiness stung me to make a nasty sneering speech; and she – well, she just shook me a little, as you saw.

PARAMORE [*chivalrously*] I shall never forget that you helped me to win her, Charteris. [*Julia turns quickly, a spasm of fury in her face*].

CHARTERIS. Sh! For Heaven's sake dont mention it.

CRAVEN. This is a very different story to the one you told Cuthbertson and myself this morning. Youll excuse my saying that it sounds much more like the truth. Come! you were humbugging us, werent you?

CHARTERIS [*enigmatically*] Ask Julia.

    Paramore and Craven turn to Julia. Charteris remains dog-gedly looking straight before him.

JULIA. It's quite true. He has been in love with me; he has persecuted me; and I utterly despise him.

CRAVEN. Dont rub it in, Julia: it's not kind. No man is quite himself when he's crossed in love. [*To Charteris*] Now listen to me, Charteris. When I was a young fellow, Cuthbertson and I fell in love with the same woman. She preferred Cuthbertson. I was taken aback: I wont deny it. But I knew my duty; and I did it. I gave her up, and wished Cuthbertson joy. He told me this morning, when we met after many years, that he has respected and liked me ever since for it. And I believe him, and feel the better for it. [*Impressively*] Now, Charteris: Paramore and you stand today where Cuthbertson and I stood on a certain July evening thirty-five years ago. How are you going to take it?

JULIA [*indignantly*] How is he going to take it, indeed! Really, papa, this is too much. If Mrs Cuthbertson wouldnt have you, it may have been very noble of you to make a virtue of giving her up, just as you made a virtue of being a teetotaller when Percy cut off your wine. But he shant be virtuous over me. I have refused him; and if he doesnt like it he can – he can –

CHARTERIS. I can lump it. Precisely. Craven: you can depend on me. I'll lump it. [*He moves off nonchalantly, and leans against the bookcase with his hands in his pockets*].

CRAVEN [*hurt*] Julia: you dont treat me respectfully. I dont wish to complain; but that was not a becoming speech.

JULIA [*bursting into tears, and throwing herself into the easy chair*] Is there any one in the world who has any feeling for me? who does not think me utterly vile?

    Craven and Paramore hurry to her in the greatest consternation.

CRAVEN [*remorsefully*] My pet: I didnt for a moment mean –

JULIA. Must I stand to be bargained for by two men –

passed from one to the other like a slave in the market, and not say a word in my own defence?

CRAVEN. But, my love –

JULIA. Oh, go away, all of you. Leave me. I – oh – [*she gives way to a passion of tears*].

PARAMORE [*reproachfully to Craven*] Youve wounded her cruelly, Colonel Craven. Cruelly.

CRAVEN. But I didnt mean to: I said nothing. Charteris: was I harsh?

CHARTERIS. You forget the revolt of the daughters, Craven. And you certainly wouldnt have gone on like that to any grown-up woman who was not your daughter.

CRAVEN. Do you mean to say that I am expected to treat my daughter the same as I would any other girl?

PARAMORE. I should say certainly, Colonel Craven.

CRAVEN. Well, dash me if I will. There!

PARAMORE. If you take that tone, I have nothing more to say. [*He crosses the room with offended dignity, and posts himself with his back to the bookcase beside Charteris*].

JULIA [*with a sob*] Daddy.

CRAVEN [*turning solicitously to her*] Yes, my love.

JULIA [*looking up at him tearfully, and kissing his hand*] Dont mind them. You didnt mean it, Daddy, did you?

CRAVEN. No, no, my precious. Come: dont cry.

PARAMORE [*to Charteris, looking at Julia with delight*] How beautiful she is!

CHARTERIS [*throwing up his hands*] Oh, Lord help you, Paramore! [*He leaves the bookcase, and sits at the end of the couch farthest from the fire*].

    Sylvia arrives.

SYLVIA [*contemplating Julia*] Crying again! Well you are a womanly one!

CRAVEN. Dont worry your sister, Sylvia. You know she cant bear it.

SYLVIA. I speak for her good, Dad. All the world cant be expected to know that she's the family baby.

JULIA. You will get your ears boxed presently, Silly.

CRAVEN. Now! now! now! my dear children, really now! Come, Julia: put up your handkerchief before Mrs Tranfield sees you. She's coming along with Jo.

JULIA [*rising*] That woman again!

SYLVIA. Another row! Go it, Julia!

CRAVEN. Hold your tongue, Sylvia. [*He turns commandingly to Julia*]. Now look here, Julia.

CHARTERIS. Hello! A revolt of the fathers!

CRAVEN. Silence, Charteris. [*To Julia, unanswerably*] The test of a man's or woman's breeding is how they behave in a quarrel. Anybody can behave well when things are going smoothly. Now you said today, at that iniquitous club, that you were not a womanly woman. Very well: I dont mind. But if you are not going to behave like a lady when Mrs Tranfield comes into this room, youve got to behave like a gentleman; or fond as I am of you, I'll cut you dead exactly as I would if you were my son.

PARAMORE [*remonstrating*] Colonel Craven –

CRAVEN [*cutting him short*] Dont be a fool, Paramore.

JULIA [*tearfully excusing herself*] I'm sure, Daddy –

CRAVEN. Stop snivelling. I'm not speaking as your Daddy now: I'm speaking as your commanding officer.

SYLVIA. Good old Victoria Cross! [*Craven turns sharply on her; and she darts away behind Charteris, and presently seats herself on the couch, so that she and Charteris are shoulder to shoulder, facing opposite ways*].

Cuthbertson arrives with Grace, who remains near the door whilst her father joins the others.

CRAVEN. Ah, Jo, here you are. Now, Paramore: tell em the news.

PARAMORE. Mrs Tranfield: Cuthbertson: allow me to introduce you to my future wife.

CUTHBERTSON [*coming forward to shake hands with Paramore*] My heartiest congratulations! Miss Craven: you will accept Grace's congratulations as well as mine, I hope.

CRAVEN. She will, Jo. [*Peremptorily*] Now, Julia.

> *Julia slowly rises.*

CUTHBERTSON. Now, Grace. [*He conducts her to Julia's right, then posts himself on the heathrug, with his back to the fire, watching them, whilst the Colonel keeps guard on the other side*].

GRACE [*speaking in a low voice to Julia alone*] So you have shewn him that you can do without him! Now I take back everything I said. Will you shake hands with me? [*Julia gives her hand painfully, with her face averted*]. They think this a happy ending, Julia, these men: our lords and masters! *The two stand silent hand in hand.*

SYLVIA [*leaning back across the couch, aside to Charteris*] Has she really chucked you? [*He nods assent. She looks at him dubiously, and adds*] I expect you chucked her.

CUTHBERTSON. And now, Paramore, mind you dont stand any chaff from Charteris about this. He's in the same predicament himself. He's engaged to Grace.

JULIA [*dropping Grace's hand, and speaking with breathless anguish, but not violently*] Again!

CHARTERIS [*rising hastily*] Dont be alarmed. It's all off.

SYLVIA [*rising indignantly*] What! Youve chucked Grace too! What a shame! [*She goes to the other side of the room, fuming*].

CHARTERIS [*following her, and putting his hand soothingly on her shoulder*] She wont have me, old chap. That is [*turning to the others*] unless Mrs Tranfield has changed her mind again.

GRACE. No: we shall remain very good friends, I hope; but nothing would induce me to marry you. [*She takes the easy chair at the fireplace, and sits down with perfect composure*].

JULIA. Ah! [*She sits down on the couch with a great sigh of relief*].

SYLVIA [*consoling Charteris*] Poor old Leonard!

CHARTERIS. Yes: this is the doom of the philanderer. I shall have to go on philandering now all my life. No domesticity, no firesides, no little ones, nothing at all in

Cuthbertson's line! Nobody will marry me – unless you, Sylvia: eh?

SYLVIA. Not if I know it, Charteris.

CHARTERIS [*to them all*] You see!

CRAVEN [*coming between Charteris and Sylvia*] Now you really shouldnt make a jest of these things: upon my life and soul you shouldnt, Charteris.

CUTHBERTSON [*on the hearthrug*] The only use he can find for sacred things is to make a jest of them. Thats the New Order. Thank Heaven, we belong to the Old Order, Dan!

CHARTERIS. Cuthbertson: dont be symbolic.

CUTHBERTSON [*outraged*] Symbolic! That is an accusation of Ibsenism. What do you mean?

CHARTERIS. Symbolic of the Old Order. Dont persuade yourself that you represent the Old Order. There never was any Old Order.

CRAVEN. There I flatly contradict you, and stand up for Jo. I'd no more have behaved as you do when I was a young man than I'd have cheated at cards. *I* belong to the Old Order.

CHARTERIS. Youre getting old, Craven; and you want to make a merit of it, as usual.

CRAVEN. Come now, Charteris: youre not offended, I hope. [*With a conciliatory outburst*] Well, perhaps I shouldnt have said that about cheating at cards. I withdraw it [*offering his hand*].

CHARTERIS [*taking Craven's hand*] No offence, my dear Craven: none in the world. I didnt mean to shew any temper. But [*aside, after looking round to see whether the others are listening*] only just consider! the spectacle of a rival's happiness! the –

CRAVEN [*aloud, decisively*] Charteris: now youve got to behave like a man. Your duty's plain before you. [*To Cuthbertson*] Am I right, Jo?

CUTHBERTSON [*firmly*] You are, Dan.

176

CRAVEN [*to Charteris*] Go straight up and congratulate Julia. And do it like a gentleman, smiling.

CHARTERIS. Colonel: I will. Not a quiver shall betray the conflict within.

CRAVEN. Julia: Charteris has not congratulated you yet. He's coming to do it.

Julia rises, and fixes a dangerous look on Charteris.

SYLVIA [*whispering quickly behind Charteris as he is about to advance*] Take care. She's going to hit you. I know her.

Charteris stops and looks cautiously at Julia, measuring the situation. They regard one another steadfastly for a moment. Grace softly rises and gets close to Julia.

CHARTERIS [*whispering over his shoulder to Sylvia*] I'll chance it. [*He walks confidently up to Julia*]. Julia? [*He proffers his hand*].

JULIA [*exhausted, allowing herself to take it*] You are right. I am a worthless woman.

CHARTERIS [*triumphant, and gaily remonstrating*] Oh, Why?

JULIA. Because I am not brave enough to kill you.

GRACE [*taking her in her arms as she sinks, almost fainting, away from him*] Oh no. Never make a hero of a philanderer.

Charteris, amused and untouched, shakes his head laughingly. The rest look at Julia with concern, and even a little awe, feeling for the first time the presence of a keen sorrow.

MRS WARREN'S PROFESSION

A Play

1894

PREFACE

MRS WARREN'S PROFESSION was written in 1894 to draw attention to the truth that prostitution is caused, not by female depravity and male licentiousness, but simply by underpaying, undervaluing, and overworking women so shamefully that the poorest of them are forced to resort to prostitution to keep body and soul together. Indeed all attractive unpropertied women lose money by being infallibly virtuous or contracting marriages that are not more or less venal. If on the large social scale we get what we call vice instead of what we call virtue it is simply because we are paying more for it. No normal woman would be a professional prostitute if she could better herself by being respectable, nor marry for money if she could afford to marry for love.

Also I desired to expose the fact that prostitution is not only carried on without organization by individual enterprise in the lodgings of solitary women, each her own mistress as well as every customer's mistress, but organized and exploited as a big international commerce for the profit of capitalists like any other commerce, and very lucrative to great city estates, including Church estates, through the rents of the houses in which it is practised.

I could not have done anything more injurious to my prospects at the outset of my career. My play was immediately stigmatized by the Lord Chamberlain, who by Act of Parliament has despotic and even supermonarchical power over our theatres, as 'immoral and otherwise improper for the stage'. Its performance was prohibited, I myself being branded by implication, to my great damage, as an unscrupulous and blackguardly author. True, I have lived this defamation down, and am apparently none the worse. True too that the stage under the censorship became so licentious after the war that the ban on a comparatively prudish play like mine became ridiculous and had to be lifted. Also I admit that my career as a revolutionary critic of our most respected social institutions kept me so continually in hot water that the addition of another jugful of boiling fluid by the Lord Chamberlain troubled me too little to entitle me to personal commiseration, especially as the play greatly strengthened my repute among serious readers. Besides, in 1894 the ordinary commercial theatres would have nothing to say to me, Lord Chamberlain or no Lord Chamberlain. None the less the injury done me now admittedly indefensible, was real and considerable, and the injury to society much greater; for when the White Slave Traffic, as Mrs Warren's profession came to be called, was dealt with legislatively, all that Parliament did was to enact that prostitutes' male bullies and parasites should be flogged, leaving Mrs Warren in complete command of the situation, and its true nature more effectually masked than ever. It was the fault of the Censorship that our legislators and journalists were not better instructed.

In 1902 the Stage Society, technically a club giving private performances for the entertainment of its own members, and therefore exempt from the Lord Chamberlain's jurisdiction, resolved to perform the play. None of the public theatres dared brave his displeasure (he has absolute power to close them if they offend him) by harboring the performance; but another club which had a little stage, and which rather courted a pleasantly scandalous reputation, opened its doors for one night and one afternoon. Some idea of the resultant sensation may be gathered from the following polemic, which appeared as a preface to a special edition of the play, and was headed.

The Author's Apology

Mrs Warren's Profession has been performed at last, after a delay of only eight years; and I have once more shared with Ibsen the triumphant amusement of startling all but the strongest-headed of the London theatre critics clean out of the practice of their profession. No author who has ever known the exultation of sending the Press into an hysterical tumult of protest, of moral panic, of involuntary and frantic confession of sin, of a horror of conscience in which the power of distinguishing between the work of art on the stage and the real life of the spectator is confused and overwhelmed, will ever care for the stereotyped compliments which every successful farce or melodrama elicits from the newspapers. Give me that critic who rushed from my play to declare furiously that Sir George Crofts ought to be kicked. What a triumph for the actor, thus to reduce a jaded London journalist to the condition of the simple sailor in the Wapping gallery, who shouts execrations at Iago and warnings to Othello not to believe him! But dearer still than such simplicity is that sense of the sudden earthquake shock to the foundations of morality which sends a pallid crowd of critics into the street shrieking that the pillars of society are cracking and the ruin of the State at hand. Even the Ibsen champions of ten years ago remonstrate with me just as the veterans of those brave days remonstrated with them. Mr Grein, the hardy iconoclast who first launched my plays on the stage alongside Ghosts and The Wild Duck, exclaims that I have shattered his ideals. Actually his ideals! What would Dr Relling say? And Mr William Archer himself disowns me because I 'cannot touch pitch without wallowing in it.' Truly my play must be more needed than I knew; and yet I thought I knew how little the others know.

Do not suppose, however, that the consternation of the Press reflects any consternation among the general public. Anybody can upset the theatre critics, in a turn of the wrist, by substituting for the romantic commonplaces of the stage the moral commonplaces of the pulpit, the platform, or the library. Play Mrs Warren's Profession to an audience of clerical members of the Christian Social Union and of women well experienced in Rescue, Temperance, and Girls' Club work, and no moral panic will arise: every man and woman present will know that as long as poverty makes virtue hideous and the spare pocket-money of rich bachelordom makes vice dazzling, their daily hand-to-hand fight against prostitution with prayer and persuasion, shelters and scanty alms, will be a losing one. There was a time when they were able to urge that though 'the white-lead factory where Anne Jane was poisoned' may be a far more terrible place than Mrs Warren's house, yet hell is still more dreadful. Nowadays they no longer believe in hell; and the girls among whom they are working know that they do not believe in it, and would laugh at them if they did. So well have the rescuers learnt that Mrs Warren's defence of herself and indictment of society is the thing that most needs saying, that those who know me personally reproach me, not for writing this play, but for wasting my energies on 'pleasant plays' for the amusement of frivolous people, when I can build up such excellent stage sermons on their own work. Mrs Warren's Profession is the one play of mine which I could submit to a censorship without doubt of the result; only, it must not be the censorship of the minor theatre critic, nor of an innocent court official like the Lord Chamberlain's Examiner, much less of people who consciously profit by Mrs Warren's profession, or who personally make use of it, or who hold the widely whispered view that it is an indispensable safety-valve for the protection of domestic virtue, or, above all, who are smitten with a sentimental affection for our fallen sister, and would 'take her up tenderly, lift her with care, fashioned so slenderly, young, and *so* fair.' Nor am I prepared to accept the verdict of the medical gentlemen who would compulsorily examine and register Mrs Warren, whilst leaving Mrs Warren's patrons, especially her military patrons, free to destroy her health and anybody else's without fear of reprisals. But I should be quite content to have my play judged by, say, a joint committee of the Central Vigilance Society and the Salvation Army. And the sterner moralists the members of the committee were, the better.

Some of the journalists I have shocked reason so unripely that they will gather nothing from this but a confused notion that I am accusing the National Vigilance Association and the Salvation Army of complicity in my own scandalous immorality. It will seem to them that people who would stand this play would stand anything. They are quite mistaken. Such an audience as I have described would be revolted by many of our fashionable plays. They would leave the theatre convinced that the Plymouth Brother who still regards the playhouse as one of the gates of hell is perhaps the safest adviser on the subject of which he knows so little. If I do not draw the same conclusion, it is not because I am one of those who claim that art is exempt from moral obligations, and deny that the writing or performance of a play is a moral act, to be treated on exactly the same footing as theft or murder if it produces equally mischievous consequences. I am convinced that fine art is the subtlest, the most seductive, the most effective instrument of moral propaganda in the world, excepting only the example of personal conduct; and I waive even this exception in favour of the art of the stage, because it works by exhibiting examples of personal conduct made intelligible and moving to crowds of unobservant unreflecting people to whom real life means nothing. I have pointed out again and again that the influence of the theatre in England is growing so great that private conduct, religion, law, science, politics, and morals are becoming more and more theatrical, whilst the theatre itself remains impervious to common sense, religion, science, politics, and morals. That is why I fight the theatre, not with pamphlets and sermons and treatises, but with plays; and so effective do I find the dramatic method that I have no doubt I shall at last persuade even London to take its conscience and its brains with it when it goes to the theatre, instead of leaving them at home with its prayer-book as it does at present. Consequently, I am the last man to deny that if the net effect of performing Mrs Warren's Profession were an increase in the number of persons entering that profession or employing it, its performance might well be made an indictable offence.

Now let us consider how such recruiting can be encouraged by the theatre. Nothing is easier. Let the Lord Chamberlain's Examiner of Plays, backed by the Press, make an unwritten but perfectly well understood regulation that members of Mrs Warren's profession shall be tolerated on the stage only when they are beautiful, exquisitely dressed, and sumptuously lodged and fed; also that they shall, at the end of the play, die of consumption to the sympathetic tears of the whole audience, or step into the next room to commit suicide, or at least be turned out by their protectors, and passed on to be 'redeemed' by old and faithful lovers who have adored them in spite of all their levities. Naturally, the poorer girls in the gallery will believe in the beauty, in the exquisite dresses, and the luxurious living, and will see that there is no real necessity for the consumption, the suicide, or the ejectment: mere pious forms, all of them, to save the Censor's face. Even if these purely official catastrophes carried any conviction, the majority of English girls remain so poor, so dependent, so well aware that the drudgeries of such honest work as is within their reach are likely enough to lead them eventually to lung disease, premature death, and domestic desertion or brutality, that they would still see reason to prefer the primrose path to the stony way of virtue, since both, vice at worst and virtue at best, lead to the same end in poverty and overwork. It is true, that the Elementary School mistress will tell you that only girls of a certain kind will reason in this way. But alas! that certain kind turns out on inquiry to be simply the pretty, dainty kind: that is, the only kind that gets the chance of acting on such reasoning. Read the first report of the Commission on the Housing of the Working Classes (Bluebook C 4402, 1889); read the Report on Home Industries (sacred word, Home!) issued by the Women's Industrial Council (Home Industries of Women in London, 1897, 1s); and ask yourself whether, if the lot in life therein described were your lot in life, you would not rather be a jewelled Vamp. If you can go deep enough into things to be able to say no, how many ignorant half-starved girls will believe you are speaking sincerely? To them the lot of the stage courtesan is heavenly in comparison with their own. Yet the Lord Chamberlain's Examiner, being an officer of the Royal Household, places the King in the position of saying to the dramatist 'Thus, and thus only, shall you present Mrs Warren's profession on the stage, or you shall starve. Witness Shaw, who told the untempting truth about it, and whom We, by the Grace of God, accordingly disallow and suppress, and do what in Us lies to silence.' Fortunately, Shaw cannot be silenced. 'The harlot's cry from street to street' is louder than the voices of all the kings. I am not dependent on the theatre, and cannot be starved into making my play a standing advertisement of the attractive side of Mrs Warren's business.

Here I must guard myself against a misunderstanding. It is not the fault of their authors that the long string of wanton's tragedies, from Antony and Cleopatra to Iris, are snares to poor girls, and are objected to on that account by many earnest men and women who consider Mrs Warren's Profession an excellent sermon. Pinero is in no way bound to suppress the fact that his Iris is a person to be envied by millions of better women. If he made his play false to life by inventing fictitious disadvantages for her, he would be acting as unscrupulously as any tract-writer. If society chooses to provide for its Irises better than for its working women, it must not expect honest playwrights to manufacture spurious evidence to save its credit. The mischief lies in the deliberate suppression of the other side of the case: the refusal to allow Mrs Warren to expose the drudgery and repulsiveness of plying for hire among coarse tedious drunkards. All that, says the Examiner in effect, is horrifying, loathsome. Precisely: what does he expect it to be? would he have us represent it as beautiful and gratifying? His answer to this question amounts, I fear, to a blunt Yes; for it seems impossible to root out of an Englishman's mind the notion that vice is delightful, and that abstention from it is privation. At all events, as long as the tempting side of it is kept towards the public, and softened by plenty of sentiment and sympathy, it is welcomed by our Censor, whereas the slightest attempt to place it in the light of the policeman's lantern or the Salvation Army shelter is checkmated at once as not merely disgusting, but, if you please, unnecessary.

Everybody will, I hope, admit that this state of things is intolerable; that the subject of Mrs Warren's profession must be either tapu altogether, or else exhibited with the warning side as freely displayed as the tempting side. But many persons will vote for a complete tapu, and an impartial clean sweep from the boards of Mrs Warren and Gretchen and the rest: in short, for banishing the sexual instincts from the stage altogether. Those who think this impossible can hardly have considered the number and importance of the subjects which are actually banished from the stage. Many plays, among them Lear, Hamlet, Macbeth, Coriolanus, Julius Ceasar, have no sex complications: the thread of their action can be followed by children who could not understand a single scene of Mrs Warren's Profession or Iris. None of our plays rouse the sympathy of the audience by an exhibition of the pains of maternity, as Chinese plays constantly do. Each nation has its particular set of tapus in addition to the common human stock; and though each of these tapus limits the scope of the dramatist, it does not make drama impossible. If the Examiner were to refuse to license plays with female characters in them, he would only be doing to the stage what our tribal customs already do to the pulpit and the bar. I have myself written a rather entertaining play with only one woman in it, and she quite heartwhole; and I could just as easily write a play without a woman in it at all. I will even go as far as to promise the Examiner my support if he will introduce this limitation for part of the year, say during Lent, so as to make a close season for that dullest of stock dramatic subjects, adultery, and force our managers and authors to find out what all great dramatists find out spontaneously: to wit, that people who sacrifice every other consideration to love are as hopelessly unheroic on the stage as lunatics or dipsomaniacs. Hector and Hamlet are the world's heroes; not Paris and Antony.

But though I do not question the possibility of a drama in which love should be as effectively ignored as cholera is at present, there is not the slightest chance of that way out of the difficulty being taken by the Examiner. If he attempted it there would be a revolt in which he would be swept away, in spite of my singlehanded efforts to defend him. A complete tapu is politically impossible. A complete toleration is equally impossible to the Examiner, because his occupation would be gone if there were no tapu to enforce. He is therefor compelled to maintain the present compromise of a partial tapu, applied, to the best of his judgment, with a careful respect to persons and to public opinion. And a very sensible English solution of the difficulty, too, most readers will say. I should not dispute it if dramatic poets really were what English public opinion generally assumes them to be during their lifetime: that is, a licentiously irregular group to be kept in order in a rough and ready way by a magistrate who will stand no nonsense from them. But I cannot admit that the class represented by Eschylus, Sophocles, Aristophanes, Euripides, Shakespear, Goethe, Ibsen, and Tolstoy, not to mention our own contemporary playwrights, is as much in place in the Examiner's office as a pickpocket is in Bow Street. Further, it is not true that the Censorship, though it certainly suppresses Ibsen and Tolstoy, and would suppress Shakespear but for the absurd rule that a play once licensed is always licensed (so that Wycherly is permitted and Shelley prohibited), also suppresses unscrupulous playwrights. I challenge the Examiner to mention any extremity of sexual misconduct which any manager in his senses would risk presenting on the London stage that has not been presented under his license and that of his predecessor. The compromise, in fact, works out in practice in favor of loose plays as against earnest ones.

To carry conviction on this point, I will take the extreme course of narrating the plots of two plays witnessed within the last ten years by myself at London West End theatres, one licensed under Queen Victoria, the other under her successor. Both plots conform to the strictest rules of the period when La Dame aux Camellias was still a forbidden play, and when The Second Mrs Tanqueray would have been tolerated only on condition that she carefully explained to the audience that when she met Captain Ardale she sinned 'but in intention.'

Play number one. A prince is compelled by his parents to marry the daughter of a neighboring king, but loves another maiden. The scene represents a hall in the king's palace at night. The wedding has taken place that day; and the closed door of the nuptial chamber is in view of the audience. Inside, the princess awaits her bridegroom. A duenna is in attendance. The bridegroom enters. His sole desire is to escape from a marriage which is hateful to him. A means occurs to him. He will assault the duenna, and be ignominiously expelled from the palace by his indignant father-in-law. To his horror, when he proceeds to carry out this stratagem, the duenna, far from raising an alarm is flattered, delighted, and compliant. The assaulter becomes the assaulted. He flings her angrily to the ground, where she remains placidly. He flies. The father enters; dismisses the duenna; and listens at the keyhole of his daughter's nuptial chamber, uttering various pleasantries, and declaring, with a shiver, that a sound of kissing, which he supposes to proceed from within, makes him feel young again.

Story number two. A German officer finds himself in an inn with a French lady who has wounded his national vanity.

He resolves to humble her by committing a rape upon her.
He announces his purpose. She remonstrates, implores, flies
to the doors and finds them locked, calls for help and finds
none at hand, runs screaming from side to side, and, after a
harrowing scene, is overpowered and faints. Nothing further
being possible on the stage without actual felony, the officer
then relents and leaves her. When she recovers, she believes
that he has carried out his threat; and during the rest of the
play she is represented as vainly vowing vengeance upon
him, whilst she is really falling in love with him under the
influence of his imaginary crime against her. Finally she
consents to marry him; and the curtain falls on their
happiness.

This story was certified by the Examiner, acting for the
Lord Chamberlain, as void in its general tendency of 'anything immoral or otherwise improper for the stage.' But let
nobody conclude therefore that the Examiner is a monster,
whose policy it is to deprave the theatre. As a matter of fact,
both the above stories are strictly in order from the official
point of view. The incidents of sex which they contain,
though carried in both to the extreme point at which another
step would be dealt with, not by the Examiner, but by the
police, do not involve adultery, nor any allusion to Mrs
Warren's profession, nor to the fact that the children of any
polyandrous group will, when they grow up, inevitably be
confronted, as those of Mrs Warren's group are in my play,
with the insoluble problem of their own possible con-
sanguinity. In short, by depending wholly on the coarse
humors and the physical fascination of sex, they comply
with all the formulable requirements of the Censorship,
whereas plays in which these humors and fascinations are
discarded, and the social problems created by sex seriously
faced and dealt with, inevitably ignore the official formula
and are suppressed. If the old rule against the exhibition of
illicit sex relations on the stage were revived, and the subject
absolutely barred, the only result would be that Antony and

Cleopatra, Othello (because of the Bianca episode), Troilus and Cressida, Henry IV, Measure for Measure, Timon of Athens, La Dame aux Camellias, The Profligate, The Second Mrs Tanqueray, The Notorious Mrs Ebbsmith, The Gay Lord Quex, Mrs Dane's Defence, and Iris would be swept from the stage, and placed under the same ban as Tolstoy's Dominion of Darkness and Mrs Warren's Profession, whilst such plays as the two described above would have a monopoly of the theatre as far as sexual interest is concerned.

What is more, the repulsiveness of the worst of the certified plays would protect Censorship against effective exposure and criticism. Not long ago an American Review of high standing asked me for an article on the Censorship of the English Stage. I replied that such an article would involve passages too disagreeable for publication in a magazine for general family reading. The editor persisted nevertheless; but not until he had declared his readiness to face this, and had pledged himself to insert the article unaltered (the particularity of the pledge extending even to a specification of the exact number of words in the article) did I consent to the proposal. What was the result? The editor, confronted with the two stories given above, threw his pledge to the winds, and, instead of returning the article, printed it with the illustrative examples omitted, and nothing left but the argument from political principle against the Censorship. In doing this he fired my broadside after withdrawing the cannon balls; for neither the Censor nor any other Englishman, except perhaps a few veterans of the dwindling old guard of Benthamism, cares a dump about political principle. The ordinary Briton thinks that if every other Briton is not under some form of tutelage, the more childish the better, he will abuse his freedom viciously. As far as its principle is concerned, the Censorship is the most popular institution in England; and the playwright who criticizes it is slighted as a blackguard agitating for impunity. Consequently nothing can really shake the confidence of the public in the Lord

Chamberlain's department except a remorseless and un-bowdlerized narration of the licentious fictions which slip through its net, and are hallmarked by it with the approval of the royal household. But as such stories cannot be made public without great difficulty, owing to the obligation an editor is under not to deal unexpectedly with matters that are not *virginibus puerisque*, the chances are heavily in favor of the Censor escaping all remonstrance. With the exception of such comments as I was able to make in my own critical articles in The World and The Saturday Review when the pieces I have described were first produced, and a few ignorant protests by churchmen against much better plays which they confessed they had not seen nor read, nothing has been said in the press that could seriously disturb the easygoing notion that the stage would be much worse than it admittedly is but for the vigilance of the Examiner. The truth is, that no manager would dare produce on his own responsi-bility the pieces he can now get royal certificates for at two guineas per piece.

I hasten to add that I believe these evils to be inherent in the nature of all censorship, and not merely a consequence of the form the institution takes in London. No doubt there is a staggering absurdity in appointing an ordinary clerk to see that the leaders of European literature do not corrupt the morals of the nation, and to restrain Sir Henry Irving from presuming to impersonate Samson or David on the stage, though any other sort of artist may daub these scriptural figures on a signboard or carve them on a tombstone without hindrance. If the General Medical Council, the Royal Col-lege of Physicians, the Royal Academy of Arts, the Incor-porated Law Society, and Convocation were abolished, and their functions handed over to the Examiner, the Concert of Europe would presumably certify England as mad. Yet, though neither medicine nor painting nor law nor the Church moulds the character of the nation as potently as the theatre does, nothing can come on the stage unless its dimensions

admit of its first passing through the Examiner's mind! Pray
do not think that I question his honesty. I am quite sure
that he sincerely thinks me a blackguard, and my play a
grossly improper one, because, like Tolstoy's Dominion of
Darkness, it produces, as they are both meant to produce, a
very strong and very painful impression of evil. I do not
doubt for a moment that the rapine play which I have described, and which he licensed, was quite incapable in
manuscript of producing any particular effect on his mind
at all, and that when he was once satisfied that the ill-
conducted hero was a German and not an English officer, he
passed the play without studying its moral tendencies. Even
if he had undertaken that study, there is no more reason to
suppose that he is a competent moralist than there is to suppose that I am a competent mathematician. But truly it does
not matter whether he is a moralist or not. Let nobody
dream for a moment that what is wrong with the Censorship
is the shortcoming of the gentleman who happens at any
moment to be acting as Censor. Replace him tomorrow by
an Academy of Letters and an Academy of Dramatic Poetry,
and the new filter will still exclude original and epoch-
making work, whilst passing conventional, old-fashioned, and
vulgar work. The conclave which compiles the expurgatory
index of the Roman Catholic Church is the most august,
ancient, learned, famous, and authoritative censorship in
Europe. Is it more enlightened, more liberal, more tolerant
than the comparatively unqualified office of the Lord
Chamberlain? On the contrary, it has reduced itself to a
degree of absurdity which makes a Catholic university a con-
tradiction in terms. All censorships exist to prevent anyone
from challenging current conceptions and existing institutions. All progress is initiated by challenging current conceptions, and executed by supplanting existing institutions.
Consequently the first condition of progress is the removal of
censorships. There is the whole case against censorships in a
nutshell.

It will be asked whether theatrical managers are to be allowed to produce what they like, without regard to the public interest. But that is not the alternative. The managers of our London music-halls are not subject to any censorship. They produce their entertainments on their own responsibility, and have no two-guinea certificates to plead if their houses are conducted viciously. They know that if they lose their character, the County Council will simply refuse to renew their license at the end of the year; and nothing in the history of popular art is more amazing than the improvement in music-halls that this simple arrangement has produced within a few years. Place the theatres on the same footing, and we shall promptly have a similar revolution: a whole class of frankly blackguardly plays, in which unscrupulous low comedians attract crowds to gaze at bevies of girls who have nothing to exhibit but their prettiness, will vanish like the obscene songs which were supposed to enliven the squalid dulness, incredible to the younger generation, of the music-halls fifteen years ago. On the other hand, plays which treat sex questions as problems for thought instead of as aphrodisiacs will be freely performed. Gentlemen of the Examiner's way of thinking will have plenty of opportunity of protesting against them in Council; but the result will be that the Examiner will find his natural level; Ibsen and Tolstoy theirs; so no harm will be done.

This question of the Censorship reminds me that I have to apologize to those who went to the recent performance of Mrs Warren's Profession expecting to find it what I have just called an aphrodisiac. That was not my fault: it was the Examiner's. After the specimens I have given of the tolerance of his department, it was natural enough for thoughtless people to infer that a play which overstepped his indulgence must be a very exciting play indeed. Accordingly, I find one critic so explicit as to the nature of his disappointment as to say candidly that 'such airy talk as there is upon the matter is utterly unworthy of acceptance as being a representation of what people with blood in them think or do on such occasions.' Thus am I crushed between the upper millstone of the Examiner, who thinks me a libertine, and the nether popular critic, who thinks me a prude. Critics of all grades and ages, middle-aged fathers of families no less than ardent young enthusiasts, are equally indignant with me. They revile me as lacking in passion, in feeling, in manhood. Some of them even sum the matter up by denying me any dramatic power: a melancholy betrayal of what dramatic power has come to mean on our stage under the Censorship! Can I be expected to refrain from laughing at the spectacle of a number of respectable gentlemen lamenting because a playwright lures them to the theatre by a promise to excite their senses in a very special and sensational manner, and then, having successfully trapped them in exceptional numbers, proceeds to ignore their senses and ruthlessly improve their minds? But I protest again that the lure was not mine. The play had been in print for four years; and I have spared no pains to make known that my plays are built to induce, not voluptuous reverie but intellectual interest, not romantic rhapsody but humane concern. Accordingly, I do not find those critics who are gifted with intellectual appetite and political conscience complaining of want of dramatic power. Rather do they protest, not altogether unjustly, against a few relapses into staginess and caricature which betray the young playwright and the old playgoer in this early work of mine. As to the voluptuaries, I can assure them that the playwright, whether he be myself or another, will always disappoint them. The drama can do little to delight the senses: all the apparent instances to the contrary are instances of the personal fascination of the performers. The drama of pure feeling is no longer in the hands of the playwright: it has been conquered by the musician, after whose enchantments all the verbal arts seem cold and tame. Romeo and Juliet with the loveliest Juliet is dry, tedious, and rhetorical in comparison with Wagner's Tristan, even though Isolde be both fourteen stone and forty, as she often is in Germany. Indeed, it needed no Wagner to convince the public of this. The voluptuous sentimentality of Gounod's Faust and Bizet's Carmen has captured the common playgoer; and there is, flatly, no future now for any drama without music except the drama of thought. The attempt to produce a genus of opera without music (and this absurdity is what our fashionable theatres have been driving at for a long time past without knowing it) is far less hopeful than my own determination to accept problem as the normal material of the drama.

That this determination will throw me into a long conflict with our theatre critics, and with the few playgoers who go to the theatre as often as the critics, I well know; but I am too well equipped for the strife to be deterred by it, or to bear malice towards the losing side. In trying to produce the sensuous effects of opera, the fashionable drama has become so flaccid in its sentimentality, and the intellect of its frequenters so atrophied by disuse, that the reintroduction of problem, with its remorseless logic and iron framework of fact, inevitably produces at first an overwhelming impression of coldness and inhuman rationalism. But this will soon pass away. When the intellectual muscle and moral nerve of the critics has been developed in the struggle with modern problem plays, the pettish luxuriousness of the clever ones, and the sulky sense of disadvantaged weakness in the sentimental ones, will clear away; and it will be seen that only in the problem play is there any real drama, because drama is no mere setting up of the camera to nature: it is the presentation in parable of the conflict between Man's will and his environment: in a word, of problem. The vapidness of such drama as the pseudo-operatic plays contain lies in the fact that in them animal passion, sentimentally diluted, is shewn in conflict, not with real circumstances, but with a set of conventions and assumptions half of which do not exist off the stage, whilst the other half can either be evaded by a pretence of compliance or defied with complete impunity by any reasonably strong-minded person. Nobody can feel that such conventions are really compulsory; and consequently nobody can believe in the stage pathos that accepts them as an inexorable fate, or in the reality of the figures who indulge in such pathos. Sitting at such plays we do not believe: we make-believe. And the habit of make-believe becomes at last so rooted, that criticism of the theatre insensibly ceases to be criticism at all, and becomes more and more a chronicle of the fashionable enterprises of the only realities left on the stage: that is, the performers in their own persons. In this phase the playwright who attempts to revive genuine drama produces the disagreeable impression of the pedant who attempts to start a serious discussion at a fashionable at-home. Later on, when he has driven the tea services out and made the people who had come to use the theatre as a drawing-room understand that it is they and not the dramatists who are the intruders, he has to face the accusation that his plays ignore human feeling, an illusion produced by that very resistance of fact and law to human feeling which creates drama. It is the *deus ex machina* who, by suspending that resistance, makes the fall of the curtain an immediate necessity, since drama ends exactly where resistance ends. Yet the introduction of this resistance produces so strong an impression of heartlessness nowadays that a distinguished critic has summed up the impression made on him by Mrs Warren's Profession, by declaring that 'the difference between the spirit of Tolstoy and the spirit of Mr Shaw is the difference between the spirit of Christ and the spirit of Euclid.' But the epigram would be as good if Tolstoy's name were put in place of mine and D'Annunzio's in place of Tolstoy's. At the same time I accept the enormous compliment to my reasoning powers with sincere complacency; and I promise my flatterer that when he is sufficiently accustomed to and therefore undazzled by problem on the stage to be able to attend to the familiar factor of humanity in it as well as to the

unfamiliar one of a real environment, he will both see and feel
that Mrs Warren's Profession is no mere theorem, but a play
of instincts and temperaments in conflict with each other and
with a flinty social problem that never yields an inch to mere
sentiment.

I go further than this. I declare that the real secret of the
cynicism and inhumanity of which shallower critics accuse
me is the unexpectedness with which my characters behave
like human beings, instead of conforming to the romantic
logic of the stage. The axioms and postulates of that dreary
mimanthropometry are so well known that it is almost impossible for its slaves to write tolerable last acts to their
plays, so conventionally do their conclusions follow from
their premises. Because I have thrown this logic ruthlessly
overboard, I am accused of ignoring, not stage logic, but, of
all things, human feeling. People with completely theatrified
imaginations tell me that no girl would treat her mother as
Vivie Warren does, meaning that no stage heroine would
in a popular sentimental play. They say this just as they
might say that no two straight lines would enclose a space.
They do not see how completely inverted their vision has
become even when I throw its preposterousness in their
faces, as I repeatedly do in this very play. Praed, the sentimental artist (fool that I was not to make him a theatre critic
instead of an architect!), burlesques them by expecting all
through the piece that the feelings of the others will be
logically deducible from their family relationships and from
his 'conventionally unconventional' social code. The sar-
casm is lost on the critics: they, saturated with the same
logic, only think him the sole sensible person on the stage.
Thus it comes about that the more completely the dramatist
is emancipated from the illusion that men and women are
primarily reasonable beings, and the more powerfully he
insists on the ruthless indifference of their great dramatic
antagonist, the external world, to their whims and emotions,
the surer he is to be denounced as blind to the very distinc-

tion on which his whole work is built. Far from ignoring idiosyncrasy, will, passion, impulse, whim, as factors in human action, I have placed them so nakedly on the stage that the elderly citizen, accustomed to see them clothed with the veil of manufactured logic about duty, and to disguise even his own impulses from himself in this way, finds the picture as unnatural as Carlyle's suggested painting of parliament sitting without its clothes.

I now come to those critics who, intellectually baffled by the problem in Mrs Warren's Profession, have made a virtue of running away from it on the gentlemanly ground that the theatre is frequented by women as well as by men, and that such problems should not be discussed or even mentioned in the presence of women. With that sort of chivalry I cannot argue: I simply affirm that Mrs Warren's Profession is a play for women; that it was written for women; that it has been performed and produced mainly through the determination of women that it should be performed and produced; that the enthusiasm of women made its first performance excitingly successful; and that not one of these women had any inducement to support it except their belief in the timeliness and the power of the lesson the play teaches. Those who were 'surprised to see ladies present' were men; and when they proceeded to explain that the journals they represented could not possibly demoralize the public by describing such a play, their editors cruelly devoted the space saved by their delicacy to reporting at unusual length an exceptionally abominable police case.

My old Independent Theatre manager, Mr Grein, besides that reproach to me for shattering his ideals, complains that Mrs Warren is not wicked enough, and names several romancers who would have clothed her black soul with all the terrors of tragedy. I have no doubt they would; but that is just what I did not want to do. Nothing would please our sanctimonious British public more than to throw the whole guilt of Mrs Warren's profession on Mrs Warren herself.

Now the whole aim of my play is to throw that guilt on the British public itself. Mr Grein may remember that when he produced my first play, Widowers' Houses, exactly the same misunderstanding arose. When the virtuous young gentleman rose up in wrath against the slum landlord, the slum landlord very effectually shewed him that slums are the product, not of individual Harpagons, but of the indifference of virtuous young gentlemen to the condition of the city they live in, provided they live at the west end of it on money earned by somebody else's labor. The notion that prostitution is created by the wickedness of Mrs Warren is as silly as the notion – prevalent, nevertheless, to some extent in Temperance circles – that drunkenness is created by the wickedness of the publican. Mrs Warren is not a whit a worse woman than the reputable daughter who cannot endure her. Her indifference to the ultimate social consequence of her means of making money, and her discovery of that means by the ordinary method of taking the line of least resistance to getting it, are too common in English society to call for any special remark. Her vitality, her thrift, her energy, her outspokenness, her wise care of her daughter, and the managing capacity which has enabled her and her sister to climb from the fried fish shop down by the Mint to the establishments of which she boasts, are all high English social virtues. Her defence of herself is so overwhelming that it provokes the St James's Gazette to declare that 'the tendency of the play is wholly evil' because 'it contains one of the boldest and most specious defences of an immoral life for poor women that has ever been penned.' Happily the St James's Gazette here speaks in its haste. Mrs Warren's defence of herself is not only bold and specious, but valid and unanswerable. But it is no defence at all of the vice which she organizes. It is no defence of an immoral life to say that the alternative offered by society collectively to poor women is a miserable life, starved, overworked, fetid, ailing, ugly. Though it is quite natural and *right* for Mrs Warren to choose what is, according to her lights, the least immoral alternative, it is none the less infamous of society to offer such alternatives. For the alternatives offered are not morality and immorality, but two sorts of immorality. The man who cannot see that starvation, overwork, dirt, and disease are as anti-social as prostitution – that they are the vices and crimes of a nation, and not merely its misfortunes – is (to put it as politely as possible) a hopelessly Private Person.

The notion that Mrs Warren must be a fiend is only an example of the violence and passion which the slightest reference to sex rouses in undisciplined minds, and which makes it seem natural to our lawgivers to punish silly and negligible indecencies with a ferocity unknown in dealing with, for example, ruinous financial swindling. Had my play been entitled Mr Warren's Profession, and Mr Warren been a bookmaker, nobody would have expected me to make him a villain as well. Yet gambling is a vice, and bookmaking an institution, for which there is absolutely nothing to be said. The moral and economic evil done by trying to get other people's money without working for it (and this is the essence of gambling) is not only enormous but uncompensated. There are no two sides to the question of gambling, no circumstances which force us to tolerate it lest its suppression lead to worse things, no consensus of opinion among responsible classes, such as magistrates and military commanders, that it is a necessity, no Athenian records of gambling made splendid by the talents of its professors, no contention that instead of violating morals it only violates a legal institution which is in many respects oppressive and unnatural, no possible plea that the instinct on which it is founded is a vital one. Prostitution can confuse the issue with all these excuses: gambling has none of them. Consequently, if Mrs Warren must needs be a demon, a bookmaker must be a cacodemon. Well, does anybody who knows the sporting world really believe that bookmakers are worse than their neighbors? On the contrary, they have to be a good deal better; for in that world nearly everybody whose social rank does not exclude such an occupation would be a bookmaker if he could; but the strength of character required for handling large sums of money and for strict settlements and unflinching payment of losses is so rare that successful bookmakers are rare too. It may seem that at least public spirit cannot be one of a bookmaker's virtues; but I can testify from personal experience that excellent public work is done with money subscribed by bookmakers. It is true that there are abysses in bookmaking: for example, welshing. Mr Grein hints that there are abysses in Mrs Warren's profession also. So there are in every profession: the error lies in supposing that every member of them sounds these depths. I sit on a public body which prosecutes Mrs Warren zealously; and I can assure Mr Grein that she is often leniently dealt with because she has conducted her business 'respectably' and held herself above its vilest branches. The degrees in infamy are as numerous and as scrupulously observed as the degrees in the peerage: the moralist's notion that there are depths at which the moral atmosphere ceases is as delusive as the rich man's notion that there are no social jealousies or snobberies among the very poor. No: had I drawn Mrs Warren as a fiend in human form, the very people who now rebuke me for flattering her would probably be the first to deride me for deducing character logically from occupation instead of observing it accurately in society.

One critic is so enslaved by this sort of logic that he calls my portraiture of the Reverend Samuel Gardner an attack on religion. According to this view Subaltern Iago is an attack on the army, Sir John Falstaff an attack on knighthood, and King Claudius an attack on royalty. Here again the clamor for naturalness and human feeling, raised by so many critics when they are confronted by the real thing on the stage, is really a clamor for the most mechanical and superficial sort of logic. The dramatic reason for making the clergyman what Mrs Warren calls 'an old stick-in-the-mud', whose son, in spite of much capacity and charm, is a cynically worthless member of society, is to set up a mordant contrast between him and the woman of infamous profession, with her well brought-up, straightforward, hardworking daughter. The critics who have missed the contrast have doubtless observed often enough that many clergymen are in the Church through no genuine calling, but simply because, in circles which can command preferment, it is the refuge of the fool of the family; and that clergymen's sons are often conspicuous reactionists against the restraints imposed on them in childhood by their father's profession. These critics must know, too, from history if not from experience, that women as unscrupulous as Mrs Warren have distinguished themselves as administrators and rulers, both commercially and politically. But both observation and knowledge are left behind when journalists go to the theatre. Once in their stalls, they assume that it is 'natural' for clergymen to be saintly, for soldiers to be heroic, for lawyers to be hard-hearted, for sailors to be simple and generous, for doctors to perform miracles with little bottles, and for Mrs Warren to be a beast and a demon. All this is not only not natural, but not dramatic. A man's profession only enters into the drama of his life when it comes into conflict with his nature. The result of this conflict is tragic in Mrs Warren's case, and comic in the clergyman's case (at least we are savage enough to laugh at it); but in both cases it is illogical, and in both cases natural. I repeat, the critics who accuse me of sacrificing nature to logic are so sophisticated by their profession that to them logic is nature, and nature absurdity.

Many friendly critics are too little skilled in social questions and moral discussions to be able to conceive that respectable gentlemen like themselves, who would instantly call the police to remove Mrs Warren if she ventured to canvass them personally, could possibly be in any way responsible for her proceedings. They remonstrate sincerely, asking me what good such painful exposures can possibly do.

They might as well ask what good Lord Shaftesbury did by devoting his life to the exposure of evils (by no means yet remedied) compared to which the worst things brought into view or even into surmise in this play are trifles. The good of mentioning them is that you make people so extremely uncomfortable about them that they finally stop blaming 'human nature' for them, and begin to support measures for their reform. Can anything be more absurd than the copy of The Echo which contains a notice of the performance of my play? It is edited by a gentleman who, having devoted his life to work of the Shaftesbury type, exposes social evils and clamors for their reform in every column except one; and that one is occupied by the declaration of the paper's kindly theatre critic, that the performance left him 'wondering what useful purpose the play was intended to serve.' The balance has to be redressed by the more fashionable papers, which usually combine capable art criticism with West-End solecism on politics and sociology. It is very noteworthy, however, on comparing the press explosion produced by Mrs Warren's Profession in 1902 with that produced by Widowers' Houses about ten years earlier, that whereas in 1892 the facts were frantically denied and the persons of the drama flouted as monsters of wickedness, in 1902 the facts are admitted, and the characters recognized, though it is suggested that this is exactly why no gentleman should mention them in public. Only one writer has ventured to imply this time that the poverty mentioned by Mrs Warren has since been quietly relieved, and need not have been dragged back to the footlights. I compliment him on his splendid mendacity, in which he is unsupported, save by a little plea in a theatrical paper which is innocent enough to think that ten guineas a year with board and lodging is an impossibly low wage for a barmaid. It goes on to cite Mr Charles Booth as having testified that there are many laborers' wives who are happy and contented on eighteen shillings a week. But I can go further than that myself. I have seen an Oxford agricultural laborer's wife looking cheerful on eight shillings a week; but that does not console me for the fact that agriculture in England is a ruined industry. If poverty does not matter as long as it is contented, then crime does not matter as long as it is unscrupulous. The truth is that it is only then that it does matter most desperately. Many persons are more comfortable when they are dirty than when they are clean; but that does not recommend dirt as a national policy.

In 1905 Arnold Daly produced Mrs Warren's Profession in New York. The press of that city instantly raised a cry that such persons as Mrs Warren are 'ordure' and should not be mentioned in the presence of decent people. This hideous repudiation of humanity and social conscience so took possession of the New York journalists that the few among them who kept their feet morally and intellectually could do nothing to check the epidemic of foul language, gross suggestion, and raving obscenity of word and thought that broke out. The writers abandoned all self-restraint under the impression that they were upholding virtue instead of outraging it. They infected each other with their hysteria until they were for all practical purposes indecently mad. They finally forced the police to arrest Daly and his company and led the magistrate to express his loathing of the duty thus forced upon him of reading an unmentionable and abominable play. Of course the convulsion soon exhausted itself. The magistrate, naturally somewhat impatient when he found that what he had to read was a strenuously ethical play forming part of a book which had been in circulation unchallenged for eight years, and had been received without protest by the whole London and New York Press, gave the journalists a piece of his mind as to their moral taste in plays. By consent, he passed the case on to a higher court, which declared that the play was not immoral; acquitted Daly; and made an end of the attempt to use the law to declare living women to be 'ordure,' and thus enforce silence as to the far-reaching fact that you cannot cheapen women in the market for industrial purposes without cheapening them for other purposes as well. I hope Mrs Warren's Profession will be played everywhere, in season and out of season, until Mrs Warren has bitten that fact into the public conscience, and shamed the newspapers which support a tariff to keep up the price of every American commodity except American manhood and womanhood.

Unfortunately, Daly had already suffered the usual fate of those who direct public attention to the profits of the sweater or the pleasures of the voluptuary. He was morally lynched side by side with me. Months elapsed before the decision of the courts vindicated him; and even then, since his vindication implied the condemnation of the Press, which was by that time sober again, and ashamed of its orgy, his triumph received a rather sulky and grudging publicity. In the meantime he had hardly been able to approach an American city, including even those cities which had heaped applause on him as the defender of hearth and home when he produced Candida, without having to face articles discussing whether mothers could allow their daughters to attend such plays as You Never Can Tell, written by the infamous author of Mrs Warren's Profession, and acted by the monster who produced it. What made this harder to bear was that though no fact is better established in theatrical business than the financial disastrousness of moral discredit, the journalists who had done all the mischief kept paying vice the homage of assuming that it is enormously popular and lucrative, and that Daly and I, being exploiters of vice, must therefore be making colossal fortunes out of the abuse heaped on us, and had in fact provoked it and welcomed it with that express object. Ignorance of real life could hardly go further.

I was deeply disgusted by this unsavory mobbing. And I have certain sensitive places in my soul: I do not like that word 'ordure'. Apply it to my work, and I can afford to smile, since the world, on the whole, will smile with me. But to apply it to the woman in the street, whose spirit is of one substance with your own and her body no less holy: to look your women folk in the face afterwards and not go out and hang yourself: that is not on the list of pardonable sins.

Shortly after these events a leading New York newspaper, which was among the most abusively clamorous for the suppression of Mrs Warren's Profession, was fined heavily for deriving part of its revenue from advertisements of Mrs Warren's houses.

Many people have been puzzled by the fact that whilst stage entertainments which are frankly meant to act on the spectators as aphrodisiacs are everywhere tolerated, plays which have an almost horrifying contrary effect are fiercely attacked by persons and papers notoriously indifferent to public morals on all other occasions. The explanation is very simple. The profits of Mrs Warren's profession are shared not only by Mrs Warren and Sir George Crofts, but by the landlords of their houses, the newspapers which advertise them, the restaurants which cater for them, and, in short, all the trades to which they are good customers, not to mention the public officials and representatives whom they silence by complicity, corruption, or blackmail. Add to these the employers who profit by cheap female labor, and the shareholders whose dividends depend on it (you find such people everywhere, even on the judicial bench and in the highest places in Church and State), and you get a large and powerful class with a strong pecuniary incentive to protect Mrs Warren's profession, and a correspondingly strong incentive to conceal, from their own consciences no less than from the world, the real sources of their gain. These are the people who declare that it is feminine vice and not poverty that drives women to the streets, as if vicious women with independent incomes ever went there. These are the people who, indulgent or indifferent to aphrodisiac plays, raise the moral hue and cry against performances of Mrs Warren's Profession, and drag actresses to the police court to be in-

sulted, bullied, and threatened for fulfilling their engagements. For please observe that the judicial decision in New
York State in favour of the play did not end the matter. In
Kansas City, for instance, the municipality, finding itself
restrained by the courts from preventing the performance,
fell back on a local bye-law against indecency. It summoned the actress who impersonated Mrs Warren to the
police court, and offered her and her colleagues the alternative of leaving the city or being prosecuted under this
bye-law.

Now nothing is more possible than that the city councillors who suddenly displayed such concern for the morals
of the theatre were either Mrs Warren's landlords, or employers of women at starvation wages, or restaurant keepers,
or newspaper proprietors, or in some other more or less
direct way sharers of the profits of her trade. No doubt it is
equally possible that they were simply stupid men who
thought that indecency consists, not in evil, but in mentioning it. I have, however, been myself a member of a municipal
council, and have not found municipal councillors quite so
simple and inexperienced as this. At all events I do not propose to give the Kansas councillors the benefit of the doubt.
I therefore advise the public at large, which will finally
decide the matter, to keep a vigilant eye on gentlemen who
will stand anything at the theatre except a performance of
Mrs Warren's Profession, and who assert in the same breath
that (a) the play is too loathsome to be bearable by civilized
people, and (b) that unless its performance is prohibited the
whole town will throng to see it. They may be merely excited
and foolish; but I am bound to warn the public that it is
equally likely that they may be collected and knavish.

At all events, to prohibit the play is to protect the evil
which the play exposes; and in view of that fact, I see no
reason for assuming that the prohibitionists are disinterested
moralists, and that the author, the managers, and the performers, who depend for their livelihood on their personal

reputations and not on rents, advertisements, or dividends, are grossly inferior to them in moral sense and public responsibility.

It is true that in Mrs Warren's Profession, Society, and not any individual, is the villain of the piece; but it does not follow that the people who take offence at it are all champions of society. Their credentials cannot be too carefully examined.

PICCARD'S COTTAGE, *January* 1902 [*revised 1930*]

P.S (1930) On reading the above after a lapse of 28 years, with the ban on Mrs Warren withdrawn and forgotten, I should have discarded it as an overdone fuss about nothing that now matters were it not for a recent incident. Before describing this I must explain that with the invention of the cinematograph a new censorship has come into existence, created, not this time by Act of Parliament, but by the film manufacturers to provide themselves with the certificates of propriety which have proved so useful to the theatre managers. This private censorship has acquired public power through its acceptance by the local authorities, without whose licence the films cannot be exhibited in places of public entertainment.

A lady who has devoted herself to the charitable work of relieving the homeless and penniless people who are to be found every night in London on the Thames Embankment had to deal largely with working men who had come to London from the country under the mistaken impression that there is always employment there for everybody, and with young women, also from the provinces, who had been lured to London by offers of situations which were really traps set for them by the agents of the White Slave traffic. The lady rightly concluded that much the best instrument for warning the men, and making known to the women the addresses of the organization for befriending unprotected

girl travellers, is the cinema. She caused a film to be made
for this purpose. The Film Censor immediately banned the
part of the film which gave the addresses to the girls and
shewed them the risks they ran. The lady appealed to me to
help her to protest. After convincing myself by witnessing a
private exhibition of the film that it was quite innocent I
wrote to the Censor, begging him to examine the film personally, and remedy what seemed to be a rule-of-thumb mistake by his examiners. He not only confirmed their veto, but
left uncontradicted a report in all the papers that he had
given as his reason that the lady had paraded the allurements of vice, and that such parades could not be tolerated by him. The sole allurements were the smart motor
car in which the heroine of the film was kidnapped, and
the fashionable clothes of the two very repulsive agents
who drugged her in it. In every other respect her experi-
ences were as disagreeable as the sternest moralist could
desire.

I then made a tour of the picture houses to see what the
Film Censor considers allowable. Of the films duly licensed
by him two were so nakedly pornographic that their exhibition could hardly have been risked without the Censor's
certificate of purity. One of them presented the allurements
of a supposedly French brothel so shamelessly that I rose
and fled in disgust long before the end, though I am as
hardened to vulgar salacity in the theatre as a surgeon is to
a dissecting room.

The only logical conclusion apparent is that the White
Slave traffickers are in complete control of our picture
theatres, and can close them to our Rescue workers as
effectively as they can reserve them for advertisements of
their own trade. I spare the Film Censor that conclusion.
The conclusion I press upon him and on the public is my old
one of twenty-eight years ago: that all the evil effects of such
corrupt control are inevitably produced gratuitously by
Censors with the best intentions.

POSTSCRIPT 1933. In spite of the suppression of my play for so many years by the censorship the subject broke out into a campaign for the abolition of the White Slave Traffic which still occupies the League of Nations at Geneva. But my demonstration that the root of the evil is economic was ruthlessly ignored by the profiteering Press (that is, by the entire Press); and when at last parliament proceeded to legislate, its contribution to the question was to ordain that Mrs Warren's male competitors should be flogged instead of fined. This had the double effect of stimulating the perverted sexuality which delights in flogging, and driving the traffic into female hands, leaving Mrs Warren triumphant.

The ban on performances of the play has long since been withdrawn; and when it is performed the critics hasten to declare that the scandal of underpaid virtue and overpaid vice is a thing of the past. Yet when the war created an urgent demand for women's labor in 1914 the Government proceeded to employ women for twelve hours a day at a wage of five ha'pence an hour. It is amazing how the grossest abuses thrive on their reputation for being old unhappy far-off things in an age of imaginary progress.

MRS WARREN'S PROFESSION

ACT 1

Summer afternoon in a cottage garden on the eastern slope of a hill a little south of Haslemere in Surrey. Looking up the hill, the cottage is seen in the left hand corner of the garden, with its thatched roof and porch, and a large latticed window to the left of the porch. A paling completely shuts in the garden, except for a gate on the right. The common rises uphill beyond the paling to the sky line. Some folded canvas garden chairs are leaning against the side bench in the porch. A lady's bicycle is propped against the wall, under the window. A little to the right of the porch a hammock is slung from two posts. A big canvas umbrella, stuck in the ground, keeps the sun off the hammock, in which a young lady lies reading and making notes, her head towards the cottage and her feet towards the gate. In front of the hammock, and within reach of her hand, is a common kitchen chair, with a pile of serious-looking books and a supply of writing paper on it.

A gentleman walking on the common comes into sight from behind the cottage. He is hardly past middle age, with something of the artist about him, unconventionally but carefully dressed, and clean-shaven except for a moustache, with an eager susceptible face and very amiable and considerate manners. He has silky black hair, with waves of grey and white in it. His eyebrows are white, his moustache black. He seems not certain of his way. He looks over the paling; takes stock of the place; and sees the young lady.

THE GENTLEMAN [*taking off his hat*] I beg your pardon. Can you direct me to Hindhead View – Mrs Alison's?

THE YOUNG LADY [*glancing up from her book*] This is Mrs Alison's. [*She resumes her work*].

THE GENTLEMAN. Indeed! Perhaps – may I ask are you Miss Vivie Warren?

THE YOUNG LADY [*sharply, as she turns on her elbow to get a good look at him*] Yes.

THE GENTLEMAN [*daunted and conciliatory*] I'm afraid I

appear intrusive. My name is Praed. [*Vivie at once throws her books upon the chair, and gets out of the hammock*]. Oh, pray dont let me disturb you.

VIVIE [*striding to the gate and opening it for him*] Come in, Mr Praed. [*He comes in*]. Glad to see you. [*She proffers her hand and takes his with a resolute and hearty grip. She is an attractive specimen of the sensible, able, highly-educated young middle-class Englishwoman. Age 22. Prompt, strong, confident, self-possessed. Plain business-like dress, but not dowdy. She wears a chatelaine at her belt, with a fountain pen and a paper knife among its pendants*].

PRAED. Very kind of you indeed, Miss Warren. [*She shuts the gate with a vigorous slam. He passes in to the middle of the garden, exercising his fingers, which are slightly numbed by her greeting*]. Has your mother arrived?

VIVIE [*quickly, evidently scenting aggression*] Is she coming?

PRAED [*surprised*] Didnt you expect us?

VIVIE. No.

PRAED. Now, goodness me, I hope Ive not mistaken the day. That would be just like me, you know. Your mother arranged that she was to come down from London and that I was to come over from Horsham to be introduced to you.

VIVIE [*not at all pleased*] Did she? Hm! My mother has rather a trick of taking me by surprise – to see how I behave myself when she's away, I suppose. I fancy I shall take my mother very much by surprise one of these days, if she makes arrangements that concern me without consulting me beforehand. She hasnt come.

PRAED [*embarrassed*] I'm really very sorry.

VIVIE [*throwing off her displeasure*] It's not your fault, Mr Praed, is it? And I'm very glad youve come. You are the only one of my mother's friends I have ever asked her to bring to see me.

PRAED [*relieved and delighted*] Oh, now this is really very good of you, Miss Warren!

VIVIE. Will you come indoors; or would you rather sit out here and talk?

PRAED. It will be nicer out here, dont you think?

VIVIE. Then I'll go and get you a chair. [*She goes to the porch for a garden chair*].

PRAED [*following her*] Oh, pray, pray! Allow me. [*He lays hands on the chair*].

VIVIE [*letting him take it*] Take care of your fingers: theyre rather dodgy things, those chairs. [*She goes across to the chair with the books on it; pitches them into the hammock; and brings the chair forward with one swing*].

PRAED [*who has just unfolded his chair*] Oh, now do let me take that hard chair. I like hard chairs.

VIVIE. So do I. Sit down, Mr Praed. [*This invitation she gives with genial peremptoriness, his anxiety to please her clearly striking her as a sign of weakness of character on his part. But he does not immediately obey*].

PRAED. By the way, though, hadnt we better go to the station to meet your mother?

VIVIE [*coolly*] Why? She knows the way.

PRAED [*disconcerted*] Er – I suppose she does [*he sits down*].

VIVIE. Do you know, you are just like what I expected. I hope you are disposed to be friends with me.

PRAED [*again beaming*] Thank you, my dear Miss Warren: thank you. Dear me! I'm so glad your mother hasnt spoilt you!

VIVIE. How?

PRAED. Well, in making you too conventional. You know, my dear Miss Warren, I am a born anarchist. I hate authority. It spoils the relations between parent and child: even between mother and daughter. Now I was always afraid that your mother would strain her authority to make you very conventional. It's such a relief to find that she hasnt.

VIVIE. Oh! have I been behaving unconventionally?

PRAED. Oh no: oh dear no. At least not conventionally unconventionally, you understand. [*She nods and sits down. He goes on, with a cordial outburst*] But it was so charming of you to say that you were disposed to be friends with me! You modern young ladies are splendid: perfectly splendid!

VIVIE [*dubiously*] Eh? [*watching him with dawning disappointment as to the quality of his brains and character*].

PRAED. When I was your age, young men and women were afraid of each other: there was no good fellowship. Nothing real. Only gallantry copied out of novels, and as vulgar and affected as it could be. Maidenly reserve! gentlemanly chivalry! always saying no when you meant yes! simple purgatory for shy and sincere souls.

VIVIE. Yes, I imagine there must have been a frightful waste of time. Especially women's time.

PRAED. Oh, waste of life, waste of everything. But things are improving. Do you know, I have been in a positive state of excitement about meeting you ever since your magnificent achievements at Cambridge: a thing unheard of in my day. It was perfectly splendid, your tieing with the third wrangler. Just the right place, you know. The first wrangler is always a dreamy, morbid fellow, in whom the thing is pushed to the length of a disease.

VIVIE. It doesnt pay. I wouldnt do it again for the same money!

PRAED [*aghast*] The same money!

VIVIE. I did it for £50.

PRAED. Fifty pounds!

VIVIE. Yes. Fifty pounds. Perhaps you dont know how it was. Mrs Latham, my tutor at Newnham, told my mother that I could distinguish myself in the mathematical tripos if I went in for it in earnest. The papers were full just then of Phillipa Summers beating the senior wrangler. You remember about it, of course.

PRAED [*shakes his head energetically*] ! ! !

VIVIE. Well anyhow she did: and nothing would please my mother but that I should do the same thing. I said flatly it was not worth my while to face the grind since I was not going in for teaching; but I offered to try for fourth wrangler or thereabouts for £50. She closed with me at that, after a little grumbling; and I was better than my bargain. But I wouldnt do it again for that. £200 would have been nearer the mark.

PRAED [*much damped*] Lord bless me! Thats a very practical way of looking at it.

VIVIE. Did you expect to find me an unpractical person?

PRAED. But surely it's practical to consider not only the work these honors cost, but also the culture they bring.

VIVIE. Culture! My dear Mr Praed: do you know what the mathematical tripos means? It means grind, grind, grind for six to eight hours a day at mathematics, and nothing but mathematics. I'm supposed to know something about science; but I know nothing except the mathematics it involves. I can make calculations for engineers, electricians, insurance companies, and so on; but I know next to nothing about engineering or electricity or insurance. I dont even know arithmetic well. Outside mathematics, lawn-tennis, eating, sleeping, cycling, and walking, I'm a more ignorant barbarian than any woman could possibly be who hadnt gone in for the tripos.

PRAED [*revolted*] What a monstrous, wicked, rascally system! I knew it! I felt at once that it meant destroying all that makes womanhood beautiful.

VIVIE. I dont object to it on that score in the least. I shall turn it to very good account, I assure you.

PRAED. Pooh! in what way?

VIVIE. I shall set up chambers in the City, and work at actuarial calculations and conveyancing. Under cover of that I shall do some law, with one eye on the Stock Exchange all the time. Ive come down here by myself to read law: not for a holiday, as my mother imagines. I hate holidays.

PRAED. You make my blood run cold. Are you to have no romance, no beauty in your life?

VIVIE. I dont care for either, I assure you.

PRAED. You cant mean that.

VIVIE. Oh yes I do. I like working and getting paid for it. When I'm tired of working, I like a comfortable chair, a cigar, a little whisky, and a novel with a good detective story in it.

PRAED [*rising in a frenzy of repudiation*] I dont believe it. I am an artist; and I cant believe it: I refuse to believe it. It's only that you havnt discovered yet what a wonderful world art can open up to you.

VIVIE. Yes I have. Last May I spent six weeks in London with Honoria Fraser. Mamma thought we were doing a round of sightseeing together; but I was really at Honoria's chambers in Chancery Lane every day, working away at actuarial calculations for her, and helping her as well as a greenhorn could. In the evenings we smoked and talked, and never dreamt of going out except for exercise. And I never enjoyed myself more in my life. I cleared all my expenses, and got initiated into the business without a fee into the bargain.

PRAED. But bless my heart and soul, Miss Warren, do you call that discovering art?

VIVIE. Wait a bit. That wasnt the beginning. I went up to town on an invitation from some artistic people in Fitzjohn's Avenue: one of the girls was a Newnham chum. They took me to the National Gallery –

PRAED [*approving*] Ah ! ! [*He sits down, much relieved*].

VIVIE [*continuing*] – to the Opera –

PRAED [*still more pleased*] Good!

VIVIE. – and to a concert where the band played all the evening: Beethoven and Wagner and so on. I wouldnt go through that experience again for anything you could offer me. I held out for civility's sake until the third day; and then I said, plump out, that I couldnt stand any more of it, and went off to Chancery Lane. Now you know the sort of perfectly splendid modern young lady I am. How do you think I shall get on with my mother?

PRAED [*startled*] Well, I hope – er –

VIVIE. It's not so much what you hope as what you believe, that I want to know.

PRAED. Well, frankly, I am afraid your mother will be a little disappointed. Not from any shortcoming on your part, you know: I dont mean that. But you are so different from her ideal.

VIVIE. Her what?!

PRAED. Her ideal.

VIVIE. Do you mean her ideal of ME?

PRAED. Yes.

VIVIE. What on earth is it like?

PRAED. Well, you must have observed, Miss Warren, that people who are dissatisfied with their own bringing-up generally think that the world would be all right if everybody were to be brought up quite differently. Now your mother's life has been – er – I suppose you know –

VIVIE. Dont suppose anything, Mr Praed. I hardly know my mother. Since I was a child I have lived in England, at school or college, or with people paid to take charge of me. I have been boarded out all my life. My mother has lived in Brussels or Vienna and never let me go to her. I only see her when she visits England for a few days. I dont complain: it's been very pleasant; for people have been very good to me; and there has always been plenty of money to make things smooth. But dont imagine I know anything about my mother. I know far less than you do.

PRAED [very ill at ease] In that case – [He stops, quite at a loss. Then, with a forced attempt at gaiety] But what nonsense we are talking! Of course you and your mother will get on capitally. [He rises, and looks abroad at the view]. What a charming little place you have here!

VIVIE [unmoved] Rather a violent change of subject, Mr Praed. Why wont my mother's life bear being talked about?

PRAED. Oh, you really mustnt say that. Isnt it natural that I should have a certain delicacy in talking to my old friend's daughter about her behind her back? You and she will have plenty of opportunity of talking about it when she comes.

VIVIE. No: s h e wont talk about it either. [*Rising*] However, I daresay you have good reasons for telling me nothing. Only, mind this, Mr Praed. I expect there will be a battle royal when my mother hears of my Chancery Lane project.

PRAED [*ruefully*] I'm afraid there will.

VIVIE. Well, I shall win, because I want nothing but my fare to London to start there to-morrow earning my own living by devilling for Honoria. Besides, I have no mysteries to keep up; and it seems she has. I shall use that advantage over her if necessary.

PRAED [*greatly shocked*] Oh no! No, pray. Youd not do such a thing.

VIVIE. Then tell me why not.

PRAED. I really cannot. I appeal to your good feeling. [*She smiles at his sentimentality*]. Besides, you may be too bold. Your mother is not to be trifled with when she's angry.

VIVIE. You cant frighten me, Mr Praed. In that month at Chancery Lane I had opportunities of taking the measure of one or two women very like my mother. You may back me to win. But if I hit harder in my ignorance than I need, remember that it is you who refuse to enlighten me. Now, let us drop the subject. [*She takes her chair and replaces it near the hammock with the same vigorous swing as before*].

PRAED [*taking a desperate resolution*] One word, Miss Warren. I had better tell you. It's very difficult; but –

Mrs Warren and Sir George Crofts arrive at the gate. Mrs Warren is between 40 and 50, formerly pretty, showily dressed in a brilliant hat and a gay blouse fitting tightly over her bust and flanked by fashionable sleeves. Rather spoilt and domineering, and decidedly vulgar, but, on the whole, a genial and fairly presentable old blackguard of a woman.

Crofts is a tall powerfully-built man of about 50, fashionably dressed in the style of a young man. Nasal voice, reedier than might be expected from his strong frame. Clean-shaven bulldog jaws,

*large flat ears, and thick neck: gentlemanly combination of the
most brutal types of city man, sporting man, and man about town.*

VIVIE. Here they are. [*Coming to them as they enter the garden*]
How do, mater? Mr Praed's been here this half hour
waiting for you.

MRS WARREN. Well, if youve been waiting, Praddy, it's
your own fault: I thought youd have had the gumption to
know I was coming by the 3.10 train. Vivie: put your hat
on, dear: youll get sunburnt. Oh, I forgot to introduce
you. Sir George Crofts: my little Vivie.

*Crofts advances to Vivie with his most courtly manner. She nods,
but makes no motion to shake hands.*

CROFTS. May I shake hands with a young lady whom I
have known by reputation very long as the daughter of
one of my oldest friends?

VIVIE [*who has been looking him up and down sharply*] If you like.
[*She takes his tenderly proffered hand and gives it a squeeze that
makes him open his eyes; then turns away and says to her mother*]
Will you come in, or shall I get a couple more chairs?
[*She goes into the porch for the chairs*].

MRS WARREN. Well, George, what do you think of her?

CROFTS [*ruefully*] She has a powerful fist. Did you shake
hands with her, Praed?

PRAED. Yes: it will pass off presently.

CROFTS. I hope so. [*Vivie reappears with two more chairs. He
hurries to her assistance*]. Allow me.

MRS WARREN [*patronizingly*] Let Sir George help you with
the chairs, dear.

VIVIE [*pitching them into his arms*] Here you are. [*She dusts
her hands and turns to Mrs Warren*]. Youd like some tea,
wouldnt you?

MRS WARREN [*sitting in Praed's chair and fanning herself*] I'm
dying for a drop to drink.

VIVIE. I'll see about it. [*She goes into the cottage*].

*Sir George has by this time managed to unfold a chair and plant
it beside Mrs Warren, on her left. He throws the other on the*

*grass and sits down, looking dejected and rather foolish, with th
handle of his stick in his mouth. Praed, still very uneasy, fidgets
about the garden on their right.*

MRS WARREN [*to Praed, looking at Crofts*] Just look at him,
Praddy: he looks cheerful, dont he? He's been worrying
my life out these three years to have that little girl of mine
shewn to him; and now that Ive done it, he's quite out of
countenance. [*Briskly*] Come! sit up, George; and take
your stick out of your mouth. [*Crofts sulkily obeys*].

PRAED. I think, you know – if you dont mind my saying so
– that we had better get out of the habit of thinking of her
as a little girl. You see she has really distinguished herself;
and I'm not sure, from what I have seen of her, that she is
not older than any of us.

MRS WARREN [*greatly amused*] Only listen to him, George!
Older than any of us! Well, she has been stuffing you
nicely with her importance.

PRAED. But young people are particularly sensitive about
being treated in that way.

MRS WARREN. Yes; and young people have to get all that
nonsense taken out of them, and a good deal more besides.
Dont you interfere, Praddy: I know how to treat my own
child as well as you do. [*Praed, with a grave shake of his head,
walks up the garden with his hands behind his back. Mrs Warren
pretends to laugh, but looks after him with perceptible concern.
Then she whispers to Crofts*] Whats the matter with him?
What does he take it like that for?

CROFTS [*morosely*] Youre afraid of Praed.

MRS WARREN. What! Me! Afraid of dear old Praddy! Why,
a fly wouldnt be afraid of him.

CROFTS. Youre afraid of him.

MRS WARREN [*angry*] I'll trouble you to mind your own
business, and not try any of your sulks on me. I'm not
afraid of you, anyhow. If you cant make yourself agreeable, youd better go home. [*She gets up, and, turning her back
on him, finds herself face to face with Praed*]. Come, Praddy, I

know it was only your tender-heartedness. Youre afraid
I'll bully her.

PRAED. My dear Kitty: you think I'm offended. Dont imagine that: pray dont. But you know I often notice things
that escape you; and though you never take my advice,
you sometimes admit afterwards that you ought to have
taken it.

MRS WARREN. Well, what do you notice now?

PRAED. Only that Vivie is a grown woman. Pray, Kitty,
treat her with every respect.

MRS WARREN [*with genuine amazement*] Respect! Treat my
own daughter with respect! What next, pray!

VIVIE [*appearing at the cottage door and calling to Mrs Warren*]
Mother: will you come to my room before tea?

MRS WARREN. Yes, dearie. [*She laughs indulgently at Praed's
gravity, and pats him on the cheek as she passes him on her way to
the porch*]. Dont be cross, Praddy. [*She follows Vivie in to the
cottage*].

CROFTS [*furtively*] I say, Praed.

PRAED. Yes.

CROFTS. I want to ask you a rather particular question.

PRAED. Certainly. [*He takes Mrs Warren's chair and sits close
to Crofts*].

CROFTS. Thats right: they might hear us from the window.
Look here: did Kitty ever tell you who that girl's father is?

PRAED. Never.

CROFTS. Have you any suspicion of who it might be?

PRAED. None.

CROFTS [*not believing him*] I know, of course, that you perhaps
might feel bound not to tell if she had said anything to
you. But it's very awkward to be uncertain about it now
that we shall be meeting the girl every day. We wont
exactly know how we ought to feel towards her.

PRAED. What difference can that make? We take her on her
own merits. What does it matter who her father was?

CROFTS [*suspiciously*] Then you know who he was?

223

PRAED [*with a touch of temper*] I said no just now. Did you not hear me?

CROFTS. Look here, Praed. I ask you as a particular favor. If you do know [*movement of protest from Praed*] – I only say, if you know, you might at least set my mind at rest about her. The fact is, I feel attracted.

PRAED [*sternly*] What do you mean?

CROFTS. Oh, dont be alarmed: it's quite an innocent feeling. Thats what puzzles me about it. Why, for all I know *I* might be her father.

PRAED. You! Impossible!

CROFTS [*catching him up cunningly*] You know for certain that I'm not?

PRAED. I know nothing about it, I tell you, any more than you. But really, Crofts – oh no, it's out of the question. Theres not the least resemblance.

CROFTS. As to that, theres no resemblance between her and her mother that I can see. I suppose she's not *your* daughter, is she?

PRAED [*rising indignantly*] Really, Crofts –!

CROFTS. No offence, Praed. Quite allowable as between two men of the world.

PRAED [*recovering himself with an effort and speaking gently and gravely*] Now listen to me, my dear Crofts. [*He sits down again*]. I have nothing to do with that side of Mrs Warren's life, and never had. She has never spoken to me about it; and of course I have never spoken to her about it. Your delicacy will tell you that a handsome woman needs some friends who are not – well, not on that footing with her. The effect of her own beauty would become a torment to her if she could not escape from it occasionally. You are probably on much more confidential terms with Kitty than I am. Surely you can ask her the question yourself.

CROFTS. I have asked her, often enough. But she's so determined to keep the child all to herself that she would

deny that it ever had a father if she could. [*Rising*] I'm
thoroughly uncomfortable about it, Praed.

PRAED [*rising also*] Well, as you are, at all events, old
enough to be her father, I dont mind agreeing that we both
regard Miss Vivie in a parental way, as a young girl whom
we are bound to protect and help. What do you say?

CROFTS [*aggressively*] I'm no older than you, if you come to
that.

PRAED. Yes you are, my dear fellow: you were born old. I
was born a boy: Ive never been able to feel the assurance
of a grown-up man in my life. [*He folds his chair and carries it
to the porch*].

MRS WARREN [*calling from within the cottage*] Prad-dee!
George! Tea-ea-ea-ea!

CROFTS [*hastily*] She's calling us. [*He hurries in*].

> *Praed shakes his head bodingly, and is following Crofts when
> he is hailed by a young gentleman who has just appeared on the
> common, and is making for the gate. He is pleasant. pretty,
> smartly dressed, cleverly good-for-nothing, not long turned 20,
> with a charming voice and agreeably disrespectful manners. He
> carries a light sporting magazine rifle.*

THE YOUNG GENTLEMAN. Hallo! Praed!

PRAED. Why, Frank Gardner! [*Frank comes in and shakes
hands cordially*]. What on earth are you doing here?

FRANK. Staying with my father.

PRAED. The Roman father?

FRANK. He's rector here. I'm living with my people this
autumn for the sake of economy. Things came to a crisis in
July: the Roman father had to pay my debts. He's stony
broke in consequence; and so am I. What are you up to in
these parts? Do you know the people here?

PRAED. Yes: I'm spending the day with a Miss Warren.

FRANK [*enthusiastically*] What! Do you know Vivie? Isnt she
a jolly girl? I'm teaching her to shoot with this [*putting
down the rifle*]. I'm so glad she knows you: youre just the
sort of fellow she ought to know. [*He smiles, and raises the*

charming voice almost to a singing tone as he exclaims] It's ever
so jolly to find you here, Praed.

PRAED. I'm an old friend of her mother. Mrs Warren
brought me over to make her daughter's acquaintance.

FRANK. The mother! Is she here?

PRAED. Yes: inside, at tea.

MRS WARREN [*calling from within*] Prad-dee-ee-ee-eee! The
tea-cake'll be cold.

PRAED [*calling*] Yes, Mrs Warren. In a moment. Ive just
met a friend here.

MRS WARREN. A what?

PRAED [*louder*] A friend.

MRS WARREN. Bring him in.

PRAED. All right. [*To Frank*] Will you accept the invitation?

FRANK [*incredulous, but immensely amused*] Is that Vivie's
mother?

PRAED. Yes.

FRANK. By Jove! What a lark! Do you think she'll like me?

PRAED. Ive no doubt youll make yourself popular, as usual.
Come in and try [*moving towards the house*].

FRANK. Stop a bit. [*Seriously*] I want to take you into my
confidence.

PRAED. Pray dont. It's only some fresh folly, like the barmaid at Redhill.

FRANK. It's ever so much more serious than that. You say
youve only just met Vivie for the first time?

PRAED. Yes.

FRANK [*rhapsodically*] Then you can have no idea what a
girl she is. Such character! Such sense! And her clever-
ness! Oh, my eye, Praed, but I can tell you she is clever!
And – need I add? – she loves me.

CROFTS [*putting his head out of the window*] I say, Praed: what
are you about? Do come along. [*He disappears*].

FRANK. Hallo! Sort of chap that would take a prize at a
dog show, aint he? Who's he?

226

PRAED. Sir George Crofts, an old friend of Mrs Warren's. I think we had better come in.

On their way to the porch they are interrupted by a call from the gate. Turning, they see an elderly clergyman looking over it.

THE CLERGYMAN [*calling*] Frank!

FRANK. Hallo! [*To Praed*] The Roman father. [*To the clergyman*] Yes, gov'nor: all right: presently. [*To Praed*] Look here, Praed: youd better go in to tea. I'll join you directly.

PRAED. Very good. [*He goes into the cottage*].

The clergyman remains outside the gate, with his hands on the top of it. The Rev. Samuel Gardner, a beneficed clergyman of the Established Church, is over 50. Externally he is pretentious, booming, noisy, important. Really he is that obsolescent social phenomenon the fool of the family dumped on the Church by his father the patron, clamorously asserting himself as father and clergyman without being able to command respect in either capacity.

REV. S. Well, sir. Who are your friends here, if I may ask?

FRANK. Oh, it's all right, gov'nor! Come in.

REV. S. No, sir; not until I know whose garden I am entering.

FRANK. It's all right. It's Miss Warren's.

REV. S. I have not seen her at church since she came.

FRANK. Of course not: she's a third wrangler. Ever so intellectual. Took a higher degree than you did; so why should she go to hear you preach?

REV. S. Dont be disrespectful, sir.

FRANK. Oh, it dont matter: nobody hears us. Come in. [*He opens the gate, unceremoniously pulling his father with it into the garden*]. I want to introduce you to her. Do you remember the advice you gave me last July, gov'nor?

REV. S. [*severely*] Yes. I advised you to conquer your idleness and flippancy, and to work your way into an honorable profession and live on it and not upon me.

FRANK. No: thats what you thought of afterwards. What you actually said was that since I had neither brains nor

227

money, I'd better turn my good looks to account by marrying somebody with both. Well, look here, Miss Warren has brains: you cant deny that.

REV. S. Brains are not everything.

FRANK. No, of course not: theres the money –

REV. S. [*interrupting him austerely*] I was not thinking of money sir. I was speaking of higher things. Social position, for instance.

FRANK. I dont care a rap about that.

REV. S. But I do, sir.

FRANK. Well, nobody wants you to marry her. Anyhow she has what amounts to a high Cambridge degree; and she seems to have as much money as she wants.

REV. S. [*sinking into a feeble vein of humor*] I greatly doubt whether she has as much money as you will want.

FRANK. Oh, come: I havnt been so very extravagant. I live ever so quietly; I dont drink; I dont bet much; and I never go regularly on the razzle-dazzle as you did when you were my age.

REV. S. [*booming hollowly*] Silence, sir.

FRANK. Well, you told me yourself, when I was making ever such an ass of myself about the barmaid at Redhill, that you once offered a woman £50 for the letters you wrote to her when –

REV. S. [*terrified*] Sh-sh-sh, Frank, for Heaven's sake! [*He looks round apprehensively. Seeing no one within earshot he plucks up courage to boom again, but more subduedly*]. You are taking an ungentlemanly advantage of what I confided to you for your own good, to save you from an error you would have repented all your life long. Take warning by your father's follies, sir; and dont make them an excuse for your own.

FRANK. Did you ever hear the story of the Duke of Wellington and his letters?

REV. S. No, sir; and I dont want to hear it.

FRANK. The old Iron Duke didnt throw away £50: not he.

He just wrote: 'Dear Jenny: publish and be damned! Yours affectionately, Wellington.' Thats what you should have done.

REV. S. [*piteously*] Frank, my boy: when I wrote those letters I put myself into that woman's power. When I told you about them I put myself, to some extent, I am sorry to say, in your power. She refused my money with these words, which I shall never forget. 'Knowledge is power,' she said; 'and I never sell power'. Thats more than twenty years ago; and she has never made use of her power or caused me a moment's uneasiness. You are behaving worse to me than she did, Frank.

FRANK. Oh yes I dare say! Did you ever preach at her the way you preach at me every day?

REV. S. [*wounded almost to tears*] I leave you, sir. You are incorrigible. [*He turns towards the gate*].

FRANK [*utterly unmoved*] Tell them I shant be home to tea, will you, gov'nor, like a good fellow? [*He moves towards the cottage door and is met by Praed and Vivie coming out*].

VIVIE [*to Frank*] Is that your father, Frank? I do so want to meet him.

FRANK. Certainly. [*Calling after his father*] Gov'nor. Youre wanted. [*The parson turns at the gate, fumbling nervously at his hat. Praed crosses the garden to the opposite side, beaming in anticipation of civilities*]. My father: Miss Warren.

VIVIE [*going to the clergyman and shaking his hand*] Very glad to see you here, Mr Gardner. [*Calling to the cottage*] Mother: come along: youre wanted.

Mrs Warren appears on the threshold, and is immediately transfixed recognizing the clergyman.

VIVIE [*continuing*] Let me introduce –

MRS WARREN [*swooping on the Reverend Samuel*] Why, it's Sam Gardner, gone into the Church! Well, I never! Dont you know us, Sam? This is George Crofts, as large as life and twice as natural. Dont you remember me?

REV. S. [*very red*] I really – er –

MRS WARREN. Of course you do. Why, I have a whole album of your letters still: I came across them only the other day.

REV. S. [*miserably confused*] Miss Vavasour, I believe.

MRS WARREN [*correcting him quickly in a loud whisper*] Tch! Nonsense! Mrs Warren: dont you see my daughter there?

ACT II

Inside the cottage after nightfall. Looking eastward from within instead of westward from without, the latticed window, with its curtains drawn, is now seen in the middle of the front wall of the cottage, with the porch door to the left of it. In the left-hand side wall is the door leading to the kitchen. Farther back against the same wall is a dresser with a candle and matches on it, and Frank's rifle standing beside them, with the barrel resting in the plate-rack. In the centre a table stands with a lighted lamp on it. Vivie's books and writing materials are on a table to the right of the window, against the wall. The fireplace is on the right, with a settle: there is no fire. Two of the chairs are set right and left of the table.

The cottage door opens, shewing a fine starlit night without; and Mrs Warren, her shoulders wrapped in a shawl borrowed from Vivie, enters, followed by Frank, who throws his cap on the window seat. She has had enough of walking, and gives a gasp of relief as she unpins her hat; takes it off; sticks the pin through the crown; and puts it on the table.

MRS WARREN. O Lord! I dont know which is the worst of the country, the walking or the sitting at home with nothing to do. I could do with a whisky and soda now very well, if only they had such a thing in this place.

FRANK. Perhaps Vivie's got some.

MRS WARREN. Nonsense! What would a young girl like her be doing with such things! Never mind: it dont matter. I wonder how she passes her time here! I'd a good deal rather be in Vienna.

FRANK. Let me take you there. [*He helps her to take off her shawl, gallantly giving her shoulders a very perceptible squeeze as he does so*].

MRS WARREN. Ah! would you? I'm beginning to think youre a chip of the old block.

FRANK. Like the gov'nor, eh? [*He hangs the shawl on the nearest chair and sits down*].

MRS WARREN. Never you mind. What do you know about such things? Youre only a boy. [*She goes to the hearth, to be farther from temptation*].

FRANK. Do come to Vienna with me? It'd be ever such larks.

MRS WARREN. No, thank you. Vienna is no place for you – at least not until youre a little older. [*She nods at him to emphasize this piece of advice. He makes a mock-piteous face, belied by his laughing eyes. She looks at him; then comes back to him*]. Now, look here, little boy [*taking his face in her hands and turning it up to her*]: I know you through and through by your likeness to your father, better than you know yourself. Dont you go taking any silly ideas into your head about me. Do you hear?

FRANK [*gallantly wooing her with his voice*] Cant help it, my dear Mrs Warren: it runs in the family.

She pretends to box his ears; then looks at the pretty laughing upturned face for a moment, tempted. At last she kisses him, and immediately turns away, out of patience with herself.

MRS WARREN. There! I shouldnt have done that. I am wicked. Never mind, my dear: it's only a motherly kiss. Go and make love to Vivie.

FRANK. So I have.

MRS WARREN [*turning on him with a sharp note of alarm in her voice*] What!

FRANK. Vivie and I are ever such chums.

MRS WARREN. What do you mean? Now see here: I wont have any young scamp tampering with my little girl. Do you hear? I wont have it.

FRANK [*quite unabashed*] My dear Mrs Warren: dont you be alarmed. My intentions are honorable: ever so honorable; and your little girl is jolly well able to take care of herself. She dont need looking after half so much as her mother. She aint so handsome, you know.

MRS WARREN [*taken aback by his assurance*] Well, you have got a nice healthy two inches thick of cheek all over you. I dont know where you got it. Not from your father, anyhow.

CROFTS [*in the garden*] The gipsies, I suppose?

REV. S. [*replying*] The broomsquires are far worse.

MRS WARREN [*to Frank*] S-sh! Remember! youve had your warning.

    Crofts and the Reverend Samuel come in from the garden, the clergyman continuing his conversation as he enters.

REV. S. The perjury at the Winchester assizes is deplorable.

MRS WARREN. Well? what became of you two? And wheres Praddy and Vivie?

CROFTS [*putting his hat on the settle and his stick in the chimney corner*] They went up the hill. We went to the village. I wanted a drink. [*He sits down on the settle, putting his legs up along the seat*].

MRS WARREN. Well, she oughtnt go off like that without telling me. [*To Frank*] Get your father a chair, Frank: where are your manners? [*Frank springs up and gracefully offers his father his chair; then takes another from the wall and sits down at the table, in the middle, with his father on his right and Mrs Warren on his left*]. George: where are you going to stay tonight? You cant stay here. And whats Praddy going to do?

CROFTS. Gardner'll put me up.

MRS WARREN. Oh, no doubt youve taken care of yourself! But what about Praddy?

CROFTS. Dont know. I suppose he can sleep at the inn.

MRS WARREN. Havnt you room for him, Sam?

REV. S. Well – er – you see, as rector here, I am not free to do as I like. Er – what is Mr Praed's social position?

MRS WARREN. Oh, he's all right: he's an architect. What an old stick-in-the-mud you are, Sam!

FRANK. Yes, it's all right, gov'nor. He built that place down in Wales for the Duke. Caernarvon Castle they call it. You must have heard of it. [*He winks with lightning smartness at Mrs Warren, and regards his father blandly*].

REV. s. Oh, in that case, of course we shall only be too happy. I suppose he knows the Duke personally.

FRANK. Oh, ever so intimately! We can stick him in Georgina's old room.

MRS WARREN. Well, thats settled. Now if those two would only come in and let us have supper. Theyve no right to stay out after dark like this.

CROFTS [*aggressively*] What harm are they doing you?

MRS WARREN. Well, harm or not, I dont like it.

FRANK. Better not wait for them, Mrs Warren. Praed will stay out as long as possible. He has never known before what it is to stray over the heath on a summer night with my Vivie.

CROFTS [*sitting up in some consternation*] I say, you know! Come!

REV. s. [*rising, startled out of his professional manner into real force and sincerity*] Frank, once for all, it's out of the question. Mrs Warren will tell you that it's not to be thought of.

CROFTS. Of course not.

FRANK [*with enchanting placidity*] Is that so, Mrs Warren?

MRS WARREN [*reflectively*] Well, Sam, I dont know. If the girl wants to get married, no good can come of keeping her unmarried.

REV. s. [*astounded*] But married to him! – your daughter to my son! Only think: it's impossible.

CROFTS. Of course it's impossible. Dont be a fool, Kitty.

MRS WARREN [*nettled*] Why not? Isnt my daughter good enough for your son?

REV. s. But surely, my dear Mrs Warren, you know the reasons –

MRS WARREN [*defiantly*] I know no reasons. If you know any, you can tell them to the lad, or to the girl, or to your congregation, if you like.

REV. s. [*collapsing helplessly into his chair*] You know very well that I couldnt tell anyone the reasons. But my boy will

MRS WARREN'S PROFESSION

believe me when I tell him there are reasons.

FRANK. Quite right, Dad: he will. But has your boy's conduct ever been influenced by your reasons?

CROFTS. You cant marry her; and thats all about it. [*He gets up and stands on the hearth, with his back to the fireplace, frowning determinedly*].

MRS WARREN [*turning on him sharply*] What have you got to do with it, pray?

FRANK [*with his prettiest lyrical cadence*] Precisely what I was going to ask myself, in my own graceful fashion.

CROFTS [*to Mrs Warren*] I suppose you dont want to marry the girl to a man younger than herself and without either a profession or twopence to keep her on. Ask Sam, if you dont believe me. [*To the parson*] How much more money are you going to give him?

REV. S. Not another penny. He has had his patrimony and he spent the last of it in July. [*Mrs Warren's face falls*].

CROFTS [*watching her*] There! I told you. [*He resumes his place on the settle and puts up his legs on the seat again, as if the matter were finally disposed of*].

FRANK [*plaintively*] This is ever so mercenary. Do you suppose Miss Warren's going to marry for money? If we love one another –

MRS WARREN. Thank you. Your love's a pretty cheap commodity, my lad. If you have no means of keeping a wife, that settles it: you cant have Vivie.

FRANK [*much amused*] What do you say, gov'nor, eh?

REV. S. I agree with Mrs Warren.

FRANK. And good old Crofts has already expressed his opinion.

CROFTS [*turning angrily on his elbow*] Look here: I want none of your cheek.

FRANK [*pointedly*] I'm ever so sorry to surprise you, Crofts, but you allowed yourself the liberty of speaking to me like a father a moment ago. One father is enough, thank you.

CROFTS [*contemptuously*] Yah! [*He turns away again*].

FRANK [*rising*] Mrs Warren: I cannot give my Vivie up, even for your sake.

MRS WARREN [*muttering*] Young scamp!

FRANK [*continuing*] And as you no doubt intend to hold out other prospects to her, I shall lose no time in placing my case before her. [*They stare at him, and he begins to declaim gracefully*]

> He either fears his fate too much,
> Or his deserts are small,
> That dares not put it to the touch
> To gain or lose it all.

The cottage door opens whilst he is reciting; and Vivie and Praed come in. He breaks off. Praed puts his hat on the dresser. There is an immediate improvement in the company's behavior. Crofts takes down his legs from the settle and pulls himself together as Praed joins him at the fireplace. Mrs Warren loses her ease of manner and takes refuge in querulousness.

MRS WARREN. Wherever have you been, Vivie?

VIVIE [*taking off her hat and throwing it carelessly on the table*] On the hill.

MRS WARREN. Well, you shouldnt go off like that without letting me know. How could I tell what had become of you? And night coming on too!

VIVIE [*going to the door of the kitchen and opening it, ignoring her mother*] Now, about supper? [*All rise except Mrs Warren*]. We shall be rather crowded in here, I'm afraid.

MRS WARREN. Did you hear what I said, Vivie?

VIVIE [*quietly*] Yes, mother. [*Reverting to the supper difficulty*] How many are we? [*Counting*] One, two, three, four, five, six. Well, two will have to wait until the rest are done: Mrs Alison has only plates and knives for four.

PRAED. Oh, it doesnt matter about me. I –

VIVIE. You have had a long walk and are hungry, Mr Praed: you shall have your supper at once. I can wait myself. I want one person to wait with me. Frank: are you hungry?

FRANK. Not the least in the world. Completely off my peck, in fact.

MRS WARREN [*to Crofts*] Neither are you, George. You can wait.

CROFTS. Oh, hang it, Ive eaten nothing since tea-time. Cant Sam do it?

FRANK. Would you starve my poor father?

REV. S. [*testily*] Allow me to speak for myself, sir. I am perfectly willing to wait.

VIVIE [*decisively*] Theres no need. Only two are wanted. [*She opens the door of the kitchen*]. Will you take my mother in, Mr Gardner. [*The parson takes Mrs Warren; and they pass into the kitchen. Praed and Crofts follow. All except Praed clearly disapprove of the arrangement, but do not know how to resist it. Vivie stands at the door looking in at them*]. Can you squeeze past to that corner, Mr Praed: it's rather a tight fit. Take care of your coat against the white-wash: thats right. Now, are you all comfortable?

PRAED [*within*] Quite, thank you.

MRS WARREN [*within*] Leave the door open, dearie. [*Vivie frowns; but Frank checks her with a gesture, and steals to the cottage door, which he softly sets wide open*]. Oh Lor, what a draught! Youd better shut it, dear.

    Vivie shuts it with a slam, and then, noting with disgust that her mother's hat and shawl are lying about, takes them tidily to the window seat, whilst Frank noiselessly shuts the cottage door.

FRANK [*exulting*] Aha! Got rid of em. Well, Vivvums: what do you think of my governor?

VIVIE [*preoccupied and serious*] Ive hardly spoken to him. He doesnt strike me as being a particularly able person.

FRANK. Well, you know, the old man is not altogether such a fool as he looks. You see, he was shoved into the Church rather; and in trying to live up to it he makes a much bigger ass of himself than he really is. I dont dislike him as much as you might expect. He means well. How do you think youll get on with him?

VIVIE [*rather grimly*] I dont think my future life will be much concerned with him, or with any of that old circle of my mother's, except perhaps Praed. [*She sits down on the settle*]. What do you think of my mother?

FRANK. Really and truly?

VIVIE. Yes, really and truly.

FRANK. Well, she's ever so jolly. But she's rather a caution, isnt she? And Crofts! oh, my eye, Crofts! [*He sits beside her*].

VIVIE. What a lot, Frank!

FRANK. What a crew!

VIVIE [*with intense contempt for them*] If I thought that *I* was like that – that I was going to be a waster, shifting along from one meal to another with no purpose, and no character, and no grit in me, I'd open an artery and bleed to death without one moment's hesitation.

FRANK. Oh no, you wouldnt. Why should they take any grind when they can afford not to? I wish I had their luck. No: what I object to is their form. It isnt the thing: it's slovenly, ever so slovenly.

VIVIE. Do you think your form will be any better when youre as old as Crofts, if you dont work?

FRANK. Of course I do. Ever so much better. Vivvums mustnt lecture: her little boy's incorrigible. [*He attempts to take her face caressingly in his hands*].

VIVIE [*striking his hands down sharply*] Off with you: Vivvums is not in a humor for petting her little boy this evening. [*She rises and comes forward to the other side of the room*].

FRANK [*following her*] How unkind!

VIVIE [*stamping at him*] Be serious. I'm serious.

FRANK. Good. Let us talk learnedly. Miss Warren: do you know that all the most advanced thinkers are agreed that half the diseases of modern civilization are due to starvation of the affections in the young. Now, *I* –

VIVIE [*cutting him short*] You are very tiresome. [*She opens the inner door*]. Have you room for Frank there? He's complaining of starvation.

MRS WARREN [*within*] Of course there is [*clatter of knives and glasses as she moves the things on the table*]. Here! theres room now beside me. Come along, Mr Frank.

FRANK. Her little boy will be ever so even with his Vivvums for this. [*He passes into the kitchen*].

MRS WARREN [*within*] Here, Vivie: come on you too, child. You must be famished. [*She enters, followed by Crofts, who holds the door open for Vivie with marked deference. She goes out without looking at him; and shuts the door after her*]. Why, George, you cant be done: youve eaten nothing. Is there anything wrong with you?

CROFTS. Oh, all I wanted was a drink. [*He thrusts his hands in his pockets, and begins prowling about the room, restless and sulky*].

MRS WARREN. Well, I like enough to eat. But a little of that cold beef and cheese and lettuce goes a long way. [*With a sigh of only half repletion she sits down lazily on the settle*].

CROFTS. What do you go encouraging that young pup for?

MRS WARREN [*on the alert at once*] Now see here, George: what are you up to about that girl? Ive been watching your way of looking at her. Remember: I know you and what your looks mean.

CROFTS. Theres no harm in looking at her, is there?

MRS WARREN. I'd put you out and pack you back to London pretty soon if I saw any of your nonsense. My girl's little finger is more to me than your whole body and soul. [*Crofts receives this with a sneering grin. Mrs Warren, flushing a little at her failure to impose on him in the character of a theatrically devoted mother, adds in a lower key*] Make your mind easy: the young pup has no more chance than you have.

CROFTS. Maynt a man take an interest in a girl?

MRS WARREN. Not a man like you.

CROFTS. How old is she?

MRS WARREN. Never you mind how old she is.

CROFTS. Why do you make such a secret of it?

MRS WARREN. Because I choose.

CROFTS. Well, I'm not fifty yet; and my property is as good as ever it was –

MRS WARREN [*interrupting him*] Yes; because youre as stingy as youre vicious.

CROFTS [*continuing*] And a baronet isnt to be picked up every day. No other man in my position would put up with you for a mother-in-law. Why shouldnt she marry me?

MRS WARREN. You!

CROFTS. We three could live together quite comfortably: I'd die before her and leave her a bouncing widow with plenty of money. Why not? It's been growing in my mind all the time Ive been walking with that fool inside there.

MRS WARREN [*revolted*] Yes: it's the sort of thing that would grow in your mind.

He halts in his prowling; and the two look at one another, she steadfastly, with a sort of awe behind her contemptuous disgust: he stealthily, with a carnal gleam in his eye and a loose grin.

CROFTS [*suddenly becoming anxious and urgent as he sees no sign of sympathy in her*] Look here, Kitty: youre a sensible woman: you neednt put on any moral airs. I'll ask no more questions; and you need answer none. I'll settle the whole property on her; and if you want a cheque for your-self on the wedding day, you can name any figure you like – in reason.

MRS WARREN. So it's come to that with you, George, like all the other worn-out old creatures!

CROFTS [*savagely*] Damn you!

Before she can retort the door of the kitchen is opened; and the voices of the others are heard returning. Crofts, unable to recover his presence of mind, hurries out of the cottage. The clergyman appears at the kitchen door.

REV. S. [*looking round*] Where is Sir George?

MRS WARREN. Gone out to have a pipe. [*The clergyman takes his hat from the table, and joins Mrs Warren at the fireside.*

Meanwhile Vivie comes in, followed by Frank, who collapses into the nearest chair with an air of extreme exhaustion. Mrs Warren looks round at Vivie and says, with her affection of maternal patronage even more forced than usual] Well, dearie: have you had a good supper?

VIVIE. You know what Mrs Alison's suppers are. *[She turns to Frank and pets him].* Poor Frank! was all the beef gone? did it get nothing but bread and cheese and ginger beer? *[Seriously, as if she had done quite enough trifling for one evening]* Her butter is really awful. I must get some down from the stores.

FRANK. Do, in Heaven's name!

Vivie goes to the writing-table and makes a memorandum to order the butter. Praed comes in from the kitchen, putting up his handkerchief. which he has been using as a napkin.

REV. S. Frank, my boy: it is time for us to be thinking of home. Your mother does not know yet that we have visitors.

PRAED. I'm afraid we're giving trouble.

FRANK *[rising]* Not the least in the world: my mother will be delighted to see you. She's a genuinely intellectual artistic woman; and she sees nobody here from one year's end to another except the gov'nor; so you can imagine how jolly dull it pans out for her. *[To his father]* Youre not intellectual or artistic: are you, pater? So take Praed home at once; and I'll stay here and entertain Mrs Warren. Youll pick up Crofts in the garden. He'll be excellent company for the bull-pup.

PRAED *[taking his hat from the dresser, and coming close to Frank]* Come with us, Frank. Mrs Warren has not seen Miss Vivie for a long time; and we have prevented them from having a moment together yet.

FRANK *[quite softened and looking at Praed with romantic admiration]* Of course. I forgot. Ever so thanks for reminding me. Perfect gentleman, Praddy. Always were. My ideal through life. *[He rises to go, but pauses a moment between the two older men, and puts his hand on Praed's shoulder*]. Ah, if you had only been my father instead of this unworthy old man! [*He puts his other hand on his father's shoulder*].

REV. S. [*blustering*] Silence, sir, silence: you are profane.

MRS WARREN [*laughing heartily*] You should keep him in better order, Sam. Goodnight. Here: take George his hat and stick with my compliments.

REV. S. [*taking them*] Goodnight. [*They shake hands. As he passes Vivie he shakes hands with her also and bids her goodnight. Then, in booming command, to Frank*] Come along, sir, at once. [*He goes out*].

MRS WARREN. Byebye, Praddy.

PRAED. Byebye, Kitty.

They shake hands affectionately and go out together, she accompanying him to the garden gate.

FRANK [*to Vivie*] Kissums?

VIVIE [*fiercely*] No. I hate you. [*She takes a couple of books and some paper from the writing-table, and sits down with them at the middle table, at the end next the fireplace*].

FRANK [*grimacing*] Sorry. [*He goes for his cap and rifle. Mrs Warren returns. He takes her hand*] Goodnight, dear Mrs Warren. [*He kisses her hand. She snatches it away, her lips tightening, and looks more than half disposed to box his ears. He laughs mischievously and runs off, clapping-to the door behind him*].

MRS WARREN [*resigning herself to an evening of boredom now that the men are gone*] Did you ever in your life hear anyone rattle on so? Isnt he a tease? [*She sits at the table*]. Now that I think of it, dearie, dont you go encouraging him. I'm sure he's a regular good-for-nothing.

VIVIE [*rising to fetch more books*] I'm afraid so. Poor Frank! I shall have to get rid of him; but I shall feel sorry for him, though he's not worth it. That man Crofts does not seem to me to be good for much either: is he? [*She throws the books on the table rather roughly*].

MRS WARREN [*galled by Vivie's indifference*] What do you know of men, child, to talk that way about them? Youll have to make up your mind to see a good deal of Sir George Crofts, as he's a friend of mine.

VIVIE [*quite unmoved*] Why? [*She sits down and opens a book*]. Do you expect that we shall be much together? You and I, I mean?

MRS WARREN [*staring at her*] Of course: until youre married. Youre not going back to college again.

VIVIE. Do you think my way of life would suit you? I doubt it.

MRS WARREN. Your way of life! What do you mean?

VIVIE [*cutting a page of her book with the paper knife on her chatelaine*] Has it really never occurred to you, mother, that I have a way of life like other people?

MRS WARREN. What nonsense is this youre trying to talk? Do you want to shew your independence, now that youre a great little person at school? Dont be a fool, child.

VIVIE [*indulgently*] Thats all you have to say on the subject, is it, mother?

MRS WARREN [*puzzled, then angry*] Dont you keep on asking me questions like that. [*Violently*] Hold your tongue. [*Vivie works on, losing no time, and saying nothing*]. You and your way of life, indeed! What next? [*She looks at Vivie again. No reply*]. Your way of life will be what I please, so it will. [*Another pause*]. Ive been noticing these airs in you ever since you got that tripos or whatever you call it. If you think I'm going to put up with them youre mistaken; and the sooner you find it out, the better. [*Muttering*] All I have to say on the subject, indeed! [*Again raising her voice angrily*] Do you know who youre speaking to, Miss?

VIVIE. [*looking across at her without raising her head from her book*] No. Who are you? What are you?

MRS WARREN [*rising breathless*] You young imp!

VIVIE. Everybody knows my reputation, my social standing, and the profession I intend to pursue. I know nothing about you. What is that way of life which you invite me to share with you and Sir George Crofts, pray?

243

MRS WARREN. Take care. I shall do something I'll be sorry for after, and you too.

VIVIE [*putting aside her books with cool decision*] Well, let us drop the subject until you are better able to face it. [*Looking critically at her mother*] You want some good walks and a little lawn tennis to set you up. You are shockingly out of condition: you were not able to manage twenty yards uphill today without stopping to pant; and your wrists are mere rolls of fat. Look at mine. [*She holds out her wrists*].

MRS WARREN [*after looking at her helplessly, begins to whimper*] Vivie –

VIVIE [*springing up sharply*] Now pray dont begin to cry. Anything but that. I really cannot stand whimpering. I will go out of the room if you do.

MRS WARREN [*piteously*] Oh, my darling, how can you be so hard on me? Have I no rights over you as your mother?

VIVIE. Are you my mother?

MRS WARREN [*appalled*] Am I your mother! Oh, Vivie!

VIVIE. Then where are our relatives? my father? our family friends? You claim the rights of a mother: the right to call me fool and child; to speak to me as no woman in authority over me at college dare speak to me; to dictate my way of life; and to force on me the acquaintance of a brute whom any one can see to be the most vicious sort of London man about town. Before I give myself the trouble to resist such claims, I may as well find out whether they have any real existence.

MRS WARREN [*distracted, throwing herself on her knees*] Oh no, no. Stop, stop. I am your mother: I swear it. Oh, you cant mean to turn on me – my own child! it's not natural. You believe me, dont you? Say you believe me.

VIVIE. Who was my father?

MRS WARREN. You dont know what youre asking. I cant tell you.

VIVIE [*determinedly*] Oh yes you can, if you like. I have a right to know; and you know very well that I have that right. You can refuse to tell me, if you please; but if you do, you will see the last of me tomorrow morning.

MRS WARREN. Oh, it's too horrible to hear you talk like that. You wouldnt – you couldnt leave me.

VIVIE [*ruthlessly*] Yes, without a moment's hesitation, if you trifle with me about this. [*Shivering with disgust*] How can I feel sure that I may not have the contaminated blood of that brutal waster in my veins?

MRS WARREN. No, no. On my oath it's not he, nor any of the rest that you have ever met. I'm certain of that, at least.

Vivie's eyes fasten sternly on her mother as the significance of this flashes on her.

VIVIE [*slowly*] You are certain of that, at least. Ah! You mean that that is all you are certain of. [*Thoughtfully*] I see. [*Mrs Warren buries her face in her hands*]. Dont do that, mother: you know you dont feel it a bit. [*Mrs Warren takes down her hands and looks up deplorably at Vivie, who takes out her watch and says*] Well, that is enough for tonight. At what hour would you like breakfast? Is half-past eight too early for you?

MRS WARREN [*wildly*] My God, what sort of woman are you?

VIVIE [*coolly*] The sort the world is mostly made of, I should hope. Otherwise I dont understand how it gets its business done. Come [*taking her mother by the wrist, and pulling her up pretty resolutely*]: pull yourself together. Thats right.

MRS WARREN [*querulously*] Youre very rough with me, Vivie.

VIVIE. Nonsense. What about bed? It's past ten.

MRS WARREN [*passionately*] Whats the use of my going to bed? Do you think I could sleep?

VIVIE. Why not? I shall.

MRS WARREN. You! youve no heart. [*She suddenly breaks out vehemently in her natural tongue – the dialect of a woman of the people – with all her affectations of maternal authority and conventional manners gone, and an overwhelming inspiration of true conviction and scorn in her*] Oh, I wont bear it: I wont put up with the injustice of it. What right have you to set yourself up above me like this? You boast of what you are to me – to me, who gave you the chance of being what you are. What chance had I? Shame on you for a bad daughter and a stuck-up prude!

VIVIE [*sitting down with a shrug, no longer confident; for her replies, which have sounded sensible and strong to her so far, now begin to ring rather woodenly and even priggishly against the new tone of her mother*] Dont think for a moment I set myself above you in any way. You attacked me with the conventional authority of a mother: I defended myself with the conventional superiority of a respectable woman. Frankly, I am not going to stand any of your nonsense; and when you drop it I shall not expect you to stand any of mine. I shall always respect your right to your own opinions and your own way of life.

MRS WARREN. My own opinions and my own way of life! Listen to her talking! Do you think I was brought up like you? able to pick and choose my own way of life? Do you think I did what I did because I liked it, or thought it right, or wouldnt rather have gone to college and been a lady if I'd had the chance?

VIVIE. Everybody has some choice, mother. The poorest girl alive may not be able to choose between being Queen of England or Principal of Newnham; but she can choose between ragpicking and flowerselling, according to her taste. People are always blaming their circumstances for what they are. I dont believe in circumstances. The people who get on in this world are the people who get up and look for the circumstances they want, and, if they cant find them, make them.

MRS WARREN. Oh, it's easy to talk, very easy, isnt it? Here! would you like to know what my circumstances were?

VIVIE. Yes: you had better tell me. Wont you sit down?

MRS WARREN. Oh, I'll sit down: dont you be afraid. [*She plants her chair farther forward with brazen energy, and sits down. Vivie is impressed in spite of herself*]. D'you know what your gran'mother was?

VIVIE. No.

MRS WARREN. No, you dont. I do. She called herself a widow and had a fried-fish shop down by the Mint, and kept herself and four daughters out of it. Two of us were sisters: that was me and Liz; and we were both good-looking and well made. I suppose our father was a well-fed man: mother pretended he was a gentleman; but I dont know. The other two were only half sisters: undersized, ugly, starved looking, hard working, honest poor creatures: Liz and I would have half-murdered them if mother hadnt half-murdered u s to keep our hands off them. They were the respectable ones. Well, what did they get by their respectability? I'll tell you. One of them worked in a whitelead factory twelve hours a day for nine shillings a week until she died of lead poisoning. She only expected to get her hands a little paralyzed; but she died. The other was always held up to us as a model because she married a Government laborer in the Deptford victualling yard, and kept his room and the three children neat and tidy on eighteen shillings a week – until he took to drink. That was worth being respectable for, wasnt it?

VIVIE [*now thoughtfully attentive*] Did you and your sister think so?

MRS WARREN. Liz didnt, I can tell you: she had more spirit. We both went to a church school – that was part of the ladylike airs we gave ourselves to be superior to the children that knew nothing and went nowhere – and we stayed there until Liz went out one night and never came back. I know the schoolmistress thought I'd soon follow her example; for the clergyman was always warning me that Lizzie'd end by jumping off Waterloo Bridge. Poor fool: that was all he knew about it! But I was more afraid

of the whitelead factory than I was of the river; and so
would you have been in my place. That clergyman got me
a situation as scullery maid in a temperance restaurant
where they sent out for anything you liked. Then I was
waitress; and then I went to the bar at Waterloo station:
fourteen hours a day serving drinks and washing glasses for
four shillings a week and my board. That was considered
a great promotion for me. Well, one cold, wretched night,
when I was so tired I could hardly keep myself awake, who
should come up for a half of Scotch but Lizzie, in a long fur
cloak, elegant and comfortable, with a lot of sovereigns in
her purse.

VIVIE [*grimly*] My aunt Lizzie!

MRS WARREN. Yes; and a very good aunt to have, too.
She's living down at Winchester now, close to the cathedral, one of the most respectable ladies there. Chaperones
girls at the county ball, if you please. No river for Liz,
thank you! You remind me of Liz a little: she was a first-
rate business woman – saved money from the beginning –
never let herself look too like what she was – never lost her
head or threw away a chance. When she saw I'd grown up
good-looking she said to me across the bar 'What are you
doing there, you little fool? wearing out your health and
your appearance for other people's profit!' Liz was saving
money then to take a house for herself in Brussels; and she
thought we two could save faster than one. So she lent me
some money and gave me a start; and I saved steadily and
first paid her back, and then went into business with her
as her partner. Why shouldnt I have done it? The house in
Brussels was real high class: a much better place for a
woman to be in than the factory where Anne Jane got
poisoned. None of our girls were ever treated as I was
treated in the scullery of that temperance place, or at the
Waterloo bar, or at home. Would you have had me stay in
them and become a worn out old drudge before I was forty?

VIVIE [*intensely interested by this time*] No; but why did you

MRS WARREN'S PROFESSION

choose that business? Saving money and good management will succeed in any business.

MRS WARREN. Yes, saving money. But where can a woman
get the money to save in any other business? Could you
save out of four shillings a week and keep yourself dressed
as well? Not you. Of course, if youre a plain woman and
cant earn anything more; or if you have a turn for music,
or the stage, or newspaper-writing: thats different. But
neither Liz nor I had any turn for such things: all we had
was our appearance and our turn for pleasing men. Do
you think we were such fools as to let other people trade
in our good looks by employing us as shopgirls, or bar-
maids, or waitresses, when we could trade in them ourselves and get all the profits instead of starvation wages?
Not likely.

VIVIE. You were certainly quite justified – from the business
point of view.

MRS WARREN. Yes; or any other point of view. What is any
respectable girl brought up to do but to catch some rich
man's fancy and get the benefit of his money by marrying
him? – as if a marriage ceremony could make any difference in the right or wrong of the thing! Oh, the hypocrisy
of the world makes me sick! Liz and I had to work and
save and calculate just like other people; elseways we
should be as poor as any good-for-nothing drunken waster
of a woman that thinks her luck will last for ever. [*With great
energy*] I despise such people: theyve no character; and if
theres a thing I hate in a woman, its want of character.

VIVIE. Come now, mother: frankly! Isnt it part of what you
call character in a woman that she should greatly dislike
such a way of making money?

MRS WARREN. Why, of course. Everybody dislikes having
to work and make money; but they have to do it all the
same. I'm sure Ive often pitied a poor girl, tired out and
in low spirits, having to try to please some man that she
doesnt care two straws for – some half-drunken fool that

thinks he's making himself agreeable when he's teasing and worrying and disgusting a woman so that hardly any money could pay her for putting up with it. But she has to bear with disagreeables and take the rough with the smooth, just like a nurse in a hospital or anyone else. It's not work that any woman would do for pleasure, goodness knows; though to hear the pious people talk you would suppose it was a bed of roses.

VIVIE. Still, you consider it worth while. It pays.

MRS WARREN. Of course it's worth while to a poor girl, if she can resist temptation and is good-looking and well conducted and sensible. It's far better than any other employment open to her. I always thought that oughtnt to be. It cant be right, Vivie, that there shouldnt be better opportunities for women. I stick to that: it's wrong. But it's so, right or wrong; and a girl must make the best of it. But of course it's not worth while for a lady. If you took to it youd be a fool; but I should have been a fool if I'd taken to anything else.

VIVIE [*more and more deeply moved*] Mother: suppose we were both as poor as you were in those wretched old days, are you quite sure that you wouldnt advise me to try the Waterloo bar, or marry a laborer, or even go into the factory?

MRS WARREN [*indignantly*] Of course not. What sort of mother do you take me for! How could you keep your self-respect in such starvation and slavery? And whats a woman worth? whats life worth? without self-respect! Why am I independent and able to give my daughter a first-rate education, when other women that had just as good opportunities are in the gutter? Because I always knew how to respect myself and control myself. Why is Liz looked up to in a cathedral town? The same reason. Where would we be now if we'd minded the clergyman's foolishness? Scrubbing floors for one and sixpence a day and nothing to look forward to but the workhouse infirmary.

Dont you be led astray by people who dont know the world, my girl. The only way for a woman to provide for herself decently is for her to be good to some man that can afford to be good to her. If she's in his own station of life, let her make him marry her; but if she's far beneath him she cant expect it: why should she? it wouldnt be for her own happiness. Ask any lady in London society that has daughters; and she'll tell you the same, except that I tell you straight and she'll tell you crooked. Thats all the difference.

VIVIE [*fascinated, gazing at her*] My dear mother: you are a wonderful woman: you are stronger than all England. And are you really and truly not one wee bit doubtful – or – or – ashamed?

MRS WARREN. Well, of course, dearie, it's only good manners to be ashamed of it: it's expected from a woman. Women have to pretend to feel a great deal that they dont feel. Liz used to be angry with me for plumping out the truth about it. She used to say that when every woman could learn enough from what was going on in the world before her eyes, there was no need to talk about it to her. But then Liz was such a perfect lady! She had the true instinct of it; while I was always a bit of a vulgarian. I used to be so pleased when you sent me your photos to see that you were growing up like Liz: youve just her ladylike, determined way. But I cant stand saying one thing when everyone knows I mean another. Whats the use in such hypocrisy? If people arrange the world that way for women, theres no good pretending it's arranged the other way. No: I never was a bit ashamed really. I consider I had a right to be proud of how we managed everything so respectably, and never had a word against us, and how the girls were so well taken care of. Some of them did very well: one of them married an ambassador. But of course now I darent talk about such things: whatever would they think of us! [*She yawns*]. Oh dear! I do believe I'm getting sleepy after all. [*She stretches herself lazily, thoroughly relieved by her explosion, and placidly ready for her night's rest*].

VIVIE. I believe it is I who will not be able to sleep now. [*She goes to the dresser and lights the candle. Then she extinguishes the lamp, darkening the room a good deal*]. Better let in some fresh air before locking up. [*She opens the cottage door, and finds that it is broad moonlight*]. What a beautiful night! Look! [*She draws aside the curtains of the window. The landscape is seen bathed in the radiance of the harvest moon rising over Blackdown*].

MRS WARREN [*with a perfunctory glance at the scene*] Yes, dear; but take care you dont catch your death of cold from the night air.

VIVIE [*contemptuously*] Nonsense.

MRS WARREN [*querulously*] Oh yes: everything I say is nonsense, according to you.

VIVIE [*turning to her quickly*] No: really that is not so, mother. You have got completely the better of me tonight, though I intended it to be the other way. Let us be good friends now.

MRS WARREN [*shaking her head a little ruefully*] So it has been the other way. But I suppose I must give in to it. I always got the worst of it from Liz; and now I suppose it'll be the same with you.

VIVIE. Well, never mind. Come: goodnight, dear old mother. [*She takes her mother in her arms*].

MRS WARREN [*fondly*] I brought you up well, didnt I, dearie?

VIVIE. You did.

MRS WARREN. And youll be good to your poor old mother for it, wont you?

VIVIE. I will, dear. [*Kissing her*] Goodnight.

MRS WARREN [*with unction*] Blessings on my own dearie darling! a mother's blessing!

> *She embraces her daughter protectingly, instinctively looking upward for divine sanction.*

ACT III

In the Rectory garden next morning, with the sun shining from a cloudless sky. The garden wall has a five-barred wooden gate, wide enough to admit a carriage, in the middle. Beside the gate hangs a bell on a coiled spring, communicating with a pull outside. The carriage drive comes down the middle of the garden and then swerves to its left, where it ends in a little gravelled circus opposite the Rectory porch. Beyond the gate is seen the dusty high road, parallel with the wall, bounded on the farther side by a strip of turf and an unfenced pine wood. On the lawn, between the house and the drive, is a clipped yew tree, with a garden bench in its shade. On the opposite side the garden is shut in by a box hedge; and there is a sundial on the turf, with an iron chair near it. A little path leads off through the box hedge, behind the sundial.

Frank, seated on the chair near the sundial, on which he has placed the morning papers, is reading The Standard. His father comes from the house, red-eyed and shivery, and meets Frank's eye with misgiving.

FRANK [*looking at his watch*] Half-past eleven. Nice hour for a rector to come down to breakfast!

REV. s. Dont mock, Frank: dont mock. I am a little – er – [*Shivering*] –

FRANK. Off color?

REV. s. [*repudiating the expression*] No, sir: unwell this morning. Wheres your mother?

FRANK. Dont be alarmed: she's not here. Gone to town by the 11.13 with Bessie. She left several messages for you. Do you feel equal to receiving them now, or shall I wait til youve breakfasted?

REV. s. I have breakfasted, sir. I am surprised at your mother going to town when we have people staying with us. Theyll think it very strange.

FRANK. Possibly she has considered that. At all events, if Crofts is going to stay here, and you are going to sit up every night with him until four, recalling the incidents of your fiery youth, it is clearly my mother's duty, as a prudent housekeeper, to go up to the stores and order a barrel of whisky and a few hundred siphons.

REV. S. I did not observe that Sir George drank excessively.

FRANK. You were not in a condition to, gov'nor.

REV. S. Do you mean to say that *I* – ?

FRANK [*calmly*] I never saw a beneficed clergyman less sober. The anecdotes you told about your past career were so awful that I really dont think Praed would have passed the night under your roof if it hadnt been for the way my mother and he took to one another.

REV. S. Nonsense, sir. I am Sir George Crofts' host. I must talk to him about something; and he has only one subject. Where is Mr Praed now?

FRANK. He is driving my mother and Bessie to the station.

REV. S. Is Crofts up yet?

FRANK. Oh, long ago. He hasnt turned a hair: he's in much better practice than you. He has kept it up ever since, probably. He's taken himself off somewhere to smoke.

Frank resumes his paper. The parson turns disconsolately towards the gate; then comes back irresolutely.

REV. S. Er – Frank.

FRANK. Yes.

REV. S. Do you think the Warrens will expect to be asked here after yesterday afternoon?

FRANK. Theyve been asked already.

REV. S. [*appalled*] What! ! !

FRANK. Crofts informed us at breakfast that you told him to bring Mrs Warren and Vivie over here today, and to invite them to make this house their home. My mother then found she must go to town by the 11.13 train.

REV. S. [*with despairing vehemence*] I never gave any such invitation. I never thought of such a thing.

FRANK [*compassionately*] How do you know, gov'nor, what you said and thought last night?

254

PRAED [*coming in through the hedge*] Good morning.

REV. S. Good morning. I must apologise for not having met you at breakfast. I have a touch of – of –

FRANK. Clergyman's sore throat, Praed. Fortunately not chronic.

PRAED [*changing the subject*] Well, I must say your house is in a charming spot here. Really most charming.

REV. S. Yes: it is indeed. Frank will take you for a walk, Mr Praed, if you like. I'll ask you to excuse me: I must take the opportunity to write my sermon while Mrs Gardner is away and you are all amusing yourselves. You wont mind, will you?

PRAED. Certainly not. Dont stand on the slightest ceremony with me.

REV. S. Thank you. I'll – er – er – [*He stammers his way to the porch and vanishes into the house*].

PRAED. Curious thing it must be writing a sermon every week.

FRANK. Ever so curious, if he did it. He buys em. He's gone for some soda water.

PRAED. My dear boy: I wish you would be more respectful to your father. You know you can be so nice when you like.

FRANK. My dear Praddy: you forget that I have to live with the governor. When two people live together – it dont matter whether theyre father and son or husband and wife or brother and sister – they cant keep up the polite humbug thats so easy for ten minutes on an afternoon call. Now the governor, who unites to many admirable domestic qualities the irresoluteness of a sheep and the pompousness and aggressiveness of a jackass –

PRAED. No, pray, pray, my dear Frank, remember! He is your father.

FRANK. I give him due credit for that. [*Rising and flinging down his paper*] But just imagine his telling Crofts to bring the Warrens over here! He must have been ever so drunk. You know, my dear Praddy, my mother wouldnt stand

Mrs Warren for a moment. Vivie mustnt come here until she's gone back to town.

PRAED. But your mother doesnt know anything about Mrs Warren, does she? [*He picks up the paper and sits down to read it*].

FRANK. I dont know. Her journey to town looks as if she did. Not that my mother would mind in the ordinary way: she has stuck like a brick to lots of women who had got into trouble. But they were all nice women. Thats what makes the real difference. Mrs Warren, no doubt, has her merits; but she's ever so rowdy; and my mother simply wouldnt put up with her. So – hallo! [*This exclamation is provoked by the reappearance of the clergyman, who comes out of the house in haste and dismay*].

REV. S. Frank: Mrs Warren and her daughter are coming across the heath with Crofts: I saw them from the study windows. What am I to say about your mother?

FRANK. Stick on your hat and go out and say how delighted you are to see them; and that Frank's in the garden; and that mother and Bessie have been called to the bedside of a sick relative, and were ever so sorry they couldnt stop; and that you hope Mrs Warren slept well; and – and – say any blessed thing except the truth, and leave the rest to Providence.

REV. S. But how are we to get rid of them afterwards?

FRANK. Theres no time to think of that now. Here! [*He bounds into the house*].

REV. S. He's so impetuous. I dont know what to do with him, Mr Praed.

FRANK [*returning with a clerical felt hat, which he claps on his father's head*] Now: off with you. [*Rushing him through the gate*]. Praed and I'll wait here, to give the thing an unpremeditated air. [*The clergyman, dazed but obedient, hurries off*].

FRANK. We must get the old girl back to town somehow, Praed. Come! Honestly, dear Praddy, do you like seeing them together?

PRAED. Oh, why not?

FRANK [*his teeth on edge*] Dont it make your flesh creep ever so little? that wicked old devil, up to every villainy under the sun, I'll swear, and Vivie – ugh!

PRAED. Hush, pray. Theyre coming.

The clergyman and Crofts are seen coming along the road, followed by Mrs Warren and Vivie walking affectionately together.

FRANK. Look: she actually has her arm round the old woman's waist. It's her right arm: she began it. Shè's gone sentimental, by God! Ugh! ugh! Now do you feel the creeps? [*The clergyman opens the gate; and Mrs Warren and Vivie pass him and stand in the middle of the garden looking at the house. Frank, in an ecstasy of dissimulation, turns gaily to Mrs Warren, exclaiming*] Ever so delighted to see you, Mrs Warren. This quiet old rectory garden becomes you perfectly.

MRS WARREN. Well, I never! Did you hear that, George? He says I look well in a quiet old rectory garden.

REV. S. [*still holding the gate for Crofts, who loafs through it, heavily bored*] You look well everywhere, Mrs Warren.

FRANK. Bravo, gov'nor! Now look here: lets have a treat before lunch. First lets see the church. Everyone has to do that. It's a regular old thirteenth century church, you know: the gov'nor's ever so fond of it, because he got up a restoration fund and had it completely rebuilt six years ago. Praed will be able to shew its points.

PRAED [*rising*] Certainly, if the restoration has left any to shew.

REV. S. [*mooning hospitably at them*] I shall be pleased, I'm sure, if Sir George and Mrs Warren really care about it.

MRS WARREN. Oh, come along and get it over.

CROFTS [*turning back towards the gate*] Ive no objection.

REV. S. Not that way. We go through the fields, if you dont mind. Round here. [*He leads the way by the little path through the box hedge*].

CROFTS. Oh, all right. [*He goes with the parson*].

Praed follows with Mrs Warren. Vivie does not stir: she watches them until they have gone, with all the lines of purpose in her face marking it strongly.

FRANK. Aint you coming?

VIVIE. No. I want to give you a warning, Frank. You were making fun of my mother just now when you said that about the rectory garden. That is barred in future. Please treat my mother with as much respect as you treat your own.

FRANK. My dear Viv: she wouldnt appreciate it: the two cases require different treatment. But what on earth has happened to you? Last night we were perfectly agreed as to your mother and her set. This morning I find you attitudinizing sentimentally with your arm round your parent's waist.

VIVIE [*flushing*] Attitudinizing!

FRANK. That was how it struck me. First time I ever saw you do a second-rate thing.

VIVIE [*controlling herself*] Yes, Frank: there has been a change; but I dont think it a change for the worse. Yesterday I was a little prig.

FRANK. And today?

VIVIE [*wincing; then looking at him steadily*] Today I know my mother better than you do.

FRANK. Heaven forbid!

VIVIE. What do you mean?

FRANK. Viv: theres a freemasonry among thoroughly immoral people that you know nothing of. Youve too much character. Thats the bond between your mother and me: thats why I know her better than youll ever know her.

VIVIE. You are wrong: you know nothing about her. If you knew the circumstances against which my mother had to struggle –

FRANK [*adroitly finishing the sentence for her*] I should know why she is what she is, shouldnt I? What difference would that make? Circumstances or no circumstances, Viv, you wont be able to stand your mother.

VIVIE [*very angrily*] Why not?

FRANK. Because she's an old wretch, Viv. If you ever put
your arm round her waist in my presence again, I'll shoot
myself there and then as a protest against an exhibition
which revolts me.

VIVIE. Must I choose between dropping your acquaintance
and dropping my mother's?

FRANK [*gracefully*] That would put the old lady at ever such
a disadvantage. No, Viv; your infatuated little boy will
have to stick to you in any case. But he's all the more
anxious that you shouldnt make mistakes. It's no use, Viv:
your mother's impossible. She may be a good sort; but
she's a bad lot, a very bad lot.

VIVIE [*hotly*] Frank – ! [*He stands his ground. She turns away
and sits down on the bench under the yew tree, struggling to recover
her self-command. Then she says*] Is she to be deserted by all
the world because she's what you call a bad lot? Has she
no right to live?

FRANK. No fear of that, Viv: she wont ever be deserted.
[*He sits on the bench beside her*].

VIVIE. But I am to desert her, I suppose.

FRANK [*babyishly, lulling her and making love to her with his
voice*] Musnt go live with her. Little family group of mother
and daughter wouldnt be a success. Spoil our little group.

VIVIE [*falling under the spell*] What little group?

FRANK. The babes in the wood: Vivie and little Frank. [*He
nestles against her like a weary child*]. Lets go and get
covered up with leaves.

VIVIE [*rhythmically, rocking him like a nurse*] Fast asleep, hand
in hand, under the trees.

FRANK. The wise little girl with her silly little boy.

VIVIE. The dear little boy with his dowdy little girl.

FRANK. Ever so peaceful, and relieved from the imbecility
of the little boy's father and the questionableness of the
little girl's –

VIVIE [*smothering the word against her breast*] Sh-sh-sh-sh! little girl wants to forget all about her mother. [*They are silent for some moments, rocking one another. Then Vivie wakes up with a shock, exclaiming*] What a pair of fools we are! Come: sit up. Gracious! your hair. [*She smooths it*]. I wonder do all grown up people play in that childish way when nobody is looking. I never did it when I was a child.

FRANK. Neither did I. You are my first playmate. [*He catches her hand to kiss it, but checks himself to look round first. Very unexpectedly, he sees Crofts emerging from the box hedge*]. Oh damn!

VIVIE. Why damn, dear?

FRANK [*whispering*] Sh! Heres this brute Crofts. [*He sits farther away from her with an unconcerned air*].

CROFTS. Could I have a few words with you, Miss Vivie?

VIVIE. Certainly.

CROFTS [*to Frank*] Youll excuse me, Gardner. Theyre waiting for you in the church, if you dont mind.

FRANK [*rising*] Anything to oblige you, Crofts – except church. If you should happen to want me, Vivvums, ring the gate bell. [*He goes into the house with unruffled suavity*].

CROFTS [*watching him with a crafty air as he disappears, and speaking to Vivie with an assumption of being on privileged terms with her*] Pleasant young fellow that, Miss Vivie. Pity he has no money, isnt it?

VIVIE. Do you think so?

CROFTS. Well, whats he to do? No profession. No property. Whats he good for?

VIVIE. I realize his disadvantages, Sir George.

CROFTS [*a little taken aback at being so precisely interpreted*] Oh, it's not that. But while we're in this world we're in it; and money's money. [*Vivie does not answer*]. Nice day, isnt it?

VIVIE [*with scarcely veiled contempt for this effort at conversation*] Very.

CROFTS [*with brutal good humor, as if he liked her pluck*] Well, thats not what I came to say. [*Sitting down beside her*] Now listen, Miss Vivie. I'm quite aware that I'm not a young lady's man.

VIVIE. Indeed, Sir George?

CROFTS. No; and to tell you the honest truth I dont want to be either. But when I say a thing I mean it; when I feel a sentiment I feel it in earnest; and what I value I pay hard money for. Thats the sort of man I am.

VIVIE. It does you great credit, I'm sure.

CROFTS. Oh, I dont mean to praise myself. I have my faults, Heaven knows: no man is more sensible of that than I am. I know I'm not perfect; thats one of the advantages of being a middle-aged man; for I'm not a young man, and I know it. But my code is a simple one, and, I think, a good one. Honor between man and man; fidelity between man and woman; and no cant about this religion or that religion, but an honest belief that things are making for good on the whole.

VIVIE [*with biting irony*] 'A power, not ourselves, that makes for righteousness', eh?

CROFTS [*taking her seriously*] Oh certainly. Not ourselves, of course. You understand what I mean. Well, now as to practical matters. You may have an idea that Ive flung my money about; but I havnt: I'm richer today than when I first came into the property. Ive used my knowledge of the world to invest my money in ways that other men have overlooked; and whatever else I may be, I'm a safe man from the money point of view.

VIVIE. It's very kind of you to tell me all this.

CROFTS. Oh well, come, Miss Vivie: you neednt pretend you dont see what I'm driving at. I want to settle down with a Lady Crofts. I suppose you think me very blunt, eh?

VIVIE. Not at all: I am much obliged to you for being so definite and business-like. I quite appreciate the offer: the money, the position, Lady Crofts and so on. But I think I will say no, if you dont mind. I'd rather not. [*She rises, and strolls across to the sundial to get out of his immediate neighborhood*].

CROFTS [*not at all discouraged, and taking advantage of the addi-*

261

tional room left him on the seat to spread himself comfortably, as if a few preliminary refusals were part of the inevitable routine of courtship] I'm in no hurry. It was only just to let you know in case young Gardner should try to trap you. Leave the question open.

VIVIE [*sharply*] My no is final. I wont go back from it.

Crofts is not impressed. He grins; leans forward with his elbows on his knees to prod with his stick at some unfortunate insect in the grass; and looks cunningly at her. She turns away impatiently.

CROFTS. I'm a good deal older than you. Twenty-five years: quarter of a century. I shant live for ever; and I'll take care that you shall be well off when I'm gone.

VIVIE. I am proof against even that inducement, Sir George. Dont you think youd better take your answer? There is not the slightest chance of my altering it.

CROFTS [*rising, after a final slash at a daisy, and coming nearer to her*] Well, no matter. I could tell you some things that would change your mind fast enough; but I wont, because I'd rather win you by honest affection. I was a good friend to your mother: ask her whether I wasnt. She'd never have made the money that paid for your education if it hadnt been for my advice and help, not to mention the money I advanced her. There are not many men would have stood by her as I have. I put not less than £40,000 into it, from first to last.

VIVIE [*staring at him*] Do you mean to say you were my mother's business partner?

CROFTS. Yes. Now just think of all the trouble and the explanations it would save if we were to keep the whole thing in the family, so to speak. Ask your mother whether she'd like to have to explain all her affairs to a perfect stranger.

VIVIE. I see no difficulty, since I understand that the business is wound up, and the money invested.

CROFTS [*stopping short, amazed*] Wound up! Wind up a business thats paying 35 per cent in the worst years! Not likely. Who told you that?

VIVIE [*her color quite gone*] Do you mean that it is still – ? [*She stops abruptly, and puts her hand on the sundial to support herself. Then she gets quickly to the iron chair and sits down*]. What business are you talking about?

CROFTS. Well, the fact is it's not what would be considered exactly a high-class business in my set – the county set, you know – our set it will be if you think better of my offer. Not that theres any mystery about it: dont think that. Of course you know by your mother's being in it that it's perfectly straight and honest. Ive known her for many years; and I can say of her that she'd cut off her hands sooner than touch anything that was not what it ought to be. I'll tell you all about it if you like. I dont know whether youve found in travelling how hard it is to find a really comfortable private hotel.

VIVIE [*sickened, averting her face*] Yes: go on.

CROFTS. Well, thats all it is. Your mother has a genius for managing such things. Weve got two in Brussels, one in Ostend, one in Vienna, and two in Budapest. Of course there are others besides ourselves in it: but we hold most of the capital; and your mother's indispensable as managing director. Youve noticed, I daresay, that she travels a good deal. But you see you cant mention such things in society. Once let out the word hotel and everybody says you keep a public-house. You wouldnt like people to say that of your mother, would you? Thats why we're so reserved about it. By the way, youll keep it to yourself, wont you? Since its been a secret so long, it had better remain so.

VIVIE. And this is the business you invite me to join you in?

CROFTS. Oh no. My wife shant be troubled with business. Youll not be in it more than youve always been.

VIVIE. *I* always been! What do you mean?

CROFTS. Only that youve always lived on it. It paid for your education and the dress you have on your back. Dont turn up your nose at business, Miss Vivie; where would your Newnhams and Girtons be without it?

VIVIE [*rising, almost beside herself*] Take care. I know what this business is.

CROFTS [*starting, with a suppressed oath*] Who told you?

VIVIE. Your partner. My mother.

CROFTS [*black with rage*] The old —

VIVIE. Just so.

> *He swallows the epithet and stands for a moment swearing and raging foully to himself. But he knows that his cue is to be sympathetic. He takes refuge in generous indignation.*

CROFTS. She ought to have had more consideration for you. *I*'d never have told you.

VIVIE. I think you would probably have told me when we were married: it would have been a convenient weapon to break me in with.

CROFTS [*quite sincerely*] I never intended that. On my word as a gentleman I didnt.

> *Vivie wonders at him. Her sense of the irony of his protest cools and braces her. She replies with contemptuous self-possession.*

VIVIE. It does not matter. I suppose you understand that when we leave here today our acquaintance ceases.

CROFTS. Why? Is it for helping your mother?

VIVIE. My mother was a very poor woman who had no reasonable choice but to do as she did. You were a rich gentleman; and you did the same for the sake of 35 per cent. You are a pretty common sort of scoundrel, I think. That is my opinion of you.

CROFTS [*after a stare: not at all displeased, and much more at his ease on these frank terms than on their former ceremonious ones*] Ha! ha! ha! ha! Go it, little missie, go it; it doesnt hurt me and it amuses you. Why the devil shouldnt I invest my money that way? I take the interest on my capital like other people: I hope you dont think I dirty my own hands with the work. Come! you wouldnt refuse the acquaintance of my mother's cousin the Duke of Belgravia because some of the rents he gets are earned in queer ways. You wouldnt cut the Archbishop of Canterbury, I suppose, because the Ecclesiastical Commissioners have a few publicans and sinners among their tenants. Do you remember your Crofts scholarship at Newnham? Well, that was founded by my brother the M.P. He gets his 22 per cent out of a factory with 600 girls in it, and not one of them getting wages enough to live on. How d'ye suppose they manage when they have no family to fall back on? Ask your mother. And do you expect me to turn my back on 35 per cent when all the rest are pocketing what they can, like sensible men? No such fool! If youre going to pick and choose your acquaintances on moral principles, youd better clear out of this country, unless you want to cut yourself out of all decent society.

VIVIE [*conscience stricken*] You might go on to point out that I myself never asked where the money I spent came from. I believe I am just as bad as you.

CROFTS [*greatly reassured*] Of course you are; and a very good thing too! What harm does it do after all? [*Rallying her jocularly*] So you dont think me such a scoundrel now you come to think it over. Eh?

VIVIE. I have shared profits with you; and I admitted you just now to the familiarity of knowing what I think of you.

CROFTS [*with serious friendliness*] To be sure you did. You wont find me a bad sort: I dont go in for being superfine intellectually: but Ive plenty of honest human feeling; and the old Crofts breed comes out in a sort of instinctive hatred of anything low, in which I'm sure youll sympathize with me. Believe me, Miss Vivie, the world isnt such a bad place as the croakers make out. As long as you dont fly openly in the face of society, society doesnt ask any inconvenient questions; and it makes precious short work of the cads who do. There are no secrets better kept than the secrets everybody guesses. In the class of people I can introduce you to, no lady or gentleman would so far forget themselves as to discuss my business affairs or your mother's. No man can offer you a safer position.

VIVIE [*studying him curiously*] I suppose you really think youre getting on famously with me.

CROFTS. Well, I hope I may flatter myself that you think better of me than you did at first.

VIVIE [*quietly*] I hardly find you worth thinking about at all now. When I think of the society that tolerates you, and the laws that protect you! when I think of how helpless nine out of ten young girls would be in the hands of you and my mother! the unmentionable woman and her capitalist bully –

CROFTS [*livid*] Damn you!

VIVIE. You need not. I feel among the damned already.

She raises the latch of the gate to open it and go out. He follows her and puts his hand heavily on the top bar to prevent its opening.

CROFTS [*panting with fury*] Do you think I'll put up with this from you, you young devil?

VIVIE [*unmoved*] Be quiet. Some one will answer the bell. [*Without flinching a step she strikes the bell with the back of her hand. It clangs harshly; and he starts back involuntarily. Almost immediately Frank appears at the porch with his rifle*].

FRANK [*with cheerful politeness*] Will you have the rifle, Viv; or shall I operate?

VIVIE. Frank: have you been listening?

FRANK [*coming down into the garden*] Only for the bell, I assure you; so that you shouldnt have to wait. I think I shewed great insight into your character, Crofts.

CROFTS. For two pins I'd take that gun from you and break it across your head.

FRANK [*stalking him cautiously*] Pray dont. I'm ever so careless in handling firearms. Sure to be a fatal accident, with a reprimand from the coroner's jury for my negligence.

VIVIE. Put the rifle away, Frank; it's quite unnecessary.

FRANK. Quite right, Viv. Much more sportsmanlike to catch him in a trap. [*Crofts, understanding the insult, makes a threatening movement*]. Crofts: there are fifteen cartridges in the magazine here; and I am a dead shot at the present distance and at an object of your size.

CROFTS. Oh, you neednt be afraid. I'm not going to touch you.

FRANK. Ever so magnanimous of you under the circumstances! Thank you!

CROFTS. I'll just tell you this before I go. It may interest you, since youre so fond of one another. Allow me, Mister Frank, to introduce you to your half-sister, the eldest daughter of the Reverend Samuel Gardner. Miss Vivie: your half-brother. Good morning. [*He goes out through the gate along the road*].

FRANK [*after a pause of stupefaction, raising the rifle*] Youll testify before the coroner that it's an accident, Viv. [*He takes aim at the retreating figure of Crofts. Vivie seizes the muzzle and pulls it round against her breast*].

VIVIE. Fire now. You may.

FRANK [*dropping his end of the rifle hastily*] Stop! take care. [*She lets it go. It falls on the turf*]. Oh, youve given your little boy such a turn. Suppose it had gone off! ugh! [*He sinks on the garden seat overcome*].

VIVIE. Suppose it had: do you think it would not have been a relief to have some sharp physical pain tearing through me?

FRANK [*coaxingly*] Take it ever so easy, dear Viv. Remember: even if the rifle scared that fellow into telling the truth for the first time in his life, that only makes us the babes in the wood in earnest. [*He holds out his arms to her*]. Come and be covered up with leaves again.

VIVIE [*with a cry of disgust*] Ah, not that, not that. You make all my flesh creep.

FRANK. Why, whats the matter?

VIVIE. Goodbye. [*She makes for the gate*].

FRANK [*jumping up*] Hallo! Stop! Viv! Viv! [*She turns in the gateway*] Where are you going to? Where shall we find you?

VIVIE. At Honoria Fraser's chambers, 67 Chancery Lane, for the rest of my life. [*She goes off quickly in the opposite direction to that taken by Crofts*].

FRANK. But I say – wait – dash it! [*He runs after her*].

ACT IV

Honoria Fraser's chambers in Chancery Lane. An office at the top of New Stone Buildings, with a plate-glass window, distempered walls, electric light, and a patent stove. Saturday afternoon. The chimneys of Lincoln's Inn and the western sky beyond are seen through the window. There is a double writing table in the middle of the room, with a cigar box, ash pans, and a portable electric reading lamp almost snowed up in heaps of papers and books. This table has knee holes and chairs right and left and is very untidy. The clerk's desk, closed and tidy, with its high stool, is against the wall, near a door communicating with the inner rooms. In the opposite wall is the door leading to the public corridor. Its upper panel is of opaque glass, lettered in black on the outside, FRASER AND WARREN. *A baize screen hides the corner between this door and the window.*

Frank, in a fashionable light-colored coaching suit, with his stick, gloves, and white hat in his hands, is pacing up and down the office. Somebody tries the door with a key.

FRANK [*calling*] Come in. It's not locked.

> *Vivie comes in, in her hat and jacket. She stops and stares at him.*

VIVIE [*sternly*] What are you doing here?

FRANK. Waiting to see you. Ive been here for hours. Is this the way you attend to your business? [*He puts his hat and stick on the table, and perches himself with a vault on the clerk's stool looking at her with every appearance of being in a specially restless, teasing, flippant mood*].

VIVIE. Ive been away exactly twenty minutes for a cup of tea. [*She takes off her hat and jacket and hangs them up behind the screen*]. How did you get in?

FRANK. The staff had not left when I arrived. He's gone to play cricket on Primrose Hill. Why dont you employ a woman, and give your sex a chance?

VIVIE. What have you come for?

FRANK [*springing off the stool and coming close to her*] Viv: lets go and enjoy the Saturday half-holiday somewhere, like

268

the staff. What do you say to Richmond, and then a music hall, and a jolly supper?

VIVIE. Cant afford it. I shall put in another six hours work before I go to bed.

FRANK. Cant afford it, cant we? Aha! Look here. [*He takes out a handful of sovereigns and makes them chink*]. Gold, Viv: gold!

VIVIE. Where did you get it?

FRANK. Gambling, Viv: gambling. Poker.

VIVIE. Pah! It's meaner than stealing it. No: I'm not coming. [*She sits down to work at the table, with her back to the glass door, and begins turning over the papers*].

FRANK [*remonstrating piteously*] But, my dear Viv, I want to talk to you ever so seriously.

VIVIE. Very well: sit down in Honoria's chair and talk here. I like ten minutes chat after tea. [*He murmurs*]. No use groaning: I'm inexorable. [*He takes the opposite seat disconsolately*]. Pass that cigar box, will you?

FRANK [*pushing the cigar box across*] Nasty womanly habit. Nice men dont do it any longer.

VIVIE. Yes: they object to the smell in the office; and weve had to take to cigarets. See! [*She opens the box and takes out a cigaret, which she lights. She offers him one; but he shakes his head with a wry face. She settles herself comfortably in her chair, smoking*]. Go ahead.

FRANK. Well, I want to know what youve done – what arrangements youve made.

VIVIE. Everything was settled twenty minutes after I arrived here. Honoria has found the business too much for her this year; and she was on the point of sending for me and proposing a partnership when I walked in and told her I hadnt a farthing in the world. So I installed myself and packed her off for a fortnight's holiday. What happened at Haslemere when I left?

FRANK. Nothing at all. I said youd gone to town on particular business.

269

VIVIE. Well?

FRANK. Well, either they were too flabbergasted to say anything, or else Crofts had prepared your mother. Anyhow, she didnt say anything; and Crofts didnt say anything; and Praddy only stared. After tea they got up and went; and Ive not seen them since.

VIVIE [*nodding placidly with one eye on a wreath of smoke*] Thats all right.

FRANK [*looking round disparagingly*] Do you intend to stick in this confounded place?

VIVIE [*blowing the wreath decisively away, and sitting straight up*] Yes. These two days have given me back all my strength and self-possession. I will never take a holiday again as long as I live.

FRANK [*with a very wry face*] Mps! You look quite happy. And as hard as nails.

VIVIE [*grimly*] Well for me that I am!

FRANK [*rising*] Look here, Viv: we must have an explanation. We parted the other day under a complete misunderstanding. [*He sits on the table, close to her*].

VIVIE [*putting away the cigaret*] Well: clear it up.

FRANK. You remember what Crofts said?

VIVIE. Yes.

FRANK. That revelation was supposed to bring about a complete change in the nature of our feeling for one another. It placed us on the footing of brother and sister.

VIVIE. Yes.

FRANK. Have you ever had a brother?

VIVIE. No.

FRANK. Then you dont know what being brother and sister feels like? Now I have lots of sisters; and the fraternal feeling is quite familiar to me. I assure you my feeling for you is not the least in the world like it. The girls will go their way; I will go mine; and we shant care if we never see one another again. Thats brother and sister. But as to you, I cant be easy if I have to pass a week without seeing you.

Thats not brother and sister. It's exactly what I felt an hour before Crofts made his revelation. In short, dear Viv, it's love's young dream.

VIVIE [*bitingly*] The same feeling, Frank, that brought your father to my mother's feet. Is that it?

FRANK [*so revolted that he slips off the table for a moment*] I very strongly object, Viv, to have my feelings compared to any which the Reverend Samuel is capable of harboring; and I object still more to a comparison of you to your mother. [*Resuming his perch*]. Besides, I dont believe the story. I have taxed my father with it, and obtained from him what I consider tantamount to a denial.

VIVIE. What did he say?

FRANK. He said he was sure there must be some mistake.

VIVIE. Do you believe him?

FRANK. I am prepared to take his word as against Crofts'.

VIVIE. Does it make any difference? I mean in your imagination or conscience; for of course it makes no real difference.

FRANK [*shaking his head*] None whatever to me.

VIVIE. Nor to me.

FRANK [*staring*] But this is ever so surprising! [*He goes back to his chair*]. I thought our whole relations were altered in your imagination and conscience, as you put it, the moment those words were out of that brute's muzzle.

VIVIE. No: it was not that. I didnt believe him. I only wish I could.

FRANK. Eh?

VIVIE. I think brother and sister would be a very suitable relation for us.

FRANK. You really mean that?

VIVIE. Yes. It's the only relation I care for, even if we could afford any other. I mean that.

FRANK [*raising his eyebrows like one on whom a new light has dawned, and rising with quite an effusion of chivalrous sentiment*]

My dear Viv: why didnt you say so before? I am ever so sorry for persecuting you. I understand, of course.

VIVIE [*puzzled*] Understand what?

FRANK. Oh, I'm not a fool in the ordinary sense: only in the Scriptural sense of doing all the things the wise man declared to be folly, after trying them himself on the most extensive scale. I see I am no longer Vivvum's little boy. Dont be alarmed: I shall never call you Vivvums again – at least unless you get tired of your new little boy, however he may be.

VIVIE. My new little boy!

FRANK [*with conviction*] Must be a new little boy. Always happens that way. No other way, in fact.

VIVIE. None that you know of, fortunately for you.

Someone knocks at the door.

FRANK. My curse upon yon caller, whoe'er he be!

VIVIE. It's Praed. He's going to Italy and wants to say goodbye. I asked him to call this afternoon. Go and let him in.

FRANK. We can continue our conversation after his departure for Italy. I'll stay him out. [*He goes to the door and opens it*]. How are you, Praddy? Delighted to see you. Come in.

Praed, dressed for travelling, comes in, in high spirits.

PRAED. How do you do, Miss Warren? [*She presses his hand cordially, though a certain sentimentality in his high spirits jars on her*]. I start in an hour from Holborn Viaduct. I wish I could persuade you to try Italy.

VIVIE. What for?

PRAED. Why, to saturate yourself with beauty and romance, of course.

Vivie, with a shudder, turns her chair to the table, as if the work waiting for her there were a support to her. Praed sits opposite to her. Frank places a chair near Vivie, and drops lazily and carelessly into it, talking at her over his shoulder.

FRANK. No use, Praddy. Viv is a little Philistine. She is indifferent to my romance, and insensible to my beauty.

VIVIE. Mr Praed: once for all, there is no beauty and no romance in life for me. Life is what it is; and I am prepared to take it as it is.

PRAED [*enthusiastically*] You will not say that if you come with me to Verona and on to Venice. You will cry with delight at living in such a beautiful world.

FRANK. This is most eloquent, Praddy. Keep it up.

PRAED. Oh, I assure you *I* have cried – I shall cry again, I hope – at fifty! At your age, Miss Warren, you would not need to go so far as Verona. Your spirits would absolutely fly up at the mere sight of Ostend. You would be charmed with the gaiety, the vivacity, the happy air of Brussels.

VIVIE [*springing up with an exclamation of loathing*] Agh!

PRAED [*rising*] Whats the matter?

FRANK [*rising*] Hallo, Viv!

VIVIE [*to Praed, with deep reproach*] Can you find no better example of your beauty and romance than Brussels to talk to me about?

PRAED [*puzzled*] Of course it's very different from Verona. I dont suggest for a moment that –

VIVIE [*bitterly*] Probably the beauty and romance come to much the same in both places.

PRAED [*completely sobered and much concerned*] My dear Miss Warren: I – [*looking inquiringly at Frank*] Is anything the matter?

FRANK. She thinks your enthusiasm frivolous, Praddy. She's had ever such a serious call.

VIVIE [*sharply*] Hold your tongue, Frank. Dont be silly.

FRANK [*sitting down*] Do you call this good manners, Praed?

PRAED [*anxious and considerate*] Shall I take him away, Miss Warren? I feel sure we have disturbed you at your work.

VIVIE. Sit down: I'm not ready to go back to work yet. [*Praed sits*]. You both think I have an attack of nerves. Not a bit of it. But there are two subjects I want dropped, if you dont mind. One of them [*to Frank*] is love's young dream in any shape or form: the other [*to Praed*] is the romance and beauty of life, especially Ostend and the gaiety of Brussels. You are welcome to any illusions you may have left on these subjects: I have none. If we three are to remain friends, I must be treated as a woman of business, permanently single [to Frank] and permanently unromantic [to Praed].

FRANK. I also shall remain permanently single until you change your mind. Praddy: change the subject. Be eloquent about something else.

PRAED [diffidently] I'm afraid theres nothing else in the world that I can talk about. The Gospel of Art is the only one I can preach. I know Miss Warren is a great devotee of the Gospel of Getting on; but we cant discuss that without hurting your feelings, Frank, since you are determined not to get on.

FRANK. Oh, dont mind my feelings. Give me some improving advice by all means: it does me ever so much good. Have another try to make a successful man of me, Viv. Come: lets have it all: energy, thrift, foresight, self-respect, character. Dont you hate people who have no character, Viv?

VIVIE [wincing] Oh, stop, stop: let us have no more of that horrible cant. Mr Praed: if there are really only those two gospels in the world, we had better all kill ourselves; for the same taint is in both, through and through.

FRANK [looking critically at her] There is a touch of poetry about you today, Viv, which has hitherto been lacking.

PRAED [remonstrating] My dear Frank: arnt you a little unsympathetic?

VIVIE [merciless to herself] No: it's good for me. It keeps me from being sentimental.

FRANK [bantering her] Checks your strong natural propensity that way, dont it?

VIVIE [almost hysterically] Oh yes: go on: dont spare me. I was sentimental for one moment in my life – beautifully sentimental – by moonlight; and now –

FRANK [*quickly*] I say, Viv: take care. Dont give yourself away.

VIVIE. Oh, do you think Mr Praed does not know all about my mother? [*Turning on Praed*] You had better have told me that morning, Mr Praed. You are very old fashioned in your delicacies, after all.

PRAED. Surely it is you who are a little old fashioned in your prejudices, Miss Warren. I feel bound to tell you, speaking as an artist, and believing that the most intimate human relationships are far beyond and above the scope of the law, that though I know that your mother is an un-married woman, I do not respect her the less on that account. I respect her more.

FRANK [*airily*] Hear! Hear!

VIVIE [*staring at him*] Is that all you know?

PRAED. Certainly that is all.

VIVIE. Then you neither of you know anything. Your guesses are innocence itself compared to the truth.

PRAED [*rising, startled and indignant, and preserving his politeness with an effort*] I hope not. [*More emphatically*] I hope not, Miss Warren.

FRANK [*whistles*] Whew!

VIVIE. You are not making it easy for me to tell you, Mr Praed.

PRAED [*his chivalry drooping before their conviction*] If there is anything worse – that is, anything else – are you sure you are right to tell us, Miss Warren?

VIVIE. I am sure that if I had the courage I should spend the rest of my life in telling everybody – stamping and branding it into them until they all felt their part in its abomination as I feel mine. There is nothing I despise more than the wicked convention that protects these things by forbidding a woman to mention them. And yet I cant tell you. The two infamous words that describe what my mother is are ringing in my ears and struggling on my tongue; but I cant utter them: the shame of them is too horrible for me. [*She buries her face in her hands. The two men, astonished, stare at one another and then at her. She raises her head again desperately and snatches a sheet of paper and a pen*]. Here: let me draft you a prospectus.

FRANK. Oh, she's mad. Do you hear, Viv? mad. Come! pull yourself together.

VIVIE. You shall see. [*She writes*]. 'Paid up capital: not less than £40,000 standing in the name of Sir George Crofts, Baronet, the chief shareholder. Premises at Brussels, Ostend, Vienna and Budapest. Managing director: Mrs. Warren'; and now dont let us forget her qualifications: the two words. [*She writes the words and pushes the paper to them*]. There! Oh no: dont read it: dont! [*She snatches it back and tears it to pieces; then seizes her head in her hands and hides her face on the table*].

Frank, who has watched the writing over her shoulder, and opened his eyes very widely at it, takes a card from his pocket; scribbles the two words on it; and silently hands it to Praed, who reads it with amazement, and hides it hastily in his pocket.

FRANK [*whispering tenderly*] Viv, dear: thats all right. I read what you wrote: so did Praddy. We understand. And we remain, as this leaves us at present, yours ever so devotedly.

PRAED. We do indeed, Miss Warren. I declare you are the most splendidly courageous woman I ever met.

This sentimental compliment braces Vivie. She throws it away from her with an impatient shake, and forces herself to stand up, though not without some support from the table.

FRANK. Dont stir, Viv, if you dont want to. Take it easy.

VIVIE. Thank you. You can always depend on me for two things: not to cry and not to faint. [*She moves a few steps towards the door of the inner room, and stops close to Praed to say*] I shall need much more courage than that when I tell my mother that we have come to the parting of the ways. Now I must go into the next room for a moment to make myself neat again, if you dont mind.

PRAED. Shall we go away?

VIVIE. No: I'll be back presently. Only for a moment. [*She goes into the other room, Praed opening the door for her*].

PRAED. What an amazing revelation! I'm extremely disappointed in Crofts: I am indeed.

FRANK. I'm not in the least. I feel he's perfectly accounted for at last. But what a facer for me, Praddy! I cant marry her now.

PRAED [*sternly*] Frank! [*The two look at one another, Frank unruffled, Praed deeply indignant*] Let me tell you, Gardner, that if you desert her now you will behave very despicably.

FRANK. Good old Praddy! Ever chivalrous! But you mistake: it's not the moral aspect of the case: it's the money aspect. I really cant bring myself to touch the old woman's money now.

PRAED. And was that what you were going to marry on?

FRANK. What else? *I* havnt any money, not the smallest turn for making it. If I married Viv now she would have to support me; and I should cost her more than I am worth.

PRAED. But surely a clever bright fellow like you can make something by your own brains.

FRANK. Oh yes, a little [*He takes out his money again*]. I made all that yesterday in an hour and a half. But I made it in a highly speculative business. No, dear Praddy: even if Bessie and Georgina marry millionaires and the governor dies after cutting them off with a shilling, I shall have only four hundred a year. And he wont die until he's three score and ten: he hasnt originality enough. I shall be on short allowance for the next twenty years. No short allowance for Viv, if I can help it. I withdraw gracefully and leave the field to the gilded youth of England. So thats settled. I shant worry her about it: I'll just send her a little note after we're gone. She'll understand.

PRAED [*grasping his hand*] Good fellow, Frank! I heartily beg your pardon. But must you never see her again?

FRANK. Never see her again! Hang it all, be reasonable. I shall come along as often as possible, and be her brother. I can n o t understand the absurd consequences you romantic people expect from the most ordinary transactions. [*A knock at the door*]. I wonder who this is. Would you mind opening the door? If it's a client it will look more respectable than if I appeared.

PRAED. Certainly. [*He goes to the door and opens it. Frank sits down in Vivie's chair to scribble a note*]. My dear Kitty: come in: come in.

Mrs Warren comes in, looking apprehensively round for Vivie. She has done her best to make herself matronly and dignified. The brilliant hat is replaced by a sober bonnet, and the gay blouse covered by a costly black silk mantle. She is pitiably anxious and ill at ease: evidently panic-stricken.

MRS WARREN [*to Frank*] What! You re here, are you?

FRANK [*turning in his chair from his writing, but not rising*] Here, and charmed to see you. You come like a breath of spring.

MRS WARREN. Oh, get out with your nonsense. [*In a low voice*] Wheres Vivie?

Frank points expressively to the door of the inner room, but says nothing.

MRS WARREN [*sitting down suddenly and almost beginning to cry*] Praddy: wont she see me, dont you think?

PRAED. My dear Kitty: dont distress yourself. Why should she not?

MRS WARREN. Oh, you never can see why not: youre too innocent. Mr Frank: did she say anything to you?

FRANK [*folding his note*] She must see you, if [*very expressively*] you wait til she comes in.

MRS WARREN [*frightened*] Why shouldnt I wait?

Frank looks quizzically at her; puts his note carefully on the inkbottle, so that Vivie cannot fail to find it when next she dips her pen; then rises and devotes his attention to her.

FRANK. My dear Mrs Warren: suppose you were a sparrow – ever so tiny and pretty a sparrow hopping in the roadway – and you saw a steam roller coming in your direction, would you wait for it?

MRS WARREN. Oh, dont bother me with your sparrows. What did she run away from Haslemere like that for?

FRANK. I'm afraid she'll tell you if you rashly await her return.

MRS WARREN. Do you want me to go away?

FRANK. No: I always want you to stay. But I advise you to go away.

MRS WARREN. What! And never see her again!

FRANK. Precisely.

MRS WARREN [*crying again*] Praddy: dont let him be cruel to me. [*she hastily checks her tears and wipes her eyes*]. She'll be so angry if she sees Ive been crying.

FRANK [*with a touch of real compassion in his airy tenderness*] You know that Praddy is the soul of kindness, Mrs Warren. Praddy: what do you say? Go or stay?

PRAED [*to Mrs Warren*] I really should be very sorry to cause you unnecessary pain; but I think perhaps you had better not wait. The fact is – [*Vivie is heard at the inner door*].

FRANK. Sh! Too late. She's coming.

MRS WARREN. Dont tell her I was crying. [*Vivie comes in. She stops gravely on seeing Mrs Warren, who greets her with hysterical cheerfulness*]. Well, dearie. So here you are at last.

VIVIE. I am glad you have come: I want to speak to you. You said you were going, Frank, I think.

FRANK. Yes. Will you come with me, Mrs Warren? What do you say to a trip to Richmond, and the theatre in the evening? There is safety in Richmond. No steam roller there.

VIVIE. Nonsense, Frank. My mother will stay here.

MRS WARREN [*scared*] I dont know: perhaps I'd better go. We're disturbing you at your work.

VIVIE [*with quiet decision*] Mr Praed: please take Frank away. Sit down, mother. [*Mrs Warren obeys helplessly*].

PRAED. Come, Frank. Goodbye, Miss Vivie.

279

VIVIE [*shaking hands*] Goodbye. A pleasant trip.

PRAED. Thank you: thank you. I hope so.

FRANK [*to Mrs Warren*] Goodbye: youd ever so much better have taken my advice. [*He shakes hands with her. Then airily to Vivie*] Byebye, Viv.

VIVIE. Goodbye. [*He goes out gaily without shaking hands with her*].

PRAED [*sadly*] Goodbye, Kitty.

MRS WARREN [*snivelling*] – oobye!

> *Praed goes. Vivie, composed and extremely grave, sits down in Honoria's chair, and waits for her mother to speak. Mrs Warren, dreading a pause, loses no time in beginning.*

MRS WARREN. Well, Vivie, what did you go away like that for without saying a word to me? How could you do such a thing! And what have you done to poor George? I wanted him to come with me; but he shuffled out of it. I could see that he was quite afraid of you. Only fancy: he wanted me not to come. As if [*trembling*] I should be afraid of you, dearie. [*Vivie's gravity deepens*]. But of course I told him it was all settled and comfortable between us, and that we were on the best of terms. [*She breaks down*]. Vivie: whats the meaning of this? [*She produces a commercial envelope, and fumbles at the enclosure with trembling fingers*]. I got it from the bank this morning.

VIVIE. It is my month's allowance. They sent it to me as usual the other day. I simply sent it back to be placed to your credit, and asked them to send you the lodgment receipt. In future I shall support myself.

MRS WARREN [*not daring to understand*] Wasnt it enough? Why didnt you tell me? [*With a cunning gleam in her eye*] I'll double it: I was intending to double it. Only let me know how much you want.

VIVIE. You know very well that that has nothing to do with it. From this time I go my own way in my own business and among my own friends. And you will go yours. [*She rises*]. Goodbye.

MRS WARREN [*rising, appalled*] Goodbye?

VIVIE. Yes: Goodbye. Come: dont let us make a useless scene: you understand perfectly well. Sir George Crofts has told me the whole business.

MRS WARREN [*angrily*] Silly old – [*She swallows an epithet, and turns white at the narrowness of her escape from uttering it*].

VIVIE. Just so.

MRS WARREN. He ought to have his tongue cut out. But I thought it was ended: you said you didnt mind.

VIVIE [*steadfastly*] Excuse me: I d o mind.

MRS WARREN. But I explained –

VIVIE. You explained how it came about. You did not tell me that it is still going on. [*She sits*].

> *Mrs Warren, silenced for a moment, looks forlornly at Vivie, who waits, secretly hoping that the combat is over. But the cunning expression comes back into Mrs Warren's face; and she bends across the table, sly and urgent, half whispering.*

MRS WARREN. Vivie: do you know how rich I am?

VIVIE. I have no doubt you are very rich.

MRS WARREN. But you dont know all that that means: youre too young. It means a new dress every day; it means theatres and balls every night; it means having the pick of all the gentlemen in Europe at your feet; it means a lovely house and plenty of servants; it means the choicest of eating and drinking; it means everything you like, everything you want, everything you can think of. And what are you here? A mere drudge, toiling and moiling early and late for your bare living and two cheap dresses a year. Think over it. [*Soothingly*] Youre shocked, I know. I can enter into your feelings; and I think they do you credit; but trust me, nobody will blame you: you may take my word for that. I know what young girls are; and I know youll think better of it when youve turned it over in your mind.

VIVIE. So thats how it's done, is it? You must have said all that to many a woman, mother, to have it so pat.

MRS WARREN [*passionately*] What harm am I asking you to

do? [*Vivie turns away contemptuously. Mrs Warren continues desperately*] Vivie: listen to me: you dont understand: youve been taught wrong on purpose: you dont know what the world is really like.

VIVIE [*arrested*] Taught wrong on purpose! What do you mean?

MRS WARREN. I mean that youre throwing away all your chances for nothing. You think that people are what they pretend to be: that the way you were taught at school and college to think right and proper is the way things really are. But it's not: it's all only a pretence, to keep the cowardly slavish common run of people quiet. Do you want to find that out, like other women, at forty, when youve thrown yourself away and lost your chances; or wont you take it in good time now from your own mother, that loves you and swears to you that it's truth: gospel truth? [*Urgently*] Vivie: the big people, the clever people, the managing people, all know it. They do as I do, and think what I think. I know plenty of them. I know them to speak to, to introduce you to, to make friends of for you. I dont mean anything wrong: thats what you dont understand: your head is full of ignorant ideas about me. What do the people that taught you know about life or about people like me? When did they ever meet me, or speak to me, or let anyone tell them about me? the fools! Would they ever have done anything for you if I hadnt paid them? Havnt I told you that I want you to be respectable? Havnt I brought you up to be respectable? And how can you keep it up without my money and my influence and Lizzie's friends? Cant you see that youre cutting your own throat as well as breaking my heart in turning your back on me?

VIVIE. I recognize the Crofts philosophy of life, mother. I heard it all from him that day at the Gardners'.

MRS WARREN. You think I want to force that played-out old sot on you! I dont, Vivie: on my oath I dont.

VIVIE. It would not matter if you did: you would not succeed. [*Mrs Warren winces, deeply hurt by the implied indifference towards her affectionate intention. Vivie, neither understanding
this nor concerning herself about it, goes on calmly*] Mother: you
dont at all know the sort of person I am. I dont object to
Crofts more than to any other coarsely built man of his
class. To tell you the truth, I rather admire him for being
strongminded enough to enjoy himself in his own way and
make plenty of money instead of living the usual shooting,
hunting, dining-out, tailoring, loafing life of his set merely
because all the rest do it. And I'm perfectly aware that if
I'd been in the same circumstances as my aunt Liz, I'd
have done exactly what she did. I dont think I'm more
prejudiced or straitlaced than you: I think I'm less. I'm
certain I'm less sentimental. I know very well that fashionable morality is all a pretence, and that if I took your
money and devoted the rest of my life to spending it
fashionably, I might be as worthless and vicious as the
silliest woman could possibly want to be without having a
word said to me about it. But I dont want to be worthless.
I shouldnt enjoy trotting about the park to advertise my
dressmaker and carriage builder, or being bored at the
opera to shew off a shopwindowful of diamonds.

MRS WARREN [*bewildered*] But –

VIVIE. Wait a moment: Ive not done. Tell me why you
continue your business now that you are independent of
it. Your sister, you told me, has left all that behind her.
Why dont you do the same?

MRS WARREN. Oh, it's all very easy for Liz: she likes good
society, and has the air of being a lady. Imagine me in a
cathedral town! Why, the very rooks in the trees would
find me out even if I could stand the dulness of it. I must
have work and excitement, or I should go melancholy
mad. And what else is there for me to do? The life suits
me: I'm fit for it and not for anything else. If I didnt do it
somebody else would; so I dont do any real harm by it.

And then it brings in money; and I like making money. No: it's no use: I cant give it up – not for anybody. But what need you know about it? I'll never mention it. I'll keep Crofts away. I'll not trouble you much: you see I have to ,be constantly running about from one place to another. Youll be quit of me altogether when I die.

VIVIE. No: I am my mother's daughter. I am like you: I must have work, and must make more money than I spend. But my work is not your work, and my way not your way. We must part. It will not make much difference to us: instead of meeting one another for perhaps a few months in twenty years, we shall never meet: thats all.

MRS WARREN [*her voice stifled in tears*] Vivie: I meant to have been more with you: I did indeed.

VIVIE. It's no use, mother: I am not to be changed by a few cheap tears and entreaties any more than you are, I daresay.

MRS WARREN [*wildly*] Oh, you call a mother's tears cheap.

VIVIE. They cost you nothing; and you ask me to give you the peace and quietness of my whole life in exchange for them. What use would my company be to you if you could get it? What have we two in common that could make either of us happy together?

MRS WARREN [*lapsing recklessly into her dialect*] We're mother and daughter. I want my daughter. Ive a right to you. Who is to care for me when I'm old? Plenty of girls have taken to me like daughters and cried at leaving me; but I let them all go because I had you to look forward to. I kept myself lonely for you. Youve no right to turn on me now and refuse to do your duty as a daughter.

VIVIE [*jarred and antagonized by the echo of the slums in her mother's voice*] My duty as a daughter! I thought we should come to that presently. Now once for all, mother, you want a daughter and Frank wants a wife. I dont want a mother; and I dont want a husband. I have spared neither

Frank nor myself in sending him about his business. Do
you think I will spare you?

MRS WARREN [*violently*] Oh, I know the sort you are: no
mercy for yourself or anyone else. *I* know. My experience
has done that for me anyhow: I can tell the pious, canting,
hard, selfish woman when I meet her. Well, keep yourself
to yourself: *I* dont want you. But listen to this. Do you
know what I would do with you if you were a baby again?
aye, as sure as theres a Heaven above us.

VIVIE. Strangle me, perhaps.

MRS WARREN. No: I'd bring you up to be a real daughter
to me, and not what you are now, with your pride and
your prejudices and the college education you stole from
me: yes, stole: deny it if you can: what was it but stealing?
I'd bring you up in my own house, I would.

VIVIE [*quietly*] In one of your own houses.

MRS WARREN [*screaming*] Listen to her! listen to how she
spits on her mother's grey hairs! Oh, may you live to have
your own daughter tear and trample on you as you have
trampled on me. And you will: you will. No woman ever
had luck with a mother's curse on her.

VIVIE. I wish you wouldnt rant, mother. It only hardens
me. Come: I suppose I am the only young woman you
ever had in your power that you did good to. Dont spoil it
all now.

MRS WARREN. Yes, Heaven forgive me, it's true; and you
are the only one that ever turned on me. Oh, the injustice
of it! the injustice! the injustice! I always wanted to be a
good woman. I tried honest work; and I was slave-driven
until I cursed the day I ever heard of honest work. I was
a good mother; and because I made my daughter a good
woman she turns me out as if I was a leper. Oh, if I only
had my life to live over again! I'd talk to that lying
clergyman in the school. From this time forth, so help me
Heaven in my last hour, I'll do wrong and nothing but
wrong. And I'll prosper on it.

VIVIE: Yes: it's better to choose your line and go through
with it. If I had been you, mother, I might have done as
you did: but I should not have lived one life and believed
in another. You are a conventional woman at heart. That
is why I am bidding you goodbye now. I am right, am I
not?

MRS WARREN [*taken aback*] Right to throw away all my
money?

VIVIE. No: right to get rid of you! I should be a fool not to!
Isnt that so?

MRS WARREN [*sulkily*] Oh well, yes, if you come to that, I
suppose you are. But Lord help the world if everybody
took to doing the right thing! And now I'd better go than
stay where I'm not wanted. [*She turns to the door*].

VIVIE [*kindly*] Wont you shake hands?

MRS WARREN [*after looking at her fiercely for a moment with a
savage impulse to strike her*] No, thank you. Goodbye.

VIVIE [*matter-of-factly*] Goodbye. [*Mrs Warren goes out,
slamming the door behind her. The strain on Vivie's face relaxes;
her grave expression breaks up into one of joyous content; her
breath goes out in a half sob, half laugh of intense relief. She goes
buoyantly to her place at the writing-table; pushes the electric lamp
out of the way; pulls over a great sheaf of papers; and is in the act
of dipping her pen in the ink when she finds Frank's note. She opens
it unconcernedly and reads it quickly, giving a little laugh at some
quaint turn of expression in it*]. And goodbye, Frank. [*She tears
the note up and tosses the pieces into the wastepaper basket without
a second thought. Then she goes at her work with a plunge, and
soon becomes absorbed in its figures*].

Widower's Houses

Composition begun 18 August 1884; completed 20 October 1892. Published 1893. Revised text in *Plays Pleasant and Unpleasant*, 1898. Further revision in Collected Edition, 1930

First presented by the Independent Theatre at the Royalty Theatre, London, on 9 December 1892; repeated on 13 December (matinée).

Dr Harry Trench   *W. J. Robertson*
William de Burgh Cokane   *Arthur Whittaker*
Sartorius   *T. Wigney Percyval*
Lickcheese   *James Welch*
Waiter   *E. P. Donne*
Porter   *W. Alison*
Blanche Sartorius   *Florence Farr*
Annie (parlourmaid)   *N. de Silva*

ACT I *In the Grounds of a Hotel-Restaurant at Remagen, on the Rhine*

ACT II *Library in Sartorious' House at Surbiton*

ACT III *The Drawing-Room – Evening*

The Philanderer

Composition begun 14 March 1893; completed 27 June 1893. Published in *Plays Pleasant and Unpleasant*, 1898. Revised text in Collected Edition, 1930

Copyright reading at the Victoria Hall (Bijou Theatre), London, on 30 March 1898. First presented by the New Stage Club (amateurs) at the Cripplegate Institute, London, on 20 February 1905. First professional performance presented by J. E. Vedrenne and H. Granville Barker at the Royal Court Theatre, London, on 5 February 1907 (for a series of eight matinées).

First performance of the deleted last act, Hampstead Theatre, London, on 14 November 1991.

Leonard Charteris   *Ben Webster*
Mrs Grace Tranfield   *Wynne Matthison*
Julia Craven   *Mary Barton*
Colonel Daniel Craven, V.C.   *Eric Lewis*
Joseph Cuthbertson   *Luigi Lablache*
Sylvia Craven   *Dorothy Minto*
Dr Percy Paramore   *Hubert Harben*
The Club Page   *Cyril Bruce*

ACT I *Mr Joseph Cuthbertson's Flat in Ashley Gardens*

ACTS II AND III *The Library of the Ibsen Club*

ACT IV *Dr Paramore's Rooms in Savile Row*

Mrs Warren's Profession

Composition begun 20 August 1883; completed 2 November 1893. Published in *Plays Pleasant and Unpleasant*, 1898. Separate edition, 1902 (containing a new preface 'The Author's Apology'). Revised text in Collected Edition, 1930

Copyright reading at the Victoria Hall (Bijou Theatre), London, on 30 March 1898. First presented by the Stage Society at the New Lyric Club on 5 January 1902; repeated on 6 January.

Praed *Julius Knight*
Sir George Crofts *Charles Goodhart*
The Reverend Samuel Gardner *Cosmo Stuart*
Frank Gardner *H. Granville Barker*
Vivie Warren *Madge McIntosh*
Mrs Kitty Warren *Fanny Brough*

ACT I *In Garden of Vivie Warren's Holiday Cottage at Haslemere*

ACT II *Inside the Cottage*

ACT III *The Vicarage Garden*

ACT IV *Honoria Fraser's Chambers in Chancery Lane*

PRINCIPAL WORKS OF BERNARD SHAW*

PLAYS

Widowers' Houses (1893)

Plays Pleasant and Unpleasant (1898) (including *Mrs Warren's Profession; Arms and the Man; Candida; You Never Can Tell*)

Three Plays for Puritans (1901) (including *The Devil's Disciple; Caesar and Cleopatra*)

Man and Superman (1903)

John Bull's Other Island (1907)

Major Barbara (1907)

The Doctor's Dilemma (1911)

Getting Married (1911)

Misalliance (1914)

Androcles and the Lion (1916)

Pygmalion (1916)

Heartbreak House (1919)

Back to Methuselah (1921)

Saint Joan (1924)

The Apple Cart (1930)

Too True to be Good (1934)

On the Rocks (1934)

The Millionairess (1936)

In Good King Charles's Golden Days (1939)

NOVELS AND OTHER FICTION

An Unsocial Socialist (1884)

Cashel Byron's Profession (1885–6)

The Irrational Knot (1885–7)

Love among the Artists (1887–8)

Immaturity (1830)

The Black Girl in Search of God (1932)

290

PRINCIPAL WORKS OF BERNARD SHAW

CRITICISM

Major Critical Essays (1930) (including *The Quintessence of Ibsenism*, 1891; *The Sanity of Art*, 1895 and 1908; *The Perfect Wagnerite*, 1898)
Music in London (1931; from serialization 1890–94)
Our Theatres in the Nineties (1931; from serialization 1895–98)

POLITICAL WRITINGS

Fabian Essays in Socialism (edited, 1893)
Common Sense about the War (1914)
The Intelligent Woman's Guide to Socialism and Capitalism (1928)
Everybody's Political What's What? (1944)

*Dates are of first English-language publication.
[NB This clarification is essential in Shaw, for some of his works appeared in translation two and three years before English publication.]

READ MORE IN PENGUIN

In every corner of the world, on every subject under the sun, Penguin represents quality and variety – the very best in publishing today.

For complete information about books available from Penguin – including Puffins, Penguin Classics and Arkana – and how to order them, write to us at the appropriate address below. Please note that for copyright reasons the selection of books varies from country to country.

In the United Kingdom: Please write to *Dept. EP, Penguin Books Ltd, Bath Road, Harmondsworth, West Drayton, Middlesex UB7 ODA*

In the United States: Please write to *Consumer Sales, Penguin Putnam Inc., P.O. Box 12289 Dept. B, Newark, New Jersey 07101-5289*. VISA and MasterCard holders call 1-800-788-6262 to order Penguin titles

In Canada: Please write to *Penguin Books Canada Ltd, 10 Alcorn Avenue, Suite 300, Toronto, Ontario M4V 3B2*

In Australia: Please write to *Penguin Books Australia Ltd, P.O. Box 257, Ringwood, Victoria 3134*

In New Zealand: Please write to *Penguin Books (NZ) Ltd, Private Bag 102902, North Shore Mail Centre, Auckland 10*

In India: Please write to *Penguin Books India Pvt Ltd, 11 Community Centre, Panchsheel Park, New Delhi 110017*

In the Netherlands: Please write to *Penguin Books Netherlands bv, Postbus 3507, NL-1001 AH Amsterdam*

In Germany: Please write to *Penguin Books Deutschland GmbH, Metzlerstrasse 26, 60594 Frankfurt am Main*

In Spain: Please write to *Penguin Books S. A., Bravo Murillo 19, 1° B, 28015 Madrid*

In Italy: Please write to *Penguin Italia s.r.l., Via Benedetto Croce 2, 20094 Corsico, Milano*

In France: Please write to *Penguin France, Le Carré Wilson, 62 rue Benjamin Baillaud, 31500 Toulouse*

In Japan: Please write to *Penguin Books Japan Ltd, Kaneko Building, 2-3-25 Koraku, Bunkyo-Ku, Tokyo 112*

In South Africa: Please write to *Penguin Books South Africa (Pty) Ltd, Private Bag X14, Parkview, 2122 Johannesburg*

READ MORE IN PENGUIN

A CHOICE OF CLASSICS

Matthew Arnold	**Selected Prose**
Jane Austen	**Emma**
	Lady Susan/The Watsons/Sanditon
	Mansfield Park
	Northanger Abbey
	Persuasion
	Pride and Prejudice
	Sense and Sensibility
William Barnes	**Selected Poems**
Mary Braddon	**Lady Audley's Secret**
Anne Brontë	**Agnes Grey**
	The Tenant of Wildfell Hall
Charlotte Brontë	**Jane Eyre**
	Juvenilia: 1829–35
	The Professor
	Shirley
	Villette
Emily Brontë	**Complete Poems**
	Wuthering Heights
Samuel Butler	**Erewhon**
	The Way of All Flesh
Lord Byron	**Don Juan**
	Selected Poems
Lewis Carroll	**Alice's Adventures in Wonderland**
	The Hunting of the Snark
Thomas Carlyle	**Selected Writings**
Arthur Hugh Clough	**Selected Poems**
Wilkie Collins	**Armadale**
	The Law and the Lady
	The Moonstone
	No Name
	The Woman in White
Charles Darwin	**The Origin of Species**
	Voyage of the Beagle
Benjamin Disraeli	**Coningsby**
	Sybil

READ MORE IN PENGUIN

A CHOICE OF CLASSICS

Edward Gibbon	**The Decline and Fall of the Roman Empire** (in three volumes)
	Memoirs of My Life
George Gissing	**New Grub Street**
	The Odd Women
William Godwin	**Caleb Williams**
	Concerning Political Justice
Thomas Hardy	**Desperate Remedies**
	The Distracted Preacher and Other Tales
	Far from the Madding Crowd
	Jude the Obscure
	The Hand of Ethelberta
	A Laodicean
	The Mayor of Casterbridge
	A Pair of Blue Eyes
	The Return of the Native
	Selected Poems
	Tess of the d'Urbervilles
	The Trumpet-Major
	Two on a Tower
	Under the Greenwood Tree
	The Well-Beloved
	The Woodlanders
George Lyell	**Principles of Geology**
Lord Macaulay	**The History of England**
Henry Mayhew	**London Labour and the London Poor**
George Meredith	**The Egoist**
	The Ordeal of Richard Feverel
John Stuart Mill	**The Autobiography**
	On Liberty
	Principles of Political Economy
William Morris	**News from Nowhere and Other Writings**
John Henry Newman	**Apologia Pro Vita Sua**
Margaret Oliphant	**Miss Marjoribanks**
Robert Owen	**A New View of Society and Other Writings**
Walter Pater	**Marius the Epicurean**
John Ruskin	**Unto This Last and Other Writings**

READ MORE IN PENGUIN

THE BERNARD SHAW LIBRARY

'The most influential writer of his age . . . His plays can scarcely prove other than lastingly delightful since they are the product of vigorous intelligence joined to inexhaustible comic invention' J. I. M. Stewart in the *Oxford History of English Literature*

Androcles and the Lion
The Apple Cart
Back to Methuselah
The Doctor's Dilemma
Heartbreak House
John Bull's Other Island
Last Plays
Major Barbara
Major Critical Essays
Man and Superman
Misalliance and the Fascinating Foundling
Plays Extravagant
(The Millionairess, Too True to be Good, The Simpleton of the Unexpected Isles)
Plays Pleasant
(Arms and the Man, Candida, The Man of Destiny, You Never Can Tell)
Plays Political
(The Apple Cart, On the Rocks, Geneva)
Plays Unpleasant
(Widowers' Houses, The Philanderer, Mrs Warren's Profession)
Pygmalion
Saint Joan
Selected Short Plays
(including The Admirable Bashville and Great Catherine)
Three Plays for Puritans
(The Devil's Disciple, Caesar and Cleopatra, Captain Brassbound's Conversion)